STRINDBERG ON DRAMA AND THEATRE

# STRINDBERG
## ON DRAMA AND THEATRE

## A SOURCE BOOK

Selected, translated, and edited by Egil Törnqvist
and Birgitta Steene

Amsterdam University Press

Cover illustration: August Strindberg at his writing desk. Etching
by Anders Zorn, 1910.
Cover: Geert de Koning, Ten Post
Lay-out: Het Steen Typografie, Maarssen


ISBN 9789053560204
NUR 670

© Amsterdam University Press, 2007

# Contents

# Preface

Together with Norway's Henrik Ibsen and Russia's Anton Chekhov, Sweden's August Strindberg (1849-1912) has long been recognized as a leading dramatist of the late nineteenth and early twentieth century. Of these three, Strindberg has proven the most seminal to the development of modern drama.

What is less known is that throughout his adult life, Strindberg frequently commented on drama and theatre in general and on his own plays and the staging of them in particular. Two such texts are widely distributed and frequently reprinted, the preface to *Miss Julie*, often hailed as *the* manifesto of modern drama, and the prefatory note to *A Dream Play*, outlining the techniques of what later became known as dramatic expressionism. But a host of others are virtually unknown to an English-speaking audience. This regrettable oversight motivates the present book, which is being published at an auspicious moment in Strindberg scholarship. The Swedish edition of Strindberg's letters in 22 carefully annotated volumes is now complete and most of the projected 72 volumes in a new scholarly edition of his collected works have been published, including virtually all of the plays as well as the volume entitled *Teater och Intima Teatern* (Theatre and the Intimate Theatre). Both editions provide a firm underpinning for this source book.

Selections include most of Strindberg's significant statements on drama and theatre. Most, but not all, for we have tried to avoid repetitiveness by limiting, for example, similar statements to different addressees and by leaving out certain technical descriptions related to specific productions.

Moreover, our volume does not include texts which have only thematic relevance to Strindberg's plays. A concrete example may illustrate this point. In his *A Blue Book I* (1907), one of the short pieces – there are hundreds of them – is entitled "A Whole Life in an Hour." Here the narrator describes how he one morning, "obeying an exhortation," went for a walk in town, seemingly at random. He passed the neighborhood where he was born and had been educated, where he had worked as a teacher, where he was accepted as an actor, where he handed in his first play, where he married his first wife, and where his third wife and their child had been living three years earlier. He concludes: "In an hour I had gone through my life in living pictures; another three years and I would have arrived at the present time. It was like an *agonie* or moment of death when all of life travels past."

This suggestive description can easily be related to several of Strindberg's plays. There is the telescoping of time, recognizable in *The Ghost Sonata* where the Student-narrator experiences a whole life in not much more than an hour, the playing time of the drama. There is the idea of retracing one's steps, appearing in the pilgrimage drama *To Damascus*. And there is the sense of imminent death at the end of *A Dream Play* where the Poet, commenting on what we have just witnessed in the stage action, remarks: "I read somewhere that when life approaches its end, everyone and everything passes quickly by in review ... is this the end?" To which Indra's Daughter answers: "For me, yes."

The *Blue Book* fragment obviously sheds light on all three plays. We have nevertheless refrained from including texts of this kind since doing so would not only have increased the size of this book immensely, it would also have been exceedingly difficult to find a principle for limiting the material.

Our book opens with a brief introduction, sketching Strindberg's relationship to drama and theatre and outlining some of his most important ideas on these subjects. This is followed by the main part, i.e. the relevant texts by Strindberg himself, all in chronological order with regard to the time of writing. Each item is provided with a date of composition, explanatory notes and, in the case of the letters and memos, a short presentation of the addressee the first time s/he is mentioned. It would naturally have been helpful if the letters from the addressees could have been included, but unfortunately these are, with few exceptions, no longer extant. The brief presentations of the addressees give at least an indication of the context; more comprehensive presentations can be found in Michael Robinson's edition of Strindberg's letters.

The volume concludes with a list of Strindberg's plays, plus dates when they were first published and first performed, again in chronological order with regard to the time of writing. For further reading, we have included a rather extensive list of works dealing with Strindberg's plays. A few illustrations are provided to highlight the material. Finally, there is a name and title index and a subject index to enable the reader to explore topics of particular interest.

The choice of a chronological arrangement warrants an explanation. One obvious alternative, grouping relevant material around a number of Strindberg's plays, would have had the disadvantage of leaving out much pertinent subject matter simply because it would not fit under the chosen headings. Moreover, such an organizational principle would necessarily blur the developmental aspect preserved in a chronological arrangement. With a dramatist as impulsive and protean as Strindberg, there is every reason to keep track of *when* a statement was made. Besides, as already indicated, our indexes give readers the opportunity to make their own systematization of the material.

Stylistically, Strindberg's observations on drama and theatre share the characteristics of much of his other work. His mode of expression is highly idiosyncratic, often very direct, sometimes extremely laconic, sometimes rather circumstantial, frequently drastically colorful. Bearing signs of having been written in haste, his comments may occasionally seem inconsistent and are at times ambiguous. Though we have tried to retain the author's spontaneity, we have provided brief notes or have made emendations to those passages which require clarification in order to be understood. In one case, this has resulted in a change of terms. When speaking of the individual member of the audience, Strindberg often refers to the *åhörare* (listener) rather than the *åskådare* (spectator). After the emergence of radio, and radio plays, it would be misleading to retain Strindberg's term, which might well be seen less as an expression of the spirit of the time than of the author's individual need to stress the primacy of the word. We have consistently replaced 'listener' with 'spectator.' With regard to punctuation, Strindberg's texts are characterized by the frequent use of dashes, semicolons and exclamation marks. In the interest of readability, we have often seen fit to replace these either with commas or full stops. For the same reason we have sometimes departed from Strindberg's unpredictable use of capitals, italics, brackets, and quotation marks. Throughout the volume, S stands for Strindberg, [-] indicates an omission. In the texts by S, parentheses are by the author, square brackets by the editors. Single quotation marks indicate that a word is used in a special, often non-literal sense.

Egil Törnqvist is primarily responsible for the selection and editing of the texts, Birgitta Steene for the translation into (American) English. In both cases, the editors have critically scrutinized each other's contributions and consequently carry a joint responsibility for the final result.

Part of the material included in this volume was earlier translated and annotated by the late Professor Walter Johnson (University of Washington) and by Professor Michael Robinson (University of East Anglia); see the Bibliography under Strindberg. Our translation differs somewhat from both; we are, however, very grateful to Professor Robinson for his generous offer to let us make use of his translations of Strindberg's texts. We wish to thank Professor Rochelle Wright for valuable comments on the translation and curator Erik Höök at the Strindberg Museum in Stockholm for his assistance with regard to the illustrations.

The book has been made possible by a grant from Stiftelsen Konung Gustav VI Adolfs fond för svensk kultur.

Amsterdam and Stockholm, September 2007

Egil Törnqvist, Birgitta Steene

# Introduction

August Strindberg's importance for the development of modern drama is fundamental and undeniable. Few modern playwrights have been unaffected by him. Eugene O'Neill, in 1924, already considered him "the most modern of moderns, the greatest interpreter in the theatre of the characteristic spiritual conflicts which constitute the drama – the blood! – of our lives today." Some forty years later, Martin Lamm called him "the boldest [-] experimenter in modern drama." For Ingmar Bergman, Strindberg was a lifelong companion: "I tried to write like him, dialogues, scenes, everything. I felt his vitality, his anger inside me."

Like most successful modern dramatists, Strindberg wrote his plays for two kinds of recipients – readers and spectators. All his plays were published either before or in a couple of cases about the same time as they were staged. The time lapse between publication and production could sometimes be considerable (see the play list, page 174-179). This means that, unlike those dramatists today who do not publish their plays until these have proved stageworthy, that is, after they have been tested in rehearsals or productions, Strindberg, as he himself put it, had once and for all written what he had written. This was at least true in the sense that although most of the plays were written very quickly, he made very few changes in the proofs.

August Falck, actor, manager and director at Strindberg's Intimate Theatre, has described how he once, in the spring of 1907, was an eyewitness to Strindberg's way of writing:

> I was allowed to sit in the room outside and now and then steal in on my toes to fetch a few manuscript pages. He wrote with whizzing speed, pulled away the completed pages and threw them unblotted on the floor where I got to pick them up, carry them out, and sit down to read them. [-]
>
> After dinner he 'charged' himself, you actually saw how his thoughts were working; above his eyes appeared what looked like thick calluses, and his forehead and temples seemed to grow, enlarge from the strain of finding concise expressions. Short notes, difficult to grasp, were strewn around him, on the table, in the drawers, in his pockets. The chamber plays arose like a jigsaw puzzle from these fragments.

Publication was especially important in a large but sparsely populated country like Sweden with few theatres. Publication also improved the possibilities of being translated and staged abroad. The publication-production sequence meant that Strindberg could have a reading public before he had a theatre audience. Both theatre critics and ordinary theatre goers could read the drama texts before they saw the performances based on them. This situation undoubtedly strengthened the position of the dramatist in relation to the director whose distinct role in the theatre was beginning to emerge at this time.

Most of Strindberg's plays – there are close to sixty of them – are in prose, a few are in verse and yet another few mix the two modes. They have somewhat bewilderingly been labeled realist, naturalist, symbolist, expressionist, surrealist, existentialist, and absurdist as if they were endlessly malleable. It becomes even more bewildering when different labels are given to the same play. Also in terms of dramatic genre, Strindberg might perplex us because of his versatility. He wrote comedies, tragedies, tragi-comedies, historical plays, fairy-tale plays, pilgrimage plays, dream plays, chamber plays.

When Strindberg started out as a playwright, romantic idealism in the wake of Goethe and Schiller was competing with the new French drawing-room drama (Dumas fils, Augier) in the Swedish theatres. Revolting against the romantics, the French dramatists of the Second Empire considered themselves realistic. Yet their artificial and superficial plays were found lacking in realism when the naturalists conquered the stage. Naturalism in turn was, as we know, soon to be superseded by symbolism, which in a sense meant a return to a romantic kind of drama (Maeterlinck) and to a non-illusionist form of theatre. Strindberg not only experienced these various -isms during his lifetime, he also partly adjusted to them, while at the same time pursuing his own course to the benefit of modern drama.

It took a long time, however, for Strindberg the dramatist to receive due recognition in Sweden. His first important play, the prose version of *Master Olof*, today considered the most significant historical drama in Swedish, was not performed until nine years after it was written. *Miss Julie*, the best known of his plays, had to wait eighteen years for its first professional performance in Sweden. The first production of *A Dream Play*, today hailed as one of the most remarkable dramas of the twentieth century, was a failure at the Royal Dramatic Theatre in Stockholm. And the pioneering chamber plays, first performed at Strindberg's own Intimate Theatre, were coldly received and often ridiculed by both critics and public.

Instead, it was the fairy-tale play *Lucky Peter's Journey*, now considered a minor work, that in the 1880s was the only one of Strindberg's dramas to be really successful. In the 1890s, nourished by the nationalistic spirit of that period, a few of his historical plays also succeeded on stage. And of the twenty-four Strindberg plays produced at his own Intimate Theatre between 1907 and 1910, the religious and lyrical *Easter* and the fairy-tale play *Swanwhite*, now rarely performed, were the ones with the longest runs. The examples of negative and positive reception say a great deal about how taste has changed since Strindberg's time. He suffered the fate of most pioneers: to be fully recognized only after his death.

It took a foreigner, the great Austrian director Max Reinhardt, to discover Strindberg's dramatic brilliance and to demonstrate it in performances both in Germany and in Sweden. His productions had resonance. For a few years shortly after World War I Strindberg was, after Shakespeare, the most frequently performed dramatist in Germany. It was also at this time that he, thanks to Eugene O'Neill and the Provincetown Players, was discovered in America.

Strindberg wrote many of his plays in a period dominated by realism or naturalism. When he had his breakthrough as a playwright, the theatre began to use a peepshow stage, where the actors were supposed to act as though there was no audience and as though the fourth wall supposedly facing them really existed; both conventions were intended to promote the idea that what took place on stage was *une tranche de vie*, a slice of real life. This was the key illusion offered to the voyeurs in the auditorium.

Strindberg's international reputation as a dramatist is usually linked to two enterprises. Before the Inferno crisis – so called after his novel *Inferno* based on his psychic upheaval in the mid-1890s – he was an eminent representative of illusionist drama, plays in which the protagonists are primarily in conflict with each other; *The Father* and *Miss Julie* belong to this period, which was closely connected with naturalism. After the Inferno crisis, he was an equally eminent representative of non-illusionist drama, plays in which the protagonists are more in conflict with themselves and with the supernatural than with each other; *To Damascus I, A Dream Play* and *The Ghost Sonata* are the most innovative plays in this period. The neat pattern is disturbed by the fact that *The Father* actually has much in common with the subjective dramas in the post-Inferno period, whereas conversely *The Dance of Death* has much in common with the plays of the pre-Inferno period.

Strindberg's priority was of course the writing of the plays, his indulgences at his writing desk. But naturally he also wished his works to be read and, especially, to be performed and in this sense seen. His comprehensive correspondence with theatre managers and directors testifies to this. The wish to be performed was in fact so strong that he would often willingly agree to cuts if this could help bring about a production.

Throughout his life, Strindberg remarked extensively on both drama and theatre. His autobiography, *The Son of a Servant* (1886-87), is an invaluable source of information, also with regard to his relationship to drama and theatre. It was finished, however, at such an early point in his life that the bulk of his dramatic oeuvre was still to be written.

As a commentator on drama, Strindberg is best known for his preface to *Miss Julie* (1888), his essay "On Modern Drama and Modern Theatre" (1889), his discussion of Ibsen's *Rosmersholm* in "Soul Murder" (1891), his "Author's Note" to *A Dream Play* (1902), and his five open letters to the Intimate Theatre (1908-09). He also expressed many of his thoughts on his own work and on productions of his plays in letters to publishers, translators, actors, and directors.

With regard to the letters, we have to take into account not only the situation in which they were written but also to whom they were addressed. In many cases Strindberg was dependent on the addressees to make his work visible. Functioning as his own agent, he had to 'sell' his play texts to all of them. This explains to a great extent his tendency to boost the drama at hand. The great amount of letters to a given person, such as his correspondence in 1907-08 to Emil Schering, his German translator, probably reflects his eagerness to promote himself outside of Sweden more than his need for a critical recipient and confidant.

Both *Miss Julie* and its preface were written when Strindberg had just become acquainted with Nietzsche's work. Inspired by Nietzsche's aristocratic ideas, Strindberg now began to distance himself from his earlier socialism and solidarity with the lower classes. As a result, the chief characters in the play – the plebeian Jean and the noble Julie – are, to some extent, kept in balance.

In the preface, written immediately after the play, obviously in the hope of increasing his chances of getting this daring text published and produced, Strindberg is anxious to demonstrate that his play is completely attuned to the prevailing mode of naturalism. To this end, he claims that the play serves to illustrate a law of nature. Transplanting Darwinian evolutionism from the realm of animals to the realm of human beings, he suggests that the enervated upper classes are doomed to be replaced by the more forceful lower ones.

In the preface, Strindberg also applies an evolutionary perspective when he assumes that a contemporary audience will experience Miss Julie as tragic, whereas a future, intellectually more advanced public will look upon her fate with indifference. Strindberg claims, in other words, that he has written a play especially aimed at the future. That the genre label of tragedy, which figures in the subtitle, will then become a misnomer does not seem to worry him.

Actually, the subtitle – "a naturalistic tragedy" – implies a contradiction, since naturalism presupposes that the protagonist is determined by forces of heredity and environment to act the way s/he does, whereas tragedy postulates free will. Strindberg tried to solve the problem at the end by letting Julie be hypnotized by Jean (naturalism) and then having her "*resolutely*," that is, fully awake (free will) walk out of the kitchen with the lethal instrument in her hand.

In a marked naturalistic effort Strindberg in *Miss Julie* replaces "simple stage characters" with "modern characters [-] vacillating, broken, a mixture of old and new, [-] conglomerates of past and present stages of culture." In the preface he offers no less than thirteen different reasons for Julie's succumbing to her intercourse with Jean, reasons that can easily be grouped to conform with Taine's famous triad heredity, environment and moment.

In the final, technical part of the preface Strindberg reveals, despite his limited experience of practical theatre, a marked sensitivity to vital performance questions. Here he clarifies how the one-act form is closely linked with the idea of uninterrupted emotional involvement in what is enacted. He shows that his choice of an asymmetrical setting enables the actors to be seen in semi-profile, that is, at an angle that allows contact both with the fellow actors (a naturalistic demand) and with the audience in order to visualize their mimicry (a theatrical demand).

Few nineteenth century naturalistic dramas are performed today. Thus the question may be posed: Have Strindberg's so-called naturalistic plays survived because or in spite of the fact that they are naturalistic? It has to be recognized that these plays do not agree with doctrinaire naturalism in all respects. *The Father*, Peter Szondi has said, "is an attempt to blend subjective and naturalist styles." In *Miss Julie* the sunrise at the end miraculously coincides with Kristin's departure for morning service, which logically should take place about eight hours later. And *Creditors* is much less rooted in a *visualized* environment than one expects from a naturalistic drama.

In his essay "Soul Murder," Strindberg sees Rebekka West in *Rosmersholm* as a demonic schemer who, much like Iago in *Othello*, sows the seed of doubt in Beate's mind about her husband's fidelity. This leads to Beate's suicide. Strindberg's interpretation throws an interesting light also on his own play *The Father*, where Laura commits psychic murder of her husband in a fashion akin to Rebekka's of Beate.

Strindberg, in his "On Modern Drama and Modern Theatre," notes that the naturalistic drama pays more attention to character description than to plot;

that the unities of time and place are observed; and that "when searching for the significant motif," the playwrights of this mode focus on

> life's two poles, life and death [-], the fight for the spouse, for the means of subsistence, for honor, all these struggles – with their battlefield cries of woe, wounded and dead – during which one heard a new philosophy of life conceived as a struggle blow its fertile winds from the south.
>
> These were tragedies such as had not been seen before. The young authors [-] seemed reluctant to impose their suffering on others more than was absolutely necessary. Therefore, they made the suffering as brief as possible, let the pain pour forth in one act, sometimes in a single scene.

Strindberg rejects "misconceived naturalism," comparing it to "photography which includes everything, even the speck of dust on the camera lens," and praises "the great naturalism" which "delights in the struggle between natural forces."

He sees the short one-act play, the *quart d'heure*, as the paradigmatic form for modern drama. Alternatively he regards "the fully executed one-act play" as "the formula of the drama to come." Using Musset's *proverbes* as a model one might, he declares, "by means of a table and two chairs [-] present the most powerful conflicts of life," and this by resorting to "the discoveries of modern psychology." Strindberg was at this time strongly influenced by the so-called psychology of suggestion. He was also extremely anxious to be staged in Paris, where Zola-esque naturalism was *en vogue*. But uncertain about his chances there, he was at the same time trying to establish his own Scandinavian Experimental Theatre.

The demand advocated by naturalism that the staged events should mirror reality is eminently fulfilled in most of Strindberg's one-act plays, where the unity of time and place are usually strictly adhered to, so much so that playing time sometimes matches scenic time (the time assumed to pass between the raising and the lowering of the curtain) this cannot occur in a play of more than one act.

With the one-act plays he wrote between 1888 and 1892, Strindberg created the basis for a subgenre that has proved exceedingly vital ever since. Diemut Schnetz has unequivocally stated that "since Strindberg's theoretical debut in 1889, the one-act must count as an independent genre." Not only have one-acts for various reasons – not the least economic – been relished by small theatre groups, but the appearance of new media – radio, television – has also meant an increased demand for short plays.

When, after many years abroad, Strindberg returned to Sweden in 1899 to settle there, he also returned to the genre he had cultivated in his youth: the historical drama. His early play *Master Olof* had been successfully revived and Strindberg could now expect his new historical plays to be treated with more insight than his early attempts in the genre. Moreover, historical drama was in fashion in Sweden in the 1890s. Strindberg's attitude to historical sources had hardly changed since 1872. He retained his habit of handling them very freely, picking his dramatic content from popular, anecdotal rather than scholarly history books. By the time of *Master Olof*, he had already taken the necessary liberties in telescoping time and space. Much impressed by Georg Brandes's essay on Hotspur, which stresses Shakespeare's use of minutiae, he had introduced characteristic details in depicting his *dramatis personae*. Like Shakespeare, he had juxtaposed tragic scenes with comic interludes and like him, he had striven to show his protagonist as both a public and private figure. Above all, he had adapted the historical play – once a popular traditional genre – to new moral, psychological and theatrical principles.

In his drama about royal figures, written after his return to Sweden, Strindberg did much the same. To him a theatre audience should feel that the past was also the present, that on stage 'then' always becomes 'now.' His new religious orientation made him stress the classical hubris-nemesis pattern in the protagonist's struggle with supernatural powers. The inclusion of interpretative acting directions in *Carl XII* and *Kristina*, was a technical novelty – presumably an attempt to strengthen his own position as a dramatist in relation to the director. With his cycle of historical plays about Swedish monarchs, Strindberg breathed new life into an old genre, and for mere scope we would have to go back to Shakespeare to find his counterpart in world drama.

The pilgrimage drama *To Damascus I* has been hailed as a milestone in the development of modern drama mostly for three interconnected reasons: (1) its very special circular composition – the protagonist must retrace his own steps and do penance for his earlier sins; (2) its subjective handling of the characters: the all-important protagonist is surrounded by what the Germans have called *Ausstrahlungen des Ichs* (radiations of the ego), which means that all of the other characters seem to be in part incarnations of the protagonist's psyche, especially of his guilt feelings; and (3) because the audience is made to share, also visually, the protagonist's highly subjective experience of reality.

When Strindberg, in the "Author's Note" preceding *A Dream Play*, called *To Damascus* "his former dream play," he pointed to what the two works have in common. But as the "Note" indicates, the structure of *To Damascus* with its all-dominant protagonist is much firmer than that of *A Dream Play* with its suffering collective – mankind – observed by a divine narrator. In the "Note" the author states that he "has tried to imitate the disconnected yet apparently logical form of a dream." In accordance with this statement, scholars have occasionally approached the play the way a psychoanalyst would a dream. Such an approach may seem corroborated by Strindberg's sequel to his "Note" where he states that the disconnected form of the play is "merely apparent" and that "on closer inspection" the form is "rather firm." For do we not here deal with the discrepancy between latent and manifest dream content?

However, as especially the sequel to the "Note" makes clear, it is not the dream as such that is important. It is the dream as metaphor. For what *A Dream Play* is meant to express is the feeling that life is a dream, a feeling Strindberg often voiced in his post-Inferno period. In order to give an audience this feeling the dream metaphor was needed. The seeming incoherence of the play mentioned in the "Note" mirrors our feeling of life's seeming incoherence. When the play structure on closer inspection appears to be rather firm, it corresponds to the meaningfully structured universe we may sense in happy moments, but which we can only trustfully ascribe to a benevolent Creator.

Being part of a dream, "the characters split, double, multiply, evaporate, condense, disperse, and converge" – as they might, not on the stage but in a film, the new medium that had arrived just a few years before *A Dream Play* was written. This oft-quoted passage has been of great importance for the later development of both drama and theatre. In fact, few statements in modern drama theory have been as seminal as this one.

In 1906, Strindberg met the young actor and theatre manager August Falck. Together they began to plan what Strindberg first called "a *Kleines* in Stockholm." The German word is telling. In the period 1902-04, Max Reinhardt had been the leader of the Kleines Theater in Berlin where he, influenced by its preface, had successfully produced *Miss Julie*. In June 1906, his Kammerspiel-Haus opened in the same city, a theatre which, Strindberg writes, "by its name indicates its secret program: the concept of chamber music transferred to drama. The intimate procedure, the significant motif, the careful treatment." The concept of chamber play had by that time, not least via Strindberg, come to mean a play which, by employing a limited number of characters and adhering to the three unities, would be suitable for production in an intimate theatre. Described in such general terms, the label would fit most of Strindberg's short plays. When, in 1908, he tried to clarify what he meant by the term chamber play, Strindberg alternately spoke of the drama form and the manner of presentation. About the former he notes that the dramatist must seek "the strong, significant motif, but with limitations." This is still in agreement with the ideas Strindberg held in the 1880s. But he then adds:" No predetermined form is to limit the author, for the motif determines the form. Consequently, freedom in the treatment, constrained only by the unity of the conception and the artistic sense." This is something new. It opens for a thematic drama structure based on musical principles of composition. (The chamber plays characteristically carry opus numbers.) As the Old Man in *The Ghost Sonata* puts it: "although the tales differ, they hang together on a thread, and the leitmotif constantly recurs."

*The Ghost Sonata*, the most innovative of the chamber plays, has had a strong impact on drama, whether we think of the play's 'musical' structure, that is, its intricate interweaving of thematic strands; its symbolically expansive plot; its archetypal use of the different stages in life; its employment of visionary and metaphoric characters; or its use of a subjective observer, via whom we experience and see characters and events unveiled and whose gradual disillusionment we are invited to share.

When Strindberg and Falck began to plan what on November 26, 1907 was to open in Stockholm as the Intimate Theatre, the idea was that "alternating with Strindberg's own plays, the most prominent foreign as well as young Swedish literary dramatists should be staged" there. It did not turn out that way. Out of the twenty-five plays staged, twenty-four were by Strindberg. When Falck, in September 1910, departed from the hitherto followed principle by producing Maurice Maeterlinck's *L'Intruse*, Strindberg was upset. He had a very high opinion of Maeterlinck – this may well have influenced Falck's choice – but well aware that several of his own plays had still not been performed, he felt bypassed for an admired contemporary and disregarded by his co-founder of the Intimate Theatre. As so often happened with Strindberg, the friendship came to a sudden end. In a series of newspaper articles, he now severely criticized his former theatrical partner.

In the first of these, he claims that Falck had wished to name the theatre after him, Strindberg, but that Strindberg had forbidden him to do so. This sounds credible. The twenty-five-year-old Falck was a great admirer of Strindberg. Naming the theatre after him would have also put his partner, Falck, in the limelight. On the other hand, Strindberg may well have colored his version in order to appear agreeably unpretentious. Whatever the truth may be, it is evident that Strindberg would earlier not have refrained from baptizing a planned theatre with his own name. In 1891, he expressed his desire for a Strindberg *Bühne* and when in 1893 he dreamt of opening a theatre in Berlin, he self-assuredly declared: "It will be called the Strindberg Theatre." A year later, he remarked that in this theatre "only Strindberg will be played."

A Strindberg theatre was precisely what the Intimate Theatre was, if not in name. Herein lies perhaps its greatest originality. As an experimental theatre it had several predecessors. In the wake of André Antoine's Théâtre Libre in Paris (1887), a number of more or less experimental small theatres had begun to spring up in Europe. Strindberg himself a year later had considered "founding a Théâtre Libre in miniature." But except for his own exceedingly short-lived Scandinavian Experimental Theatre (1889), none of these other theatres had limited themselves to one author.

It is often said that practical theatre experience vastly enhances a dramatist's ability to write good plays. And it has been suggested that the stage successes of Shakespeare, Molière, Goethe and Ibsen would not have been possible had the authors not had first-hand experience of theatre production.

If this is true, Strindberg presents a disturbing case because his practical experience of the stage was very limited until he got his own Intimate Theatre. Lamm points out that even the chamber plays, the most remarkable part of his dramatic work in later years, were written *before* the establishment of the Intimate Theatre, and even before Strindberg knew what it was going to be like. In view of this, it seems sensible to argue, with Lamm, that Strindberg's limited experience of the stage, rather than a shortcoming, may well have been an asset. It was precisely because he was not tied down to the practical restrictions of the living theatre that he could be innovative. Much of what could not be realized in the theatre of his time, could later, thanks to technical developments, be transformed into scenic reality. And we cannot claim that the establishment of the Intimate Theatre meant a new impetus for the creation of significant drama on Strindberg's part. The few plays he wrote at the very end of his life are neither very significant nor very theatrical. The best of them, *The Great Highway*, borders on closet drama. There are certainly reasons for this. His involvement in the so-called Strindberg feud 1910–11, followed by his eventually fatal illness, provided little time for playwriting. It nevertheless confirms the general impression that whether or not he had a theatre at his disposal, inspiration occurred at his writing desk. As Strindberg said in an interview at the end of his life in response to the question of why he had chosen to make his debut as a dramatist:

> I found it easiest to write plays. People and events took shape, wove themselves together. And I derived such pleasure from this work that I found life a

sheer delight while the writing continued, and do so still. Only then do I feel alive!

Strindberg was never a frequent theatre goer and became even less so with time. This fact has been ascribed to his unwillingness to appear in public, an unwillingness that would grow as his fame increased. However, in view of the conventionality and superficiality of the theatre in Sweden at the time – Strindberg's chapter entitled "A National Educational Establishment" in *The New Kingdom* (1882) satirizes this – one can easily understand his lack of interest in contemporary Swedish stage productions. But also during his twelve-year stay abroad, where he could be more anonymous than in Stockholm and where the repertory was more varied, he rarely went to the theatre, not even in Paris, the world's theatrical capital at the time. His often documented shyness may certainly be one reason; theatre historian Gösta M. Bergman in fact stresses this aspect. Another reason is hinted at in *Memorandum to the Members of the Intimate Theatre* where Strindberg declares:

> I have never seen Goethe's *Faust* (Part II), Schiller's *Don Carlos*, or Shakespeare's *The Tempest* performed, but I have seen them all the same when I have read them, and there are good plays that should not be performed, that cannot bear to be seen. But there are poor plays that must be played in order to live; they have to be filled out, ennobled, by the art of acting.

The above idea does not rhyme well with Strindberg's conviction that his own plays lend themselves more to be seen than to be read, and seems a discouraging message to the young theatre group that was now performing his plays. But his 'slip of the tongue' certainly reveals his own preference for the theatre of the mind to the physical theatre. With regard to his own plays, he had told Falck a year earlier, after having witnessed a rehearsal at the Intimate Theatre, that "the writer cannot bear to see his fantasies transformed into reality, for they do not correspond. The same goes to an even greater extent for the acting." In line with this, Strindberg, unlike many other playwrights, rarely shaped his characters with regard to particular actors and actresses. The exceptions are the roles intended for his wives Siri von Essen and Harriet Bosse.

As Hans Lindström's inventory lists of Strindberg's libraries, book loans, and literary references clearly demonstrate, his interest in the theory of drama and theatre was for a long time very modest. Neither the preface to *Miss Julie* nor the essay "On Modern Drama and Modern Theatre" reveal any great familiarity with these fields. An avid reader, his interest reached out in all directions but even in the late *Blue Books,* where much space is devoted to philosophy, psychology, religion, philology, botany, astronomy, chemistry and occultism, the references to art and aesthetics are exceedingly few.

When focusing on Strindberg's concern for drama and theatre, we may note that while he often refers to Aristotle, it is not to his *Poetics,* often considered the most important text on the art of drama ever written. In his youth, he says in his autobiography, he learned "from Schiller [-] about the deep significance of the theatre; from Goethe [-] how one should walk and stand, move, sit down, enter and exit; in Lessing's *Hamburgische Dramaturgie* he read a whole volume of theatre reviews full of the finest perceptions." He even translated Schiller's *Die Schaubühne als eine moralische Anstalt betrachtet* into Swedish and had it published in 1869.

In his *Open Letters to the Intimate Theatre* (1909) Strindberg notes:

> There is a whole literature about the revival of the theatre, and from it I want to single out Gordon Craig's attractive periodical *The Mask* first of all. Craig has some peculiar ideas about the theatre. He wants to have everything presented through the eye, so that the text is to be subordinated. He paints costumes and stylizes them, works with lighting effects and even with masks.
>
> Georg Fuchs has published *Die Schaubühne der Zukunft* [-]. He is strongest in what he says negatively and can therefore be read, but his positive proposals are vague. His stage is very small, lacks depth, since he finds perspective unreasonable, etc. He seems to want to return to antiquity, and to believe that the theatre is not to be permanent but is to do only festival plays on exceptional occasions.
>
> One can read a lot about theatre, too, in *Die Fackel,* published by Karl Krause in Vienna.

Craig's strong emphasis on the visual elements of a performance could not appeal to Strindberg who, for all his interest in these elements, always gave precedence to the spoken word. Despite the critical remarks above, Strindberg took great interest in Fuchs's book. The description there of the so-called Shakespeare stage at the Court Theatre in Munich, which enabled swift changes of scenery, had a direct impact on Emil Grandinson's successful production of *To Damascus I* in 1900; a plan to use sciopticon projections for the backdrops, a true novelty in the theatre, met with insurmountable lighting problems and had to be relinquished. The simplified settings on the Intimate Theatre's very small stage also owed a great deal to the Munich Shakespeare *Bühne*. And Fuchs's description of refined and *sotto voce* Japanese acting may well have inspired Strindberg's ideas in this area.

The rise of the Intimate Theatre meant that Strindberg's strong wish to have his work performed could at last be satisfied. For the aging dramatist, it must have been stimulating to come into contact with young people, as eager to perform as he wished to be performed. Strindberg now had the possibility of observing a theatrical event close at hand. In a stream of memoranda he expressed his desiderata with regard to virtually every aspect that concerned the Intimate Theatre and the productions there. Some of these recall the preface to *Miss Julie* and are in line with the naturalistic demand for a concentrated and uninterrupted viewing. Others are new, as when he suggests the exclusion of Sunday matinées, indicating his post-Inferno attitude toward Christianity, or when he expresses the wish that the text of a performed drama be available to the audience, a wish that reveals once more his eagerness to emphasize the importance of the author's contribution to the performance.

In his youth, Strindberg was for a short period of time an occasional theatre critic, but later he had no good words for members of this profession. In his essay on *Julius Caesar*, he points out that critics are often chosen on dubious grounds and are therefore often incompetent. He mocks their presumption to consider themselves, after a couple of hours in the theatre, better qualified to judge a performance than the author who knows the text thoroughly and the team that has spent weeks on its production. But above all, and contrary to his argument in the preface to *Miss Julie*, he questions the reviewers' cool, rational reception of what is presented. Unlike the average – and desirable – spectator, the critics do not allow themselves to be deluded and get emotionally involved. For Strindberg, these so-called experts did not represent the audience.

With the establishment of the Intimate Theatre, Strindberg saw more possibilities of influencing the productions of his plays than ever before. He was a director, it is true, only in name and he only attended the dress rehearsals. He would then sit alone in the auditorium and afterwards not say a word to the ensemble. A day or so later, however, he would send some of them short notes based on his impressions, with suggestions, praise and blame.

Though he rarely attended rehearsals, he was eager to have a say about both the repertoire and the casting. He took a very active interest in the shapes and colors of the scenery on the diminutive stage (6 x 4 meters), as well as the properties and costumes. He frequently advised his eleven young actors and actresses about their acting style and their diction.

Strindberg, in an article on the Odéon Theatre, had already by 1876 touched upon Diderot's much-debated *Paradox of Acting*, when asking himself "whether or not an actor should give up his personality completely and 'creep' into his role, so that he himself disappears." Strindberg responded: "We do not believe [-] that he can do the former if he has a distinct individuality. The art of letting oneself disappear is best known in the secondary theatres, where types called characters, are made; it is easier to turn invisible, if you are small." Strindberg here is leaning in the direction of Diderot. The reasoning is this: To be a talented actor you need to have a strong personality, and a strong personality neither can nor should be completely repressed. Later, when confronted with naturalism, he would take an attitude much more in agreement with what we have come to associate with Stanislavsky's pleading for the actor's total identification with his role. Even as late as his *Memorandum*, Strindberg retains this naturalistic view when he writes that "the artist falls into a trance, forgets himself, and finally *becomes* the person he is going to play."

Much of what inspired the young talented amateurs and their leaders at the Intimate Theatre later came true. The rejection of the star system, so dominant around the turn of the twentieth century, in favor of ensemble acting was a pioneering accomplishment in Sweden. The demand for a simplified scenography, partly motivated by the Intimate Theatre's limited resources, was very much in line with the general development away from the illusionist clutter of what Strindberg termed "misconceived naturalism." And when Falck writes that "the Intimate Theatre was to be the home of the art of intimation, was to open perspectives for the imagination and make the spectator cooperative in the dramatic process," these ambitions were clearly in tune with what later became a *sine qua non* for serious theatre.

Some of Strindberg's comments on theatre clearly reflect the ideological and aesthetic climate of his time and therefore now seem dated, as when he, much in the spirit of Goethe, calls for beauty in the way the actors should sit and move on stage. Similarly, beyond his remark that actors should speak slowly and clearly so that they can be heard and understood, we sense the influence of the symbolist acting style – as well as the playwright's eagerness to have the spoken word, *his* word, reach the audience. But much of what he had to say about drama and theatre – these closely knit art forms – is still both relevant and thought-provoking. And, as is characteristic of Strindberg, it is written with such verve that you cannot help but be affected.

# Strindberg
# on Drama and Theatre

# 1870-1880

To Johan Oscar Strindberg (1843-1905), S's cousin. A successful businessman, he was artistically inclined and paid for the publication of S's *The Freethinker* and *Hermione*.

> Uppsala, April 1, 1870. [-] I'm still on the third act of "Erik";[1] the first scene is set here in the Castle park with the Castle in the background. The reason I've taken a week off is the following: While in Stockholm I started, as you know, a one-act comedy, *In Rome*, which was never finished. One day I read it to a friend. He became enthusiastic and urged me to complete it. I set about to do so, rewrote it entirely, and now it's finished, in 600 *rhyming* verses [-].

To Frans Hedberg (1828–1908), actor, translator, prolific and successful dramatist. He was S's teacher during S's brief training period as an actor at the Royal Theatre in Stockholm.

> Uppsala, October 13, 1870.[2] [-] At present I am working on a five-act tragedy, "Sven the Sacrificer," perhaps the greatest subject in the whole of Swedish history. If nothing comes of it, it will at least be a study! However, I am giving myself heart and soul to my subject. Among other things, I am doing some preparatory reading in Icelandic, and every day I discover new lodes of ore in its literature. My model is Oehlenschläger.[3] I shall finish Act II tomorrow. [-]
> *Hermione* is now in the hands of eighteen wise men.[4] God be with her! [-]

To August Dörum (1841–80), actor. He is best known for his roles in Swedish historical dramas, for example as Orm in *The Outlaw*.

> Uppsala, September, 1871.[5] [-] You know I believe in you and you'll be great [-] but don't be angry if I say this: Don't overact! Understand me. Your spectator is [-] entertained by hints. This is how it works: If you make a slight gesture, a mere nuance of a facial expression, he'll understand it well enough [-]. Thus his vanity is flattered and he has a good time. The pleasure is often denied him when an actor either delivers a pointed aside with such emphasis

that it comes over as "look at this, you devils, and see what I mean!" or else is afraid his gesture will be misunderstood and makes it so grand it becomes unsightly. [-]


Review of *The Kings of Salamis*,[6] *Dagens Nyheter*, February 14, 1874.

In earlier times, the acting profession was an art with its own technique and theory, which the initiated conveyed to the uninitiated. Nowadays, it doesn't seem difficult at all to become an actor as long as you have a strong enough urge or, as it is called, talent and don't mind remaining more or less idle for a number of years without learning anything new except what you might happen to pick up from older people. What used to be required from an actor was first and foremost a good figure, an outward appearance that was not disturbing to the spectators, whose demands were quite within their rights, since they had come in order to enjoy the creations of a *beautiful* art. Furthermore, a well-modulated voice and the ability to move gracefully were basic requirements. A person equipped with such talents was instructed in dance, fencing, gymnastics, the plastic arts, recitation etc., and was molded into beautiful material capable of representing the images that the dramatist had in mind or that historical tradition had transmitted through illustrative personages. In those days, it was considered ugly to cross the stage other than diagonally, so that your face was concealed as little as possible; in those days it was thought ugly to place your hand right on your chest with the fingers spread out; in those days you weren't supposed to put your hands in your trouser pockets, and when you sat down on a chair, you did not part your legs nor did you, in order to push the chair closer to the person speaking, grab the seat with your hand exactly where it was not proper to do so; you were trained to walk on the full sole of your foot and not on the heels; through exercise you strove to walk with a straight back and, through "plasticity," to move your arms in curved lines; you could not fight with a saber when you were furnished with a rapier; [-] and the instructor was petty enough to observe the actors' pronunciation of foreign words during rehearsal, so that everybody pronounced the same word correctly – or incorrectly, etc. Studies in the creations of the fine arts led to the establishment of rules to express specific emotions (see Goethe, Lessing et al.).

All of this is deemed unnecessary nowadays and that is a shame. [-]


STRINDBERG ON DRAMA AND THEATRE

"At the Odéon Theatre," *Dagens Nyheter,* February 14, 1876.

*Les Danicheff* [7] was going to be performed for the 199th time. That a dramatic piece has been performed so many times is not very common, even in Paris. The reason for *The Danicheff Family's* success can probably be attributed to its novel idea, its novel costuming, and its novel location. The plot is simple and it is still said that in Dumas's hands the piece has taken on a free and easy form. [-]

The Odéon, situated in the Quartier Latin, was earlier regarded as belonging to the students; nowadays it is a kind of annex to the Théâtre Français, which often recruits actors from there.

What first appeals to the stranger [-] is the existence of a simple and beautiful lobby for the audience. The absence of music between the acts could have had a calming effect, were it not for the strident hawking of advertising handouts that serves as an unpleasant surrogate. That gentlemen keep their hats on in the auditorium seems odd.

The audience is not striking; you don't go to the Odéon to show off; there are other places for that. Three thumps on the floor and the curtain goes up.

[-] When looking at the actors' movements on stage, your initial feeling is that you are being totally ignored as a spectator. No glances come your way. No lines are directed at you. [-] The actors don't walk down to the footlights to hold a conversation, so that the audience may hear in what a clever way they can transmit the author's well thought-out questions and answers. In other words, they don't cover up the unnatural discrepancies in time and space that the author is guilty of. [-] They are not even afraid of turning their backs on the audience if necessary. When not expressing an agitated state of mind, they speak with an ordinary low voice but without losing a single syllable. The effect of these simple and natural means is more or less to interrupt but not ignore all communication with the audience. You feel like an eavesdropper. It's like spying through a keyhole – only there is no wall. [-]

In times past, there existed an art form that Lessing gave the Greek name [-] of that aspect of dramatic art that uses the hands to express what the vocal organ cannot . This art form is not much practiced in the North, yet there too it has its natural model. Just observe someone talking or telling a story; his hands are not at rest. This is what a French actor has observed and later studied and turned into a method. He enters, he puts away his cane, fiddles with his hat until the moment has come when he must be empty-handed. He fingers his watch chain, he moves a book, touches a chair, takes out his handkerchief – not to use it – twirls his moustache, though reluctantly, adjusts his scarf if absolutely necessary, crosses his arms, puts them behind his back, folds his hands, wipes his glasses if he has any, pats his interlocutor on the shoulder, offers to shake his hand, etc. But note carefully, all in its place and never the same thing twice and never without a purpose. And when he says something, he does so vividly, as if the noted situation were taking place right then. You see the drawing pen or the brush in his hand. He takes great pains to utilize all of the available means to make clear to the spectators what he wants to portray. The method is good but it has its risks, for if exaggerated it can easily become unnatural. [-]

When the play was over and we tried to make clear to ourselves what we had absorbed from our theatre visit that evening and made comparisons between the actual performers and those we could imagine assuming the same parts back home, we felt very clearly that our foremost dramatic stage[8] ranks very high. [-]

What had at first dazzled us– the seemingly unaffected style of performance and the unrivalled ensemble acting, rested on a shortcoming, the absence of what we call character. Everyone spoke in the same excellent way. Everyone hit the same sonorous tone of voice at similar emotional states. All the young men were alike. Not fully grown, with straight black hair and small black moustaches, they wore their fine clothes in excellent fashion. No one stood out above the rest. The ladies were the same: brilliant, tasteful costumes, elegant manners, but unlikable, lacking in character, typical. Underneath their masks, they all seemed to have lost their personalities, if they ever had any. For personality is a purely Germanic word, which is missing in the Romance languages because there is no equivalent in reality. What then is this personality that people so often toss around and which is said to be so excellent? Ah well, it is simply what makes one person different from another. It is an original quality which one has had the courage to hold on to despite all of society's attempts to wear it down. This courage might exist more often in smaller countries where the danger of losing it is less.

Here we encounter a question that so far has not been answered and that we don't think can be answered except in the Gordian way. For we have been wondering – *that* is perhaps the word – whether or not an actor should give up his personality completely and 'creep into' his role, so that he himself disappears. We simply do not believe that he can do that if he has a distinct individuality. [-]

STRINDBERG ON DRAMA AND THEATRE

# 1881-1889

To Ludvig Josephson (1832–99), actor and director. He took over the New Theatre in Stockholm in 1879, where the prose version of *Master Olof* had its successful premiere in 1881. The year after, he directed *Sir Bengt's Wife*, with Siri von Essen in the title role, and in 1883, the extremely popular *Lucky Peter's Journey*.

Stockholm, January 28, 1881. [-] In case you are still thinking of putting on my play *Master Olof*, I am enclosing the first manuscript [-] as it was written in 1872, and as it was then refused by the Royal Theatre.[9]

It is poor, I think, [-] but in this prose version there are crowd scenes which ought to work splendidly on the stage, especially if *you* were to take charge of them. [-]

Naturally, I cannot share the opinion of those who wish to turn it into a closet drama. It is written for the stage, and with cuts and additions it can, I believe, become a theatre piece. [-]


To Ludvig Josephson.

January 17, 1882. [-] Having carefully pondered the idea of restructuring *Lucky Peter*, and having paid close attention to the changes you suggest, I've arrived at the following scheme, which I'd like you to examine carefully before I do anything, since nothing ruins a play more than too much tinkering with it, witness *Master Olof*. [-]

Peter has gone out into the world and tried the best life has to offer – riches, friendship, honor, power – and found them all empty and hollow. Now he's in the Caliph's palace cursing humanity and wishing he was in the midst of nature, which is said to heal all wounds. He curses society.

Change of scene. He is lying on the seashore; awakens, becomes enraptured; waxes lyrical, gathers oysters, eats birds' eggs, catches a turtle, drinks water from a crevice in the rocks. Everything is fine, but there's a biting wind and he starts to feel cold. There's no fire. For that's something man has conquered and not part of nature. This reveals the inadequacy of nature and his Rousseauist-Robinsonian ideas are shattered. He recognizes the necessity of society, but after his recent experiences, he still hates it. The cold increases and he grows desperate. He doesn't dare to wish for anything else. Then he sees a yacht out to sea, tacking before the wind (which is thus coming straight from the auditorium), but each pass is so long that it disappears into the wings every time, where it is supposed to turn. Whenever it emerges, it gets bigger and is tacking in the other direction. Finally it arrives, strikes sail and Lisa steps ashore:

Dialogue. His discontentment with life. Lisa encourages him to see the true dark side of it: poverty, humiliation, toil, etc. He decides to become a shoemaker's apprentice! [-]

*The Shoemaker's Workshop.* [-] In the workshop he is treated in such a way that he loses all his notions of democracy and improvement of humanity, is spiritually quite bankrupt and wants to become a hermit. [-]

I think I could bring off the shoemaker's workshop *con amore* and let him get a proper drubbing as a pendant to the Caliph scene. [-]

What do you say to bells chiming in the tower in Act I? Scrape together any kind of bell from people we know, arrange them in a scale, and then play fifths on them in a slow tempo, anything you like, always assuming the New Theatre doesn't have its own chimes.

In the forest scene in Act II, couldn't there be a ballet of snowflakes, which are transformed into flowers at the scene change?

At the Caliph's the dancers can dance and then get a scolding.

Couldn't there also be some table music at the Rich Man's?

Why not have an automatic organ in the church during the last act? [-]

As for the lack of motivation where Peter's sharp-sightedness and worldly wisdom is concerned, I think that if you read it through again, you will find it is precisely his naiveté and his sound, uncorrupted commonsense that makes him notice what is wrong with the world, and which (as in Voltaire's *Candide*) tones down the satire. I'm not inflexible, and would like to meet you halfway. However, on this point I've tried the idea of the magic glasses and rejected it. I also think it would prove a mistake to make him more gifted than other people! For – and there is a psychological trap here – if he was more gifted, he would naturally see things for what they really are, that is, see their worth and therefore not *be able* to become a pessimist. As it is, his ordinary, youthful commonsense leads him to draw too hasty and narrow conclusions, which can then be corrected. [-]

"On Realism: Some Views," *Ur dagens krönika*, no. 2.

May 1882. [-] Realism is the name of that movement in all artistic fields where the practitioner seeks to convey his intended impression, that is, give an illusion of reality by executing the most important details among all those that make up an image.

Authors of a previous era could impress by making general suggestions, since their generation of spectators had been educated by minds who were receptive to such matters. The new generation, raised by the exact sciences – the natural sciences and mathematics – gains no impression from the general suggestions by earlier generations. This is a characteristic of the young and not a fault. [-]

To work from a model has always been considered highly commendable in all branches of art, since it has helped achieve the intended purpose, that is, to imitate reality by way of art. [-]

This is not permissible in the literature of our time since there is an immediate danger, especially in small communities, that the model may be recognized and that the author's characters, intended as types, become real persons who add a new unpleasant and not intended interest to his work. [-]

The world's greatest authors have been realists. [-]

We who are young were raised by parents born in an era that respected faith and honor. Then we were led into a new era that worshipped success at any cost. We experienced the new age of hoax and now live in the midst of an epoch that has gotten its name from America, the age of humbug.

Then we lost faith in success based on merit. Virtue was no merit, honesty was less than pragmatism, honor was beautiful but ridiculous. Our master idealists had betrayed us, therefore we abandoned them. [-]

The realists have been accused of primarily seeking out the ugly. It is true that we who have been raised on French comedy in our national court theatre have gained the impression that people are not presentable unless they have twenty thousand francs in interest income and that poverty is tantamount to lacking such income. We have lost faith in the social ideals of low-cut starched shirts and six yards of train. These things have taught us to despise the kind of beauty that exists at the expense of others.

It is these other people in their poor clothes that we dare love and in part pity, at times admire, even at the feared risk of not being counted as people of good standing.

Our realists have been accused of being something even worse: naturalists.

That is an honorary title to us! We love what is natural, we turn away in disgust from the new social conditions, from the police state, from the military state that claims to defend the nation but only protects those in power. Since we hate what is artificial and affected, we love to mention each thing by its true name and we believe that societies will collapse unless honesty, the first contract on which societies rest, is restored.

[-] We realists still adhere to the old belief that the purpose of literature, as well as theatre, "both at first and now, was and is to hold, as 't were, the mirror up to nature, to show virtue her own feature, scorn her own image, and the very age and body of the time his form and pressure."[10]

The realists have also been reproached for favoring a question that the idealists consider unimportant: the relationship between the sexes.

It is true that this question is favored by those who realize that this relationship constitutes one of the most important factors in human life, a relationship that is currently being investigated and the position of the involved parties clarified. The realists, however, go to the bottom with this matter, take it seriously and find the question too important to let it be treated as a joke. [-]


"A National Educational Establishment" in *The New Kingdom*, September 1882.

Spring-Summer 1882. [-] During a discussion about theatre subsidies, member of the *Riksdag*[11] Håkan Olsson [-]had his eyes opened to a national cultural institution named the Royal Theatre,[12] which was the pride and delight of all Stockholmers. According to some gentlemen, it was the best and least expensive institution for obtaining national culture and its effects were immeasurable. Besides, it would be a disgrace if the nation did not pay the theatre's annual debts.

It is true that Mr. Olsson had visited many other theatres and found both pleasure and edification there, but he had never actually felt culturally educated. [-]

So he bought tickets to the small national theatre and waited with anxious excitement for national culture to strike him and his family, turning them into enlightened patriots.

*Monsieur Jean,* a comedy in three acts, translated from the French by Cassacko, a pseudonym of the Counsel of Taste, is offered. The curtain rises on an endless Brussels carpet occupied by settees and a stove with an ornamental clock.[13]

The chambermaid enters in a silk dress, looks at a rose-colored visitor's card and says something inaudible. Mr. Anatole enters through another door and kisses her on the shoulder. Mr. Anatole is decked out with a walking cane with a golden knob, pince-nez and a cigarette maker,[14] plus an enormous watch chain. His shirt is low-cut "all the way down to the collarbones," as Håkan Olsson put it when he returned home. Anatole rolls a cigarette and says something to the chambermaid.

Then the Marquise enters, motions to the chambermaid who immediately takes the hint and leaves. The two are alone.

- Sir!

- Madame!

Anatole puts away his cigarette maker and grabs his cane.

- What gives me the honor of such an early visit?

Anatole beats his trousers with his cane.

- To tell you the truth, Madame, I don't know what entitles you to ask such a question.

- Your absence would entitle you to ask me why your presence does not entitle me to ask you!

("What a dialogue! Charming!" Weak applause.)

Anatole walks diagonally across the Brussels carpet, puts on his pince-nez, beats a sofa with his cane and says with his back turned to the M:

- Because I love you!

The Marquise turns her back to him, swirling the train of her dress around her feet. Then she turns her head while her body remains still, twisting her neck until her chin is directly above her spine and says with a sphinx-like smile:

- The weather is beautiful today.

Anatole bursts into convulsive laughter and brings out his cigarette maker again. The Marquise wraps the train around her arm and exits. Stopping in the middle of the carpet, she opens her mouth as if intending to say something, but says nothing and exits.

A roar of applause beckons her to soon re-enter to receive the audience's ovation. The Count, who has been standing behind the door to make his first entrance of the fall season, [-] is foaming with rage. He waits for a moment to air out the applause for the Marquise, also letting Anatole stand there, desperate. When there is dead silence and a faint whisper – "Now he is coming." – is heard, the Count enters slowly, casually, indifferently. [-]

He is greeted by thunderous applause; but at first he does not hear it, his eyes staring into empty space. Finally he wakes up, looks around with surprise: "What does this mean?" He had not expected anything like this. A faint smile of recognition hovers on his pale lips, he is moved, goes down to the prompt box and bows, his hand on his heart.

The noise subsides and Anatole who has suffered the torments of hell in trying in vain to interrupt the applause now parries with a line:

- Jean, decent old fellow! Is it really you? What good fortune has brought us together!

Jean, deeply moved, embraces Anatole and calls him his old chap. Anatole, noting his unhappy mien asks him to sit down to tell him why.

Jean sinks down to his shoulders in an armchair. Anatole offers him a cigarette, which he declines politely, whereupon he begins to tell his story. Håkan Olsson dozes off and wakes up just in time to hear the end of the story. Jean is ruined; all he has left is 6000 francs in interest income and no longer knows how he can go on living, now that he has been deprived of all his illusions.

Anatole encourages him to seek a ministerial post[15] in Naples, but Jean is too proud to work.

- So now you are going to shoot yourself, says Anatole.

- I would consider it my holy duty to the family whose name I have the honor to bear but I can no longer go through with it, for ... I ... am in love. (*He gets up and stands by the stove.*)

- You are in love? And with whom?

- The Marquise de Carambole.

- The Marquise de Carambole!

Anatole leaps up and paces the carpet in his shining leather boots. Jean lets his head sink down between his collarbones, lifts his left front foot, beats lightly on the carpet and whispers a barely audible:

- Ah well.

Noticing Anatole's emotional state, he slowly raises his head again on his shoulders, rolls his eyes toward both front boxes[16] and exclaims:

- What's the matter with you! You're so agitated.

- Nothing! Nothing! An attack of dizziness! It will soon pass!

Jean runs forward, grasps Anatole by the shoulders, looks him straight in the eyes and cries out:

- You love the Marquise!

Anatole wriggles out of his arms, collects his cigarette maker, cane and hat, prepares to leap out the doorway and cries out:

- I love her!

But Jean, who suspects a nasty trick and wants to forestall Anatole's applaud-ed exit, falls down backwards onto the carpet, hitting his head against a bol-stered piece of furniture.

The curtain comes down. Jean is called in and gets a bouquet of flowers, but Anatole does not dare re-enter. [-]

At du Nord, a small but stunning supper had been arranged, and Jean and Anatole played hosts. Håkan Olsson, who had honestly paid for his ticket, did not understand that actors on the national stage were to be thanked for their performances. This did not seem to affect their mood, however, for they were in unusually lively spirits. Jean went up to Olsson at once and embraced him.

- Well, were you pleased with us this evening, sir? [-]

- Yes, I was very pleased with my evening and I now realize there is a thing or two to be learned from a show like this that I didn't know before.

- Well, now! You realize then, sir, that it is a cultivating pleasure?

- Yes, I must say I've never felt so cultivated as tonight, and this national theatre event is indeed a blessing. [-]

- What was his name, asked Håkan Olsson, the fellow who pushed the la-dy onto the sofa?

Anatole was astonished.

- I'm the one who played Anatole, he said offended.

- Oh, were you the actor? You really pulled out the stops.

- Didn't you have a program, sir, asked Jean.

- No, you see I never use a program. I go to the theatre to watch the play and not to look at the actors' names.

- Not at those of the actresses either? Anatole added acidly.

- No, not at them either. I always prefer to think who they are  and not what they represent.

- Idiot! Jean whispered, and Anatole agreed.

After supper Jean gave a brilliant speech full of Gustav III's dramatic cre-ations, his shrines, plundering and scandals. Håkan Olsson responded: [-] Gentlemen, the theatre is a cultural institution. It is a rather dangerous weapon and, therefore, it shouldn't be left in the hands of uncultured people. Consequently, the state should handle the matter and carefully oversee that the weapon is not turned against the government. [-]

"Pantomimes from the Street," *Julkvällen*, 1883.

> If he lies around for a long time in the window recess, letting his eyes get used to watching the small figures in close-up, he will see the motif enlarged, as one always does when seeing things from above rather than standing in their midst, watching the whole thing in broad outline and being able to distinguish a trace of independent life within these illusory puppets. He will be able to see little scenes, quickly enacted, the way an impressionist's eye grasps a momentary situation. He will see people in situations when they are honest because they believe themselves to be unseen. Without having to make himself guilty of the ugly flaw of eavesdropping, for he cannot hear a word they are saying, he will see them reveal themselves in the honest language of gesture, which cannot hide the thoughts as well as can the spoken word and the deceptive eye. What he sees are splendid pantomimes and the pantomime [-] will no doubt soon become a modern form for part of dramatic art.

To Ludvig Josephson.

> Christmas Eve, 1883. [-] If this piece[17] is not a success, then I dare not write a play for many years. If it is a success, then I will come up with contemporary comedies in a jiffy. [-]

To Edvard Brandes.

> December 29, 1885. [-] Help me for Christ's sake, otherwise I shall have to sit down and write plays again, which I hate and hence will do badly! [-]

*The Son of a Servant II*,[18] September 1886.

> May 25-June 20, 1886. [-] Were he to speak up one day, painting would not express what he wanted to say. If it were to be anything at all [-], it would be the theatre. An actor could step forward, telling all these truths, no matter how bitter they were, and still not be held responsible for them. That would no doubt be a pleasant career. [-]
> Every city dweller has probably some time in his life felt the urge to step

forward as an actor. What is supposedly at work then is a cultural desire to magnify oneself, 'to stand out' and identify with greater fictional characters. To Johan who was a romantic it was also a question of stepping forth to address the people. For he thought he would get to choose his parts and he knew which ones. Like everyone else he believed he had the necessary talent. This probably had to do with an excess of unused energy caused by a lack of physical work, and with an impulse in his brain to magnify things, since mental stress made it function irregularly. He saw no difficulties in the profession itself but expected resistance from other quarters.

Assuming that the urge to act is present in most people, it would probably be too rash to presuppose an inherited aptitude derived from a mania that had existed in the family. However, his grandfather, a burgher in Stockholm, had written plays for a fraternal order, and a distant young relative was still around as a warning example. He had been an engineer [-] but had abruptly resigned to join the theatre. Johan still remembered how, in his childhood, technology students had rehearsed plays in the relative's home [-]. The engineer's decision became a family tragedy that never subsided and the unfortunate young man had never amounted to anything and was now travelling with a provincial company, having made no name for himself. That was the hardest point to face. Yes, Johan told himself, but that happened to someone else; he on the other hand would succeed. Why was that? Because he thought so. And he thought so because he wished to succeed.

As a child, Johan played a great deal with a small toy theatre. This was insufficient grounds on which to trace an inborn urge to act, [-] since all children play with such theatres. He had probably gotten the urge by seeing others act. Besides, the theatre was an unreal, better world tempting one to escape a dull reality that would probably not have seemed so dull if one's upbringing had been more harmonious, realistic, and not as romantic as it was. [-]

The decision was made and without telling anyone, he walked up to the head of the acting school, the literary adviser [Frans Hedberg] at the Royal Theatre.

When he heard his own words pronounced: I want to be an actor, he shuddered. It was like tearing down his inborn shyness and was a strong violation of his own disposition.

The teacher asked what he had been doing.

- I was going to be a doctor.

- And you abandon such a career for this one, the most difficult and worst of them all!

- Yes!

That's what all artists said about their careers, that it was the most difficult and the worst, even though they did so well. That was just to scare him.

His intent was to ask for private lessons so he could make his debut. The teacher was leaving for the countryside, since the term was over, but he asked Johan to come back again on September 1, when the theatre opened and the board would be back in town. They came to an agreement and the matter was settled. Walking down the stairs to the street he kept his eyes wide open as if staring into a bright future. His body sensed a given victory, he was already drunk on it and flew down the street, though on tottering feet.

He said nothing to the doctor's family[19] nor to anyone else. Three months now lay ahead, during which he was going to teach himself everything and then be ready. But it would be done in secret, for he was cowardly and bashful, cowardly in facing his father's and the doctor's grief, the derision of relatives, the grinning and dissuasion of friends and bashful at the thought that the entire city would learn that he believed he was fit to be an actor. [-]

For his debut he had chosen the roles of Karl Moor[20] and Wijkander's Lucidor.[21] This was not just by chance but was totally logical. In these two roles, he had found his inner self expressed and therefore he wanted to speak with their voices. He interpreted Lucidor as a wretched and discontented person of a superior nature undermined by poverty. Superior of course! In these theatrical fantasies something also emerged that he had felt when he was preaching and protested against school prayers. It was the preacher in him, the prophet, the truth-sayer.

Above all, what gave him such an elevated view of the theatre was reading Schiller's lecture *On the Theatre as an Institution of Moral Education*. Sentences like the following showed how high the goal to which he aspired was: "The theatre is the great channel into which the light of wisdom streams down from the superior-thinking part of the population and spreads its mild rays over the entire nation." – "In that artificial world we forget the real one. We find our own selves. Our sentiments are awakened. Healthy emotions stir our dormant nature, forcing our blood to surge rapidly." [-]

Thus wrote the twenty-five-year-old Schiller and the twenty-year-old youth subscribed to it.

The theatre is no doubt a cultural institution for the young and the middle class who can still be deluded by actors and painted cloth. For older and educated people, the theatre is a pleasure in which the art of acting gets the attention. Hence, it is almost a rule that old reviewers are grumpy and dissatisfied.

They are no longer caught up in the illusion and are not distracted by technical flaws. In recent times, the theatre, especially the acting profession, has been much overrated and this has caused a reaction. Having cut off their art from the drama, the actors had imagined themselves self-sufficient. Hence stardom, actor worship and – opposition. In Paris, where the trend was most obvious, the reaction showed first. *Le Figaro*[22] called the heroes at the Théâtre Français[23] to order, reminding them that they were the author's puppets. The ruining of all great European stages suggests that the theatrical art is losing its appeal. Cultured people don't attend, since their sense of reality is evolving while their imagination, a remnant from primitive times, is declining. The uncultured have neither the time nor the money to attend. Variety shows which amuse without being enlightening seem to be taking over, for they are playful and relaxing. And all important authors choose other, more suitable forms to deal with great issues. Ibsen's plays have always made their impact in printed form before being performed, and when they are performed, most of the attention has focused on how they are performed – something of secondary concern. [-]

At this time Swedish theatre was under much attack, and when has it not been? The theatre is a microcosm of society, organized in a similar way with a monarch, ministers, civil service departments and then a multitude of social classes, one above the other. Is it strange then that this society is always subject to attacks from discontented people? At this time, however, the attacks had a more practical purpose. An uncultured provincial actor had been seen bombarding the Royal Theatre with a pamphlet that neither suggested good judgment nor any lofty points of view. It resulted in the author being called in before the board. This incident was deemed worthy of imitation and there were many who now published their theses to get the Board Degree.

But the Royal Theatre was at that time probably neither worse nor better than before. A question was raised however: If the theatre is what it pretends to be, that is, a cultural institution, why are people without culture set to run it? The answer was: We've just had one of the country's most learned men, Hyltén-Cavallius,[24] on the post, and what happened? Even though he had the advantage of being a commoner, he was torn to shreds by the so-called democratic press, which pulled at his coat sleeve from below. Today we have finally seen the utopia of self-government realized and, to everybody's satisfaction, we now have a man from the lower ranks occupying the highest post.[25]

On the set date, Johan went to the theatre's secretariat to register for his debut. After some waiting he was admitted and asked about his business.

- Debut? Oh! Have you thought of any particular play?

- Karl Moor in *The Robbers*, he answered, a little more defiantly than was necessary.

People looked at each other and smiled.

- But there should be three roles; do you have any other to propose?

- Lucidor!

There was some consultation and an ensuing explanation that these plays were not in the repertoire. Johan did not find this a valid reason, but then received the very sensible answer that the theatre could not alter its repertoire and produce such major works just to give untried actors a chance. After this, the theatre manager suggested *The Fencer from Ravenna*.[26] But to follow the brilliant performance of the last actor in that role, no, that he didn't dare. The outcome was that Johan was to talk to the litterateur.[27]

Now a struggle began that probably was not the first or the last one in that room.

- Be reasonable, young man. In this profession, as in all others, you have to learn. No one is ready immediately. Crawl before you walk. Take a small part first.

- No, the part has to be big enough to carry me. In a small part, one has to be a great artist to be noticed.

- Yes, but listen to me, young man, I have experience.

- Well, but others have made their debut in big roles without ever having been on stage before.

- But you'll break your neck!

- Be that as it may. Then, I'll break my neck.

- Well, but the management will not let the country's number one stage be used as an experiment for just anyone who comes along.

- All right, that was reasonable. He would accept a small part. And so he decided on the role of Härved Boson in *The Wedding at Ulfåsa*.[28] Johan read it at home and was dumbfounded. This was not a role. It dealt with nothing. All he did was argue a couple of times with his brother-in-law and then he embraced his own wife. But he had to accept it and lower his demands.

Then the lessons began. Shouting hollow, meaningless words, that was agony.

After a couple of lessons, the teacher explained that he had no more time and told Johan to go and listen to some lessons at the acting school.

- But I won't be a student!

- All right, then.

He had heard that the acting school was some kind of children's or Sunday school where all sorts of people without education or anything were accepted and he didn't want to go there. No, he would just listen. [-]

Then, one morning he got a call to attend a rehearsal of Bjørnson's *Mary Stuart in Scotland*[29] in which he got a part. The orderly left him a small blue square notebook on which one could read: A Nobleman. And inside, on a white piece of paper, was written: "The Lords have sent a negotiator with a challenge to the Earl of Bothwell."[30] That was the entire role. And so, this was his debut.

At the appointed time he went up the small stairway facing the Stream[31] and passing the janitor he entered the stage. It was the first time he stood backstage. There was a huge storehouse with black walls, a dirty barn-like floor studded with nails, and all those gray canvas screens mounted on unpainted wood.

It was from here that wonderful scenes from world history had been performed for him. It was here Masaniello[32] had proclaimed death to the tyrants while Johan had stood trembling up there in the far back of the fourth balcony. Here Hamlet had scoffed and suffered, and it was here that Karl Moor once had blasted society and the whole world. He became frightened, for how would he himself retain any illusions at the sight of unpainted wood and coarse colorless sackcloth. Everything looked dusty and dirty and the stage-hands seemed like miserable wretches, and the actors and actresses were nothing to look at in their ordinary clothes. [-]

Then the bell rang for the rehearsal and they were pushed down onto the stage. There they lined up for the gavotte.[33] Down by the footlights stood the famous actors who had the leading roles and then the two rows of dancers extended all the way to the rear of the stage.

Bang! And the orchestra started playing. The dance began in a slow solemn rhythm. But down by the footlights the deep voices of the two Puritans were heard as they condemned the depravity of the court. [-]

He stood in the wings listening throughout the entire play. [-]

For this was something special: to live through a slice of history through these personalities. It was as solemn as church once had been. After he had entered and spoken his line, he left with the decision to put up with everything – for the sake of this holy art.

Thus the step had been taken. He had written an over-excited letter to his father, promising he would become a great success in his new choice of career or else he would quit. And he had vowed not to return home until he had succeeded. The doctor was disappointed but made no fuss, for he saw that it was impossible to stop Johan. But as a safeguard he had made other secret plans which he now began to carry out. First he persuaded Johan to translate a couple of medical booklets, for which he had found a publisher. Then he proposed that they write articles together in *Aftonbladet*.[34] Johan himself had translated Schiller's *The Theatre as a Moral Institution*, and since the theatre issue had been discussed in the *Riksdag*, the doctor wrote an introduction in which the farmers were seriously upbraided for their cultural animosity. With that the article was accepted. [-]

At the theatre things went from bad to worse. Together with some extras, Johan had been sent into the dressing room to put on his costume. People there were boozing and the room was not kept clean.

- They want to crush me, he thought, but just be patient.

By this time, he was simply called in as an extra in one opera after another. He explained that he was not afraid of the footlights or of the public since he had preached in a church. That did not help. But the worst part was having to hang around for hours during rehearsals with nothing to do. If he read a book, he got told that he seemed uninterested. If he left, the alarm went off. The pupils in the acting school now read their parts. Those who had only gone through first grade got to read Goethe's *Faust* without understanding anything of course. But strangely enough, their dauntlessness saved them and they carried on well enough. It seemed as if an actor did not really need to understand his part as long as it sounded good.

After a couple of months he was sick of the whole thing. It was workman-like. The leading actors were tired and indifferent. They never spoke about art, only about engagements and additional salaries.[35] There was not even a shred of that happy life backstage, about which so much had been written. Silent and quiet [-] they sat there waiting for their cues. Ballet dancers and female chorus singers sat in their costumes sewing or knitting. In the lobby, people tiptoed, looked at the clock, trimmed their false beards and never said a word. [-]

Since he now had free tickets to the theatre, Johan tried to make a study of it from the auditorium. But lo and behold, the illusion was gone. There he saw Mr. and Mrs. so and so. There hung the backdrop from *Quentin Durward*.[36] There Högfeldt[37] sat and there behind that wing stood Boberg.[38] The illusion had vanished.

And due to the pitiful role he kept grinding away at, his boredom grew day by day. With that came regrets and a fear that he would not be able to pull out

of this game with honor. Finally, he gathered his courage and asked to be tested. The piece had been performed more than fifty times and the leading actors were not amused at the idea but they had to come. And so the test took
place without costumes or props. He had been taught the manner of shouting which was current at the time and he shouted like a preacher. It went badly. At the end of the test, the teacher pronounced the verdict. He could enter
the acting school and wait. But no, he didn't want to. He cried in anger, went
home and ate a dose of opium that he had hidden for a long time, but to no
avail. After that, he was dragged out by a friend and got drunk [-].

He had finally found his mission, his role in life, and now his pliant nature
began to take on a firmer form. [-]

He had written his family miseries out of his system. After that, the memory of his religious struggles emerged as a three-act comedy [*The Free-
Thinker*] which made his burden considerably lighter. His creativity at this
time was enormous. The fever hit him daily and in two months he wrote two
comedies, a tragedy in verse and also shook short poems out of his sleeve.

The tragedy was his first real work of art [-], for it did not deal with anything that had occurred in his own life. Its neat little subject was *The Sinking
Hellas*. The composition was clear and complete, with a couple of worn-out
situations and much declamation. The only thing of his own invention was a
morality of strict asceticism and contempt for the uncultured demagogue. [-]
The piece was aristocratic and its proclaimed freedom was that of the sixties:
national freedom.

His comedy about the family was submitted anonymously to the board of
the Royal Theatre.

While it was there, Johan continued in good spirits as an extra. You just
wait, he thought, my time will come soon and then I'll get a say in the matter.
He was now bold on stage, and even when walking about in a peasant costume
as Wilhelm Tell, he felt like a disguised prince. "I'm certainly not a swineherd
though you might think so," he hummed to himself.

It took some time to get a response to his play. Finally he lost his patience
and disclosed his identity to the teacher who had read the piece and found
some talent in it. However, it could not be performed. Well, that was no catastrophe since Johan had his tragedy in reserve. This was better received but
had to be reworked here and there.

One evening after the end of the acting school season, the teacher asked to
talk to Johan.

- Now we've seen what you can do, he said. You have a beautiful career ahead of you. Why then would you choose a lesser one? It's likely that you can become an actor if you want to work for a few years, but why bother with this unrewarding field. Go back to Uppsala and get your degree if you can. Then become an author, for you have to be old enough and have some experience to be able to write well.

Johan agreed to the idea of becoming an author, and leaving the theatre. But to return to Uppsala, no indeed! He hated the university and could not see how the useless stuff you had to read there could benefit his authorship, which should be based directly on life. [-]

He had now drafted a tragedy with the imposing title "Jesus of Nazareth," which treated the life of Jesus in dramatic form and was meant to crush, once and for all, the image of God and abolish Christianity. But when he had completed a few scenes, he realized that the subject was too big and required lengthy research.

The theatre term was now drawing to an end. The acting school gave a presentation on the stage of the Dramatic Theatre. Johan had not been given a role but offered to be a prompter. And it was in the prompt box his career as an actor ended. That was how far he had come down from playing Karl Moor on the main stage. Did he deserve such a destiny? Was he worse equipped for the stage than the others? That wasn't likely but the matter was never investigated.

On the evening after the presentation, there was a festive gathering for the pupils.

Johan was invited and he proposed a toast in verse to make his exit less of a fiasco. He got drunk as usual, behaved like a fool and disappeared from that stage. [-]

Then *Brand* came.[39] The play had already made an appearance in 1866, but Johan and his contemporaries did not get a hold of it until 1869. It made a deep impression on his old pietist mind; it was dark and strict. The final line about *Deus Caritatis*[40] did not seem adequate and the author appeared to have been too much on his hero's side to let him go to his ruin with irony. *Brand* caused him many headaches. It had let go of the Christianity but had maintained the terrible morality of asceticism. The title figure demanded obedience to his old doctrines that were no longer applicable. He mocked contemporary striving toward humanism and compromise but ended up advocating [-] the spirit of compromise. Brand was a pietist, a fanatic who had the nerve to believe that he was right in his opposition to the whole world. Johan felt akin to this horrible egotist who on top of everything was wrong. No half measures, just push onward, break and bend anything that stands in your way, for you alone are right. Johan's sensitive conscience, which suffered with every step he took because it might hurt his father or his friends, was sedated by *Brand*. All bonds of deference, of love were to be severed for the sake of "the cause." That Johan no longer adhered to the unrighteous cause of the Hauge pietists[41] was fortunate or he too would eventually have succumbed to the avalanche.[42] But *Brand* gave him faith in a conscience purer than the one his upbringing had given him and a justice higher than the law. And he needed this iron bar in his weak spine, for there were long periods when he occasionally, out of consideration for others, took the blame himself and gave up his own right, which did himself injustice and made him quite gullible. Brand was the last Christian who fell for an old ideal and, therefore, he could not become a model to those who felt a vague rebellious spirit against all the old ideals. The play remains a beautiful plant without roots in today's world and therefore it belongs to the herbarium. [-]

In August, when the theatres opened again, Johan got the long-awaited message that his play [*In Rome*] had been accepted for production. He experienced the excitement of his first success. To have a play accepted by the Royal Dramatic Theatre at the age of twenty-one could certainly relieve the burden of all his adversities. Now his words would reach the public from the nation's first stage. The misfortunes surrounding his theatre career would soon be forgotten. His father would realize that his son had made the right choice despite his notoriously changeable nature, and everything would be fine again.

And in the fall, before the theatre season began, the play opened. It was childish and pious and worshipped art but it had one dramatic effect that saved his slender piece: Thorvaldsen standing before the statue of Jason,[43] which he wants to smash with a hammer. His impertinence, however, was his attack on the rhyming poets of the day. Which ones did the author target? And how dare a novice who himself used so many forced rhymes cast a stone at others? It was a foolishness that would soon be punished.

Johan sneaked up to the back of the third balcony to stand and watch his work be performed. [-] The audience applauded here and there, but Johan knew it was mostly relatives and friends, so he didn't let himself be fooled. Every stupidity in the verse made him shake and grated his ear. He saw nothing but imperfections in his work. At times, he felt so ashamed that his ears got hot, and before the curtain fell he ran out onto the dark square. He was completely devastated. His attack on the poets was stupid and unjust. His glorification of poverty and pride seemed wrong. His depiction of the father-son relationship was cynical. [-] It was as if he had shown himself naked, and what he felt most strongly was a sense of shame. On the other hand, he thought the actors were good and the production had more poetic sentiment than he could have dreamt of. Everything was good except the play. He wandered about down by the North Stream and wanted to drown himself. [-]

No one is as incorruptible a critic as the playwright watching his own play. He doesn't allow one word to slip through his sieve. He doesn't blame the actors, for he usually admires them since they can pronounce his stupidities with such taste. And Johan did find his piece stupid. It had been lying around for half a year. Perhaps he had outgrown it. [-]

In May, he was to take his final exam.[44] Breaking with accepted custom, he began sending in his written work, asking to get a date for the defense of his seminar paper by return mail.

His paper was called "*Earl Haakon*" and dealt with idealism versus realism. Dated 1871, it constituted an important document in the author's evolutionary history and being perhaps also a small contribution to contemporary history, it is printed below verbatim and with some necessary comments.[45] [-]

I [B speaking] once saw a twelve-year-old reading Oehlenschläger's tragedies. It went fast, for in two weeks, he became familiar with all twenty-six of them. When asked how this was possible and how he liked them, he answered that they were a great deal of "fun" to read, especially since he only had to read the list of characters and the stage directions. He then got Palmblad's translations of Sophocles,[46] but [-] they were so "boring," for they had no stage directions. Hence there is supposedly more action in Oehlenschläger's tragedies than in those of Sophocles, or Sophocles is less dramatic than Oehlenschläger! What is action then? It is the rapid development of the characters by way of changing situations. It is an inner progress or the hero's pathetic advances toward fulfillment or annihilation. You get action or movement by setting up obstacles along the way or by bringing together the contending parties as often as possible with a resultant conflict, which can be combined with a true effect. What then is a true effect? Either surprising turnabouts or unforeseen obstacles or even unexpected situations. Everything irrelevant to the action has to be weeded out, no matter how beautiful and how attractive it is on stage. [-]

[-] I consider it a criterion of good drama that it does not read very well, for it is to be seen, and so-called closet dramas are outcasts that should never be let into the dramatic genre.

As for [-] the exposition [in *Earl Haakon*], it is by no means Shakespearean [as A had claimed], for it is a part of compositional law to open a piece with the secondary characters in order to prepare for future events. However, during a seemingly indifferent conversation you should always hear the rumbling thunder in the distance that will be unleashed in the third act and kill the hero in the fifth.

The play [*The Outlaw*] was performed and had a cold reception. The subject was religious. It concerned paganism and Christianity, and Christianity was defended as a new current and not as a church doctrine. Christ himself was set aside and God, the one and only, was elevated at his expense. There was also a family conflict, and the women were elevated at the expense of the males as was the custom of the day. In a couple of lines, the author also made clear his views on a writer's position in life. "Orm, are you a man?" asks the Earl. "I only became a writer," Orm answers. [-] "Therefore you've never amounted to anything!"

Johan now believed that the life of a writer was a shadow existence and that he had no self and only lived through others. But can anyone be so sure that the writer lacks a self simply because he has more than one identity? Perhaps he who possesses more than the others is the richer one. [-] In his play, Johan had embodied himself in five different characters: the Earl fighting against time; the writer who surveys and sees through everything; the mother who rebels but loses her avenging power through her empathy; the girl leaving her father for the sake of her faith; and the lover who suffers from an unhappy love affair. Johan understood all of the characters' motives and he spoke for them all. But a play written for average people with ready-made opinions about everything has to take the sides of at least a couple of its characters in order to win over the average audience who is always passionate and opinionated. Johan had been unable to do that, since he did not believe in absolute right or wrong, for the simple reason that these concepts are relative. [-]

Returning to Uppsala he was pursued by new abusive reviews. In part, they were right, for instance, when they claimed that his form had been borrowed from *The Pretenders*.[47] This was, however, only partly true, for Johan had taken the ice-cold tone and stark language directly from the Icelandic sagas, and the play's outlook on life directly from his own experience and imagination.

*The Son of a Servant III*, February 1887.

June 21–July 27, 1886. The first days in June, he sat down to write his drama "A Renegade."[48] He had carefully studied the subject in the library[49] and had large sheets full of what he called local color, from which he now and then fetched a touch, so that his intention with the piece would not be too transparent. The subject matter was rich and well suited to be tampered with for all kinds of purposes. Emboldened by his reading of Goethe's *Götz* with its sixty or so tableaux[50], he had decided to break with current drama trends that were usually influenced by Fryxell[51] and Afzelius.[52] Hence, no verse, no recitation, no unity of place. The action itself was to determine the number of scenes and acts. People were to speak a simple everyday language, as is usually done off stage. The tragic and the comic, large and small matters were to vary as they did in life.

All that was old news, but Johan thought the time was right to bring it back.

Then he made his plan of attack. A drama was the most suitable form through which to say everything and then, in the fifth act, rescind as much as one wished or leave it open for consideration. The author hid behind the historical personages. In the guise of Olaus Petri,[53] he would appear as an idealist, in Gustav Vasa[54] as a realist; and in the anabaptist Gert[55] as a communard,[56] because Johan had discovered that the men in the Paris Commune had merely staged what Buckle[57] had proclaimed. Johan would express his three ideas from three different standpoints via the three main characters. In order to express everything he wanted to say he had to let Gert (Karl Moor) act mad, Olaus renounce his views and Gustav Vasa be right, though no one else was wrong. He also treated Hans Brask[58] with respect, the enemy from the old camp who had once been right but in the course of time had become wrong. For that reason, Johan had also intended to call his piece "What is Truth?" But in order to get it produced, both of the proposed titles were changed to the more neutral *Master Olof*. And that is when the attacks began. He began by attacking the notion of truth as something eternally evolving which would come to a halt every time someone succeeded in making the masses believe he had found it. Therefore, all useful truths are something temporary. Then he launched his attack on marriage as a divine sacrament. Olaus Petri had married against canonical law[59] but with a wedding ceremony. His marriage was not recognized either by civil law or public opinion. It was a rather clever challenge of divine law. The Whore had to be dragged in as a parallel and contrast. From experience, she was a person whom Johan neither sided with nor found pitiable.

In addition, the family was to be attacked as an anti-social institution. Matriarchal power and its obstruction of society's greater interests were savaged in the person of Olaus's mother with her overbearing and tyrannical behavior. The governing body, which Buckle had denied any good influence, was chastised in Gustav Vasa, whose Reformation work was not carried out by him but by the reformers, although the King, being a realist (Bismarck[60] perhaps) harvested the fruits and won the honor.

The people, the blind masses, were treated like cattle. They wished to be spared tithing to the church, but they wanted to preserve superstition and they were the first to cast a stone[61] at the liberator. This was not at all what our so-called democrats called democratic. With the help of Buckle, Johan had also proclaimed his conviction of the futility of working with ignorant people. [-]

The piece was also colored by the time during which it was written. The Paris Commune figures in the cultural hostility of the Anabaptists. The French-German war [1870-71] is the reason for the German's behavior at the inn where the presumptuous and arrogant Prussian has it coming to him. But to balance it all, French frivolity is made fun of in the Nobleman, while at the same time the German (not the Prussian) is praised for his moral sincerity. [-]

The author is impartial toward the hero, Olaus. In the scene where Olaus is waiting to be received by Gustav Vasa, Johan makes fun of himself and of his lower class feelings when he sat among the orderlies and the military guards in Karl XV's[62] vestibule. He turns Olaus into a weak soul, driven from below, who would rather march in the back. He makes him into an idealist who does not understand the pragmatic (realistic) King's more rational methods of crushing the church by starving it. Meanwhile, Olaus's marriage is also something strange. It is a satire on a spiritual marriage or a modern marriage of convenience. Kristina herself proposes (to Olof): "Olof," she says, "I want to become your wife; look, here is my hand. You were not the knight of my dreams and I thank God he never came, for then he would have disappeared – like a dream!"

This has a hint of Ibsen's *Love's Comedy*. But Olaus is in love with Kristina. He loves her with the kind of sound sensuous love that at least lives longer than an unsteady friendship. But Kristina is a presumptuous little featherbrain who wants to understand the makings of a strong intelligence and when she cannot, she pulls him down. [-] Excited, however, by having a great man look up to her, she imagines herself on the same level and wants to be above him. The author clearly shows that man and woman can't be compared and that each is superior in his or her own right, which was also the belief of Olaus Petri in 1872.

All the same, the author is caught, here and there, in that age-old worship of women and he supports Kristina too much against Olof, and as a bachelor, the author is of course too polite toward the young wife.[63] On the other hand, he is altogether free when he starts directing his blows at matriarchy. [-]

In the forceful King and his half-shadow, the sensible Lord High Constable, Johan had imagined himself the way he wanted to be; in Gert the way he was when he was passionate; and in Olaus, finally, the way he discovered himself to be after years of self-probing. Overly ambitious and weak in willpower, ruthless when it mattered and yielding when it didn't, very self-confident and deeply dejected, sensible and irrational, hard and soft. These dualities in his character were an inevitable consequence of his dual Christian and positivist upbringing.[64] As a transition to a new human being, he possessed old and new layers of both idealism and realism. With his double perspective – the narrow contemporary one and the expansive future one – he was bound to constantly see things from at least two sides.

His misfortune was that his rash temperament didn't always let him decide when to express one viewpoint or another. Those he regarded as enemies he had to strike out at in the usual way, that is, with the intention of crushing them. To those he regarded as fellow beings, subject to the deterministic laws of evolution, he had to be lenient, clear, and forgiving. But when would the one thing apply and when would the other?

Another source of discord in his character appears in his depiction of Olaus: the tug of war between aesthetic and ethical concerns. In the first scene of the first act, Olaus is rehearsing his play *Tobiæ Comœdia*. He calls this "to play." And at the end of the act, he looks back with regret on this period of leisurely play time,[65] which he was forced to give up to go to Stockholm to preach. This also symbolized Johan's struggle between the actor and the clergyman. Already here his vague insight into the insignificance of art versus an excessive appreciation of it could be divined.

However, the greatest importance [-] of his piece was found in the ending. Everyone is right, relatively speaking, since there is no absolute right. By asking that Olaus stay calm and continue his preaching, the Lord High Constable is right according to his own time. Olaus is correct when he admits having gone too far. The young Scholaris[66] is right when he, being young, demands the evolution of a new truth. Gert is right in calling Olaus a renegade. As a consequence of inevitable natural laws, an individual will always become a renegade – due to fatigue or an inability to develop further since his brain will stop evolving by the age of forty-five, or because of the demands of reality, according to which even a reformer must live as a human being, a husband, a father, and a member of society. [-]

To Edvard Brandes (1847–1931), Danish playwright, critic, and politician. Together with his brother Georg, he was one of the leaders of the realistic, socially engaged movement that emerged in Scandinavia during the 1870s. Acting as S's Danish agent, he used the columns of *Politiken*, the radical Copenhagen paper he co-founded in 1884, to promote S's work.

Gersau, January 3, 1887. [-] no doubt you've read my play [*Marauders*] now? As the first person to have done so (apart from the publisher), will you answer the following questions:

[-] Should I really introduce Mrs. Hall in Act V and confront her with her divorced husband? But that would make it melodramatic and sentimental, and possibly even comic, you see, since the Doctor is a so-called humorist whereas Mrs. Hall is pitiful and ridiculous.

The scene is tempting and new (?), but could be saved for another occasion. On the other hand, maybe the Doctor should have a short scene with the two Misses Hall, although he doesn't really know them, and indulge with them in trivial conversation. That might tickle the audience who expects something sensational in the fifth act. They could talk about theatre and painting, anything at all. The audience still believes it is a father and his daughters, and that's titillating. As long as it doesn't become tragicomic.

There are sharp psychological observations in the play, but I know it goes against the tide. Nevertheless, the bit about the labor market is the real point, the core of the question. But as you can see I've not labored the point one-sidedly. All it really amounts to is that those devils marry in order to get a breadwinner to support them.

Do you think that in Act V I ought to let Mrs. Starck or the Doctor say: "For heaven's sake, go, go and work, but then don't get married! One or the other, work or marriage, but not both!" [-]

Don't you think all this effeminate pampering has made men unmanly?

Isn't it a fine stroke when I let Bertha fall in love with Axel after having received a good hiding? Could I possibly save the play by letting this 'love' assume a greater significance in the final lines, thereby giving the impression that she is attacked for pushing her way into the labor market? Abel has also been aroused. How about a scene in which the two women display their jealousy? Or is it perhaps better as it is when Abel conceals Axel's confession and thereby shows the audience that she, too, is a woman who can appreciate masculinity, while Bertha is a hopelessly stingy, asexual animal! Perhaps?

However, *Marauders* is the second part of a trilogy.[67]

The first deals with the father, and Bertha's childhood. The third with Bertha's later destiny as a mother and the wife of a lard dealer. If the play remains unperformed, I'll finish all three parts and then let Engelbrecht[68] have them! [-]


## "Soul Murder: Apropos *Rosmersholm*," *Politiken*, May 30, 1887.

[-] The case [of soul murder] presented in *Rosmersholm* is [-] extremely interesting. Rebekka seems to be an unconscious cannibal who has devoured the former wife's soul. With her unconscious plans to take power in the house, her behavior has been highly suspicious. The wife [Beate] nourished suspicions against her, [-] saw through her, and Rebekka concealed matters and saved herself by making the wife believe that she was suffering from "a suspicious mind." This suspicion was naturally heightened by her further observations and the impossibility of obtaining proof. Hereby, the likelihood that the wife suffered from a suspicious mind became even greater. Therefore, it was easy for Rebekka to drive her insane. [-]

We don't get to know exactly how Rebekka went about her murder [-]. [-] Presumably, she employed the time-honored method of inducing the weaker mind to believe that she was sick, until it imagined itself so. And then she [-] made Beate believe that death was a blessing. [-]

But Rebekka probably went to work unconsciously, or persuaded herself at the outset that what she was doing was permissible, for the hitherto unexplained power of self-deception is enormous, and I believe that many cases of insanity are due to self-deception or are psychic suicides pure and simple.

When struggle passed from physical violence to legal agreements, the individual had to try to conceal his intentions. Dissimulation became necessary,

STRINDBERG ON DRAMA AND THEATRE

and developed into instinct or unconscious urge. Nor can it be denied that language, originating naturally in the need to exchange thoughts, also developed with the intention of concealing thoughts, hence the multifarious and varied meanings of words. The wisest, or he who best could mask his true purpose, was victorious in the struggle. [-]

Recalling the discovery of our time that society is a web of unconscious deceptions, we need not regard people as (conscious) scoundrels, even if one cannot deny that there *are* conscious ones, particularly in the highest quarters. Those at the top break the laws at will, and those below get around them as best they can, or get caught in the traps set for them. [-]

The necessity of hypocrisy has imposed many masks on man. The desire to tell others the truth, to reveal other people's secrets, has been hidden behind many disguises. When people noticed that freedom from responsibility was granted the madman but not the criminal, people began simulating madmen. The court fool of the Middle Ages was one such seeming madman who was used by princes both as a spy and as a teller of the truth when the prince himself lacked the courage to speak out, because he might be held responsible and be the victim of revenge. The fool became a responsible spokesman who made himself irresponsible by simulating idiocy. [-]

Hamlet feigns insanity in order to be able to both express his thoughts freely and to spy. But in so doing Hamlet commits psychic suicide, for he finally loses his will-power and his sense of judgement. [-] Hamlet's idea of protecting himself by feigning insanity was in no way original or exceptional. Danger compels people with new ideas to dissimulate [-].


To August Lindberg (1846–1916), actor and director. Staged the premiere of *Master Olof* in 1881, but declined when S (see below) invited him to help found an Experimental Theatre in Copenhagen in 1887. However, two years later he asked S to dramatize his novel *The People of Hemsö*.

Copenhagen, June 3, 1887. [-] I am hereby taking the liberty of presenting my plan.

Do you feel inclined to 'create' [-] a Swedish theatre with me on the following principles?

Embarking on a small scale tour, and perhaps later establishing a base in Stockholm, where we would in any case want to end our days.

Only performing plays by August Sg and none of his older repertoire.

Writing the plays in such a way that it won't be necessary to lug along any costumes, sets, or props.

Supplying by September 1 this year five new plays: a tragedy, a comedy, a burlesque, two *proverbes*.[69] Could even be supplied earlier.

Having a company of only eight: an old woman, a wife, two girls (blond and brunette), an old man, you, a lover (idealistic), another lover (realistic, ugly). [-]

[-] My wife must be included. She showed herself to be a great actress in Stockholm, and since I'm writing the roles for her (and you), there's no cause for anxiety.

We'd never be short of plays, for I can write a one-act in two days. I can dramatize my short stories (not *Getting Married*)[70] and besides, I've a whole case full of plans.

I have no dreams of transforming or reforming the theatre, for that's impossible. It can only be modernized a little.

If we were to finish up in Stockholm, I would create a whole series of Swedish historical plays in the genre of *Master Olof.*

What do you say to all this now?

If you want your wife to come along, I'll write alternating roles for her and my wife, but always one for you!

You can't go on much longer with Ibsen; for he probably won't write much more, and his particular genre is on the way out. You should read the Germans on *Rosmersholm.*

He can do his thing, and we ours!

Your patriotic spirit ought surely to summon you to create a Swedish theatre! [-]

N.B. The theatre will only be used for artistic ends, with no political, social or sexual aims.

Please remember that this has come entirely out of my own head, and my wife knows nothing about it. This theatre is for me – and you!


"The Battle of the Brains," *Neue Freie Presse*, July 12–13, 1887.


Doctor Charcot[71] accepts the viability of suggestion only where hypnotized hysterics are concerned; Doctor Bernheim[72] goes somewhat further and grants that anyone who can be hypnotized is susceptible to ideas from without. But the latter, on the other hand, still finds that not everyone is equally susceptible, and that one group of people is more susceptible than another. Among these he numbers the lower classes, those willing to learn, old soldiers, artisans, in short, all those whose brains are at a lower stage of development or who are accustomed to subordinating themselves to someone else's will. Although no expert or authority, my experiments have led me to conclude that suggestion is only the stronger brain's struggle with, and victory over, a weaker mind, and that this procedure is applied unconsciously in daily life. It is the mind of the politician, thinker and author which sets other people's minds automatically in motion. The actor hypnotizes his wideawake audience, forcing it to applaud, weep, and laugh. The painter is a magician who can convince the viewer that he sees a landscape where there is nothing but color on a canvas. The orator can make the masses believe any kind of nonsense if he is a gifted speaker and has a command of rhetoric. And what can a clergyman in full canonicals not achieve with all the attributes of ecclesiastical magnificence?

All political, religious and literary disputes seem to me nothing but an individual's or a party's attempt to impose their view upon others by way of suggestion, in other words, to mold opinion, which is nothing but the struggle for power, nowadays between minds since muscular battles are no longer common. The battle of the brains is no less terrible even if it isn't as bloody [-].


To Émile Zola (1840–1902), leading French novelist, pioneer of naturalism. Ever since he had first read Zola, in 1879, S admired him. Hoping that Zola's approval might lead to *The Father* being accepted for production at the Théâtre Libre, he sent him a copy of his own French translation. Zola's response was reasonably favorable but he found the characters insufficiently rooted in their environment. S used Zola's response as a preface to the French edition of the play.

August 29, 1887. [-] I hardly flatter myself that I am known to you as a writer, but the literary career which I have followed since 1869 as the acknowledged leader of the experimental and naturalist movement in Sweden, and the fate this has entailed from the obligatory trial to voluntary exile to an honorable retreat as *feuilletoniste* in the *Neue Freie Presse* in Vienna, has led me to presume that you would be willing to take the trouble of reading the enclosed work at your leisure. [-]

As you see, I have taken the liberty of submitting for your enlightened judgement a drama composed with a view to the experimental formula, aiming to show the effect of inward action at the expense of theatrical tricks, to reduce the decor to a minimum, and to preserve the unity of time as far as possible. [-][73]

To Axel Lundegård (1861–1930), Swedish novelist. For a brief period, Lundegård worked closely with S, and helped him turn *Marauders* into *Comrades*. He had been asked to translate *The Father* into Danish.

Lindau, October 17, 1887. [-] Who will play the Captain [in *The Father*] and which female wants to play Laura? The piece can easily be ruined, become ridiculous! Though I seldom interfere in the acting, I suggest that the Captain's role be given to an actor with an otherwise vigorous temperament who meets his fate in fairly good spirits, with the self-ironic, slightly skeptical tone of a man of the world. He is aware of his superiority but dies wrapping himself in those spider webs he cannot tear to pieces because of the laws of nature.

A cuckold is a comic figure to the world and especially to a theatre audience. The Captain must show that he knows this, and that he too would laugh if it concerned someone else!

This is what is modern in my tragedy, and woe to me and the actor if he goes about it by playing *The Robbers* in 1887! No shouting, no preaching. Subtly, calmly, resignedly [-].

Remember that a cavalry officer is always a rich man's son, who has been well brought up, places high demands on himself in social life and is civil also toward a lower rank soldier. Hence, he is no crude lout of military tradition or fortification policy. Besides, he is above his profession, has unmasked it, and is a man of science. It is precisely here that for me he represents a masculinity that one has tried to devalue, cheat us out of and move toward a third sex! It is only before a woman that he is unmanly, because that is how she wants him, and because the law of accommodation forces us to play the role that a mistress demands. [-]

I don't believe anything is gained by my personal presence![74] That has been tested and with poor results. My physical appearance has often hurt my case and I am satisfied with remaining at my desk. [-]

To Axel Lundegård.

Copenhagen, November 12, 1887. [-] It is as if I'm walking in my sleep; as if my life and writing have gotten all jumbled up. I don't know if *The Father* is fiction or if my life has been, but I feel as if [-] this at some moment soon will dawn upon me, and then I shall collapse either into madness and remorse or suicide. Through much writing my life has become a shadow life. I no longer feel as if I am walking the earth but floating weightless in an atmosphere not of air but darkness. If light enters into this darkness, I shall collapse and be crushed!

The strange thing is that in an often recurring nocturnal dream I feel I am flying weightless which I find quite natural, as though all notions of right and wrong, true and false, have dissolved and everything that happens, however strange, appears just as it should. [-]

To August Falck (1843–1908), actor at and manager of the New Theatre in Stockholm. His son, also named August, was to found the Intimate Theatre together with S in 1907.

Copenhagen, December 23, 1887. [-] I've just heard from August Lindberg that you have decided to stage *The Father.*

As you know from times past, I don't have much notion of scenic detail, and I'm reluctant to disrupt the work of the actor by interfering. I therefore only want to send a few general comments, based on the experience we have gained from the performance. [-]

General observation: Do the play as Lindberg did Ibsen, that is, not as tragedy, not as comedy, but something in between. Don't create too fast a tempo as we did at the start here at the Casino.[75] Rather, let it creep forward quietly, evenly, until it gathers momentum by itself toward the last act. Exception: the Captain's speeches when his *idée fixe* has broken out. They should be spoken rapidly, abruptly, spat out, repeatedly breaking the mood. Remember: the Captain isn't a coarse soldier but a scholar who has risen above his profession [-], gentle in the first act, a good child who hardens, becomes furious and ultimately goes mad. Detail: When he enters in the third act, he is in his shirt sleeves (*jäger* shirt), has his books under one arm and the saw under the other.

If Laura is played by a beautiful young woman, she should be hard, for her appearance softens her, and her influence over her husband will be motivated in that way. If she is played by someone older, the maternal aspect must be stressed, and the hardness somewhat underplayed.

The Pastor is an ordinary pastor, serious, absorbed in his role, not comical.

The Doctor is an ordinary doctor, torn between the woman's influence and his sexual comradeship with the man.

The girl must be healthy and captivating, full of life, alert, and seem like a breath of fresh air in the midst of all this misery.

An edited copy has been dispatched! Cut more if you wish. You'll no doubt hear in rehearsal what sounds awkward.

The throwing of the lamp must be contrived by some device. Here we used a wicker lamp; the glass and shade can be fastened with putty so that the lamp may be lifted without the glass falling off, and thrown past Laura's head out through the door, but not before she has exited backwards, so that the spectator is left in doubt as to whether or not it has hit her. Laura screams and the stage goes dark.

It would be a pity if Gurli Åberg[76] did not accept the role of Laura. There must be a trace of former beauty to motivate Laura's influence over her husband. [-]

Laura has a rewarding moment in Act III, Scene 1, when she sits at the same writing desk the Captain was sitting at earlier. If she then repeats or imitates some gesture of the Captain's (e.g. putting the pen between her lips and reciting a line with it there, assuming the Captain really used that gesture), the contrast will make a fine effect. [-]


To Harald Molander (1858–1900), theatre director and writer. From 1886 to 1896 he was a director at the Swedish Theatre in Helsinki, where he produced *Master Olof* (prose version), *Gustav Vasa* and *Erik XIV*. His son, Olof Molander (1892–1966), was to become the leading Strindberg director in Sweden during the first half of the twentieth century.

Klampenborg, February 4, 1888. [-] It is no surprise to me that the play [*Master Olof*] isn't a success. It will soon be twenty years old. It is an opera text, apprentice work, and nowadays only suitable for Swedes with an interest in literary history.

Why not put on my more recent pieces now, instead of waiting twenty years until they, too, become old-fashioned?

*The Father,* for example, a modern tragedy, easy to stage without expense; highly actable. The Royal Theatre in Stockholm found it too sad, as if tragedy could be merry. The straitjacket is no more deplorable than the use of poisoned foils, daggers with lingonberry juice or pipes with hard chancres.[77]

The plot is no crazier than Iago's soul murder of Othello, and the question of paternity is here treated only a little more seriously than in *The Maternity Room,*[78] where it is depicted with the usual classical crudity.

The logic is rigorous and testifies to a powerful intellect on the part of the author who therefore cannot be identified with the insane hero. [-]


To Edvard Brandes.

Klampenborg, March 13, 1888. [-] I've finished reading the play [*Superior Power*] you kindly sent me! Of everything you've written, this seems to me to have the most life, because you've given something of yourself. And what else can one give, when one knows so little of other people? [-]

You don't stick to Aristotle and the unities. I think, though, that retaining the same milieu throughout enhances the effect, not on Aristotle's stupid account but because [-] milieu plays such an important role nowadays [-]! [-]


To Karl Otto Bonnier (1856–1941), publisher. The son of Albert Bonnier, founder of what is still the major Swedish publishing house. Karl Otto became a partner in his father's firm in 1886 and was its head 1900–38. In 1911, he and S signed a contract for the publication of S's *Collected Works* which, edited by John Landquist, appeared in 55 volumes in the period 1912–20.

Skovlyst, Lyngby, July 23, 1888. [-] I believe that whatever an author does in his feverish state is right even though, upon sobering up, he thinks some things might have been done differently. Therefore I hardly ever dare change anything and when I have made changes, I've spoiled things. *Summa summarum*: what I have written, I have written! [-]

To Karl Otto Bonnier.

Skovlyst, August 10, 1888. [-] I hereby take the liberty of offering you the first Naturalistic Tragedy in Swedish Drama [*Miss Julie*]. And I beg you not to reject it lightly, so that you may later come to regret it, for as the Germans say: "*Ceci datera!*" = this play will go down in the annals. My terms are only the production costs for the manual labor [-] or 500 crowns for 1500 copies. [-]

Preface to *Miss Julie*, published by Joseph Seligmann, Stockholm, together with the play.

August 10-15, 1888. Like art in general, the theatre has long seemed to me a *Biblia pauperum*,[79] a Bible in pictures for those who cannot read what is written or printed, and the dramatist a lay preacher who peddles the ideas of the day in a popular form, so popular that the middle classes, which form the bulk of the audience, without too much mental effort can understand what it is about. That is why the theatre has always been an elementary school for the young, the semi-educated, and the women, for those who still retain the primitive capacity of deceiving themselves or letting themselves be deceived, that is, for succumbing to illusions and to the hypnotic suggestions of the author. Thus, nowadays when the rudimentary and undeveloped kind of thinking that takes the form of fantasy appears to be evolving into reflection, investigation, and examination, it seems to me that the theatre, like religion, is about to be discarded as a dying form of art, which we lack the necessary preconditions to enjoy. This supposition is supported by the pervasive theatre crisis now prevailing throughout Europe, and not least because of the fact that in England and Germany, those cultural heart-lands which have nurtured the greatest thinkers of our age, drama is dead, along with most of the other fine arts.

Again, in other countries people have believed in the possibility of creating a new drama by filling the old forms with new content [-]. But this approach has failed, partly because there has not yet been time to popularize the new ideas, and so the public has not been able to understand what was involved; partly because party differences have so inflamed emotions that pure, dispassionate enjoyment has become impossible in a situation where people's innermost thoughts have been challenged and an applauding or whistling majority has brought pressure to bear on them as openly as it can do in a theatre;

and partly because we have not yet found a new form for a new content, and the new wine has broken the old bottles.

In the following play, I have not tried to accomplish anything new, for that is impossible, but merely to modernize the form according to what I believe are the demands a contemporary audience would make of this art. To that end I have chosen, or let myself be moved by, a theme that may be said to lie outside current party strife, for the problem of rising or falling, of higher or lower, better or worse, man or woman is, has been, and always will be of lasting interest. I took this subject from a real incident that I heard about some years ago, when it made a deep impression on me. It seemed to me suitable for a tragedy, for it still strikes us as tragic to see someone favored by fortune perish, and even more to see a whole family die out. But the time may come when we shall have become so highly developed, so enlightened, that we shall be able to look with indifference at the brutal, cynical, heartless drama that life presents, when we shall have laid aside those inferior, unreliable instruments of thought called feelings, which will become superfluous and harmful once our organs of judgement have matured. That the heroine arouses our pity merely depends on our weakness in not being able to resist the fear that the same fate might overtake us. A highly sensitive spectator may still not be satisfied with such compassion, while the man with faith in the future will probably insist on some positive proposals to remedy the evil, in other words, some kind of program. But in the first place, there is no such thing as absolute evil, for when one family falls it gives another the good fortune to rise, and this alternate rising and falling is one of life's greatest pleasures, since happiness only arises from comparison. And of the man with a program to remedy the unpleasant fact that the bird of prey eats the dove and lice eat the bird of prey, I would ask: why should it be remedied? Life is not so idiotically mathematical that only the big eat the small; it is just as common for a bee to kill a lion or at least to drive it mad.

If my tragedy makes a tragic impression on many people, that is their fault. When we become as strong as the first French revolutionaries, we shall feel as much unqualified pleasure and relief at seeing the thinning out of our national parks of rotten, superannuated trees, which have stood too long in the way of others with just as much right to their time in the sun, as it does to see an incurably ill person finally die. Recently, my tragedy *The Father* was criticized for being so tragic, as if one were expecting tragedies to be merry. One also hears pretentious talk about the joy of life, and theatre managers commission farces as though this joy of life lay in behaving stupidly and depicting people as if they were all afflicted with chorea[80] or idiocy. I find the joy of life in its cruel and powerful struggles, and my enjoyment comes from getting to know something, from learning something. That is why I have chosen an unusual case but an instructive one, an exception, in other words, but an important exception that proves the rule, even though it may offend those who love the commonplace. What will also bother simple minds is that my motivation of the action is not simple, and that the point of view is not a single one. Every event in life – and this is a fairly new discovery! – is usually the result of a whole series of more or less deep-seated motives, but the spectator usually selects the one that he most easily understands or that best flatters his power of judgement. Someone commits suicide. "Business worries," says the merchant. "Unrequited love," say the ladies. "Physical illness," says the sick man. "Shattered hopes," says the derelict. But it may well be that the motive lay in all of these things, or in none of them, and that the dead man concealed his real motive by emphasizing quite a different one that shed the best possible light on his memory.

I have motivated Miss Julie's tragic fate with an abundance of circumstances: her mother's 'bad' basic instincts; her father's improper raising of the girl; her own nature and the influence her fiancé's suggestions had on her weak, degenerate brain; but also, and more immediately: the festive atmosphere of Midsummer Eve; her father's absence; her period; her preoccupation with animals; the intoxicating effect of the dance; the summer twilight; the powerful aphrodisiac influence of the flowers; and finally chance that drives the two together in a secluded room, plus the boldness of the aroused man.

So my treatment has not been one-sidedly physiological nor obsessively psychological. I have not exclusively blamed her maternal heritage; nor have I put all of the blame on her monthly period; nor just settled for 'immorality'; nor merely preached morality – lacking a clergyman, I've left that to the cook! I flatter myself that this multiplicity of motives is in tune with the times. And if others have anticipated me in this, then I flatter myself that I am not alone in my paradoxes, as all discoveries are called.

As regards characterization, I have made my figures fairly characterless for the following reasons.

Over the years, the word character has taken on many meanings. Originally it no doubt meant the dominant trait in a person's soul-complex and was confused with temperament. Later it became the middle-class expression for an automaton, so that an individual whose disposition had once and for all set firm or adapted to a certain role in life, in short someone who had stopped growing [-] was called a character, whereas someone who went on developing was called characterless. In a derogatory sense, of course, because he was so hard to catch, classify, and keep track of. This bourgeois concept of the immobility of the soul was transferred to the stage, where bourgeois values have always been dominant. There a character was a man who was fixed and set, who invariably appeared drunk or comical or sad; and all that was needed to characterize him was to give him a physical defect, a clubfoot, a wooden leg, a red nose, or some continually repeated phrase such as "That's capital"[81] or "Barkis is willin',"[82] etc. This elementary way of viewing people is still found in the great Molière. Harpagon[83] is merely a miser, although he could have been both a miser and an excellent financier, a splendid father, and a good citizen; and even worse, his 'defect' is extremely advantageous to his daughter and his son-in-law who are his heirs and therefore ought not to criticize him even if they do have to wait a while to get into bed. So I do not believe in simple stage characters, and the summary judgements that authors pass on people – this one is stupid, that one brutal, this one jealous, that one mean – ought to be challenged by naturalists, who know how complicated the soul is, and who are aware that vice has an opposite side, which is very much like virtue.

As modern characters, living in an age of transition more hectic and hysterical than the one that preceded it, I have depicted my figures as more split and vacillating, a mixture of the old and the new, and it seems to me not improbable that modern ideas may even have permeated down to the level of servants via newspapers and conversations . That is why the valet belches forth certain modern ideas from within his inherited slave's soul. And I would remind those who take exception to the characters in our modern plays talking Darwinism, holding up Shakespeare as a model, that the gravedigger in *Hamlet* talks the then fashionable philosophy of Giordano Bruno[84] (Bacon),[85] which is even more improbable since the means of disseminating ideas were fewer then than now. Besides, the fact of the matter is, 'Darwinism' has always existed, ever since Moses's successive history of creation from the lower animals up to man. It is merely that we have just not discovered and formulated it until now!

My souls (characters) are conglomerates of past and present stages of culture, bits out of books and newspapers, scraps of humanity, torn shreds of once fine clothing now turned to rags, exactly as the human soul is patched together, and I have also provided a little evolutionary history by letting the weaker repeat words stolen from the stronger, and allowed these souls to get ideas, or suggestions as they are called, from one another, from the milieu (the death of the siskin), and from the objects (the razor). And I have brought about *Gedankenübertragung*[86] via an inanimate medium (the Count's boots, the bell). Finally, I have made use of waking suggestion, a variation of the hypnotic one which is now so recognized and popularized that it cannot arouse the ridicule or skepticism it would have in Mesmer's time.[87]

Miss Julie is a modern character which does not mean that the man-hating half-woman has not existed in every age, merely that she has now been discovered, has come out into the open and made a noise about herself. [-]

The half-woman is a type who thrusts herself forward and sells herself nowadays for power, decorations, honors or diplomas as she used to for money. She represents degeneration. It is not a sound species for it does not last, but unfortunately propagates its misery in the following generation. And degenerate men unconsciously seem to select among them so that they increase in number and produce creatures of uncertain sex for whom life is a torment. Fortunately, they perish, either because they are out of harmony with reality or because their repressed instincts erupt uncontrollably or because their hopes of attaining equality with men are crushed. The type is tragic, offering the spectacle of a desperate struggle against nature, a tragic legacy of romanticism which is now being dissipated by naturalism, the only aim of which is happiness. And happiness means strong and sound species. But Miss Julie is also a relic of the old warrior nobility that is now giving way to the new aristocracy of nerve and brain; a victim of the discord which a mother's 'crime' has implanted in a family; a victim of the errors of an age, of circumstances, and of her own deficient constitution, which taken together form the equivalent of the oldfashioned concept of Fate or Universal Law. The naturalist has erased guilt along with God, but he cannot erase the consequences of an action – punishment, prison, or the fear of it – for the simple reason that they remain, regardless of whether he acquits the individual or not. For an injured party is less forbearing than the one that has not been injured, and even if her father found compelling reasons not to seek revenge, his daughter would wreak vengeance on herself, as she does here, because of her innate or acquired sense of honor which the upper classes inherit – from where? From barbarism, from their original Aryan home,[88] from the chivalry of the Middle Ages which is very beautiful but undesirable nowadays for the preservation of the species. It is the nobleman's *harakiri,* the inner law of conscience which makes a Japanese slit open his *own* stomach when someone insults him, and which survives in modified form in that privilege of the nobility, the duel. That is why Jean, the servant, lives on, whereas Miss Julie who cannot live without honor does not. The slave has this advantage over the earl that he lacks this fatal preoccupation with honor, and all of us Aryans have a little of the nobleman or Don Quixote in us,[89] which means that we sympathize with the suicide who has committed a dishonorable act and has thus lost his honor, and we are noblemen enough to suffer when we see the mighty fall and lie there as corpses, yes, even if the fallen should rise again and make amends through an honorable act. The servant Jean is a race builder, someone in whom differentiation is discernable. He is a sharecropper's son[90] and has raised himself up to become a nobleman in the future. He has been quick to learn, has finely developed senses (smell, taste, sight) and an eye for beauty. He has already come up in the world, and is strong enough not to be concerned with the exploitation of other people. He is already a stranger in his own environment which he despises as stages he has put behind him and which he fears and flees, because people there know his secrets, root out his intentions, regard his rise with envy and look forward to his fall with pleasure. Hence, his divided, indecisive character wavers between regard for high positions and hatred for those who occupy them. He calls himself an aristocrat and has learnt the secrets of good society, is polished on the surface but coarse underneath, and already wears his frock coat with style, although there is no guarantee that the body beneath it is clean.

He respects Miss Julie but is afraid of Kristin because she knows his dangerous secrets, and he is sufficiently callous not to allow the events of the night to interfere with his future plans. With the brutality of a slave and the indifference of a master he can look at blood without fainting and shake off misfortune without further ado. That is why he escapes from the struggle unscathed and will probably end up as the proprietor of a hotel. And even if *he* does not become a Romanian count, his son will probably go to a university and possibly become a bailiff.

Moreover, the information he gives about life as the lower classes see it from below is quite important – when he speaks the truth, that is, which he does not often do, for he tends to say what is to his own advantage rather than what is true. When Miss Julie supposes that everyone in the lower classes finds the pressure from above oppressive, Jean naturally agrees since his intention is to gain sympathy, but he immediately corrects himself when he sees the advantage of distinguishing himself from the common herd.

Apart from the fact that Jean is rising in the world, he is also superior to Miss Julie in that he is a man. Sexually he is the aristocrat because of his masculine strength, his more finely developed senses, and his ability to take the initiative. His inferiority arises mainly from the social milieu in which he temporarily finds himself and which he will probably discard along with his livery.

His slave mentality expresses itself in his respect for the Count (the boots) and his religious superstition. But he respects the Count mainly as the occupant of the high position that he covets, and this respect survives even when he has conquered the daughter of the house and seen how empty that pretty shell is.

I do not believe there can be any love in a higher sense between two such different dispositions, so I let Miss Julie imagine she loves Jean as a way of protecting or excusing herself, and I let Jean suppose he could fall in love with her if his social circumstances were different. I suspect that love is rather like the hyacinth which has to put its roots down into the darkness *before* it can produce a strong flower. Here it shoots up, blossoms, and goes to seed all at once, and that is why it dies so quickly.

Kristin, finally, is a female slave. Standing over the stove all day has made her subservient and dull. She is like an animal, unconscious, of her own hypocrisy, overflowing with morality and religion which serve as a cover and a scapegoat for her sins. A stronger character, someone who could bear his guilt himself or explain it away would have had no need for these. Casually and deftly she goes to church to unload her household thefts onto Jesus and to recharge herself with a new dose of guiltlessness.

Moreover, she is a minor character, and therefore I deliberately sketched her the way I did the Pastor and the Doctor in *The Father,* where I wanted to depict ordinary people as country parsons and provincial doctors usually are. If some people have found my minor characters abstract,[91] that is because ordinary people are to some extent abstract when pursuing their professions; which is to say, they lack individuality and show only one side of themselves while performing their tasks, and as long as the spectator feels no need to see them from several sides, my abstract depiction is rather correct.

Finally, I have somewhat broken with tradition where the dialogue is concerned, by not making my characters catechists who sit around asking stupid questions in order to elicit a witty reply. I have avoided the symmetrical, mathematical artificiality of French dialogue and allowed my characters' brains to work irregularly as they do in real life, where no subject is ever entirely exhausted before one mind discovers by chance in another mind a cog in which to engage. For that reason, the dialogue wanders, providing itself in the opening scenes with material that is later reworked, taken up, repeated, expanded, and developed, like the theme in a musical composition.

The action is sufficiently fecund, and since it actually only concerns two people, I have restricted myself to them, introducing only one minor character, the cook, and letting the father's unhappy spirit hover above and behind it all. I have done this because it seems to me that what most interests people today is the psychological process. Our inquiring minds are no longer satisfied with simply seeing something happen. We want to know how it happens. We want to see the strings, the machinery, examine the double-bottomed box, try the magic ring to find the seam, and watch the cards on the sly to discover how they are marked.

In this regard, I have had the monographic novels of the Goncourt brothers in mind,[92] which have attracted me more than anything else in contemporary literature.

As for the technical aspects of the composition, I have by way of experiment eliminated the act division. I have done this because it seems to me that our declining susceptibility to illusion would possibly be disturbed by intermissions, during which the spectator has time to reflect and thereby escape from the suggestive influence of the writer-hypnotist. My play probably lasts about an hour and a half, and since people can listen to a lecture, a sermon, or a conference session as long or even longer, I imagine that a ninety-minute play will not exhaust them. I already attempted this concentrated form in 1872,[93] in one of my first attempts at drama, *The Outlaw*, but with scant success. I had written the piece in five acts, but when it was finished I noticed what a disjointed and disturbing effect it had. I burned it and from the ashes arose a single, long, carefully worked-out act of fifty printed pages, which played for a full hour. Consequently, the form is not new, although it seems to belong to me, and current changes in taste may well make it timely. In due course, I hope to have an audience so educated that it could sit through a single act lasting an entire evening, but this will require some preliminary testing. Meanwhile, in order to provide resting places for the actors and the audience without breaking the illusion for the latter I have used three art forms that belong to drama, namely monologue, mime, and ballet, all originally connected with Greek tragedy, with monody[94] having become monologue and chorus ballet.

Currently, our realists have banished the monologue as implausible, but given appropriate motivation it does become plausible, and I can therefore use it to advantage. It is perfectly plausible that a speaker would walk up and down alone in his room reading his speech aloud; that an actor would run through his role aloud; a servant girl talk to her cat; a mother prattle to her child; an old maid chatter to her parrot; or a sleeper talk in his sleep. And in order to give the actor a chance, for once, to work on his own and to escape for a moment from the author's pointer, I have not written out the monologues in detail but simply suggested them. For in so far as it does not influence the action, it is quite immaterial what is said while asleep or to the cat, and a talented actor who is absorbed in the situation and mood of the play can probably improvise better than the author who cannot calculate in advance just how much needs to be said, or for how long, before the theatrical illusion is broken.

As we know, some Italian theatres have returned to improvisation, producing actors who are creative in their own right, although in accordance with the author's intentions. This could be a step forward or a fertile, new art form that may well deserve the name *creative*.

Where a monologue would be implausible, I have resorted to mime, and here I leave the actor even greater freedom to create – and so win independent acclaim. But in order to not try the audience beyond its limits, I have let the music – well-motivated by the Midsummer dance, of course – exert its beguiling power during the silent action, and I would ask the musical director to select this music with great care so that the wrong associations are not aroused by recollections of the latest operettas or dance tunes or by the use of all-too-ethnographic folk music.

I could not have substituted a so-called crowd scene for the ballet I have introduced because crowd scenes are always badly acted, with a pack of simpering idiots seeking to use the occasion to show off and thus destroy the illusion. Since ordinary people do not improvise their nasty remarks but use ready-made material that can be given a double meaning, I have not composed the peasants' malicious song but taken a little-known dance game which I noted down myself in the neighborhood of Stockholm. The words don't hit home precisely but that is the point, for the cunning (weakness) of the slave does not permit him to attack directly. So, no speaking buffoons in a serious play, no coarse smirking over a situation that puts the lid on a family's coffin.

As for the scenery, I have borrowed the asymmetry and cropped framing of impressionist painting, and believe I have thereby succeeded in strengthening the illusion; for not being able to see the whole room or all the furniture leaves us free to conjecture, that is, our imagination is set in motion and completes the picture. I have thereby gained by noting that tiresome exits through doors can be avoided, particularly since stage doors are made of canvas and sway at the slightest touch. They don't even permit an angry father to express his anger after a bad dinner by going out and slamming the door behind him "so that the whole house shakes." (In the theatre it sways!) I have likewise restricted myself to a single set, both to allow the characters time to merge with their milieu and to break with the custom of expensive scenery. But when there is only a single set, one may demand that it be credible. Yet nothing is more difficult than making a room on stage resemble a real room, no matter how easy the scene painter finds it to create erupting volcanoes and waterfalls. Even if the walls have to be of canvas, it is surely time to stop painting shelves and kitchen utensils on them. There are so many other stage conventions in which we are asked to believe that we might be spared the effort of believing in painted saucepans.

I have placed the rear wall and the table at an angle so that the actors have to play face to face or in half profile when they are seated opposite each other at the table. In a production of *Aida*[95] I saw an angled backdrop which led the eye out into an unknown perspective, but it did not give me the impression of having been put there simply to protest the boredom of straight lines.

Another perhaps desirable innovation would be the removal of the footlights. I understand that the purpose of lighting from below is to make the actors' faces fatter, but I would like to ask why all actors have to have fat faces. Does not this lighting from below obliterate a great many features in the lower parts of the face, especially around the jaws, distort the shape of the nose, and cast shadows over the eyes? Even if this is not the case, one thing is certain: it hurts the actors' eyes, so that the expressiveness of their glances is lost; for footlights strike the retina in places that are normally protected [-], and therefore we seldom see any other play of the eyes except crude glances either to the side or up to the balcony, when the white of the eye is visible. This probably also accounts for the tiresome way that actresses in particular have of fluttering their eyelashes. And when anyone on stage wants to speak with his or her eyes, the actor sadly has no alternative but to look straight at the audience, with which he or she then enters into direct contact outside the frame of the set – a bad habit rightly or wrongly called "greeting acquaintances."

Would not sufficiently strong side lighting (using parabolic reflectors or something similar) give the actor this new resource of strengthening his facial expression by means of the face's greatest asset: the play of the eyes?

I have hardly any illusions about getting the actor to play *for* the audience and not *to* it, although this would be desirable. Nor do I dream of seeing the full back of an actor[96] throughout an important scene, but I fervently wish that vital scenes were not performed next to the prompter's box as duets designed to elicit applause but were rather located to that part of the stage dictated by the action. So, no revolutions, simply some small modifications, for to turn the stage into a room with the fourth wall removed and some of the furniture consequently facing away from the audience, would probably have a distracting effect, at least for the present.

When it comes to make-up I dare not hope to be heard by the ladies who would rather be beautiful than truthful. But the actor really might consider whether it is to his advantage to paint his face with an abstract character that will sit there like a mask. Imagine an actor who gives himself a pronounced choleric expression by drawing a line with soot between his eyes, and suppose that he needs to smile on a certain line although he is in a permanently enraged state. What a horrible grimace that would be! And how can the old man get the false forehead of his wig to wrinkle with anger when it is as smooth as a billiard ball?

In a modern psychological drama, where the subtlest trembling of the soul should be mirrored more in the face than in gestures and romping, it would probably be best to experiment with strong side lighting on a small stage and with actors wearing no make-up, or at least a bare minimum.

If we could then dispense with the visible orchestra[97] with its distracting lights and faces turned toward the audience; if we could have the stalls raised so that the spectator's eyes were on a level higher than the actor's knees; if we could get rid of the private proscenium boxes with their giggling drinkers and diners; if we could have complete darkness in the auditorium;[98] and finally, and most importantly, if we had a *small* stage and a *small* auditorium, then perhaps a new drama might arise, and the theatre would again be an institution for the entertainment of cultured people. While waiting for such a theatre, we shall just have to go on writing for our desk drawers, preparing for the repertoire to come. [-]


To Karl Otto Bonnier.

Skovlyst, August 21, 1888. [-] Watch your step now, for naturalism is about to enter the Academy (not the Swedish) with the Legion of Honor, and it won't be superseded until Darwinism – whose logical consequence it is – becomes superfluous too; *hoc est*: never!

In 8 days I shall be sending you a new naturalistic tragedy, even better than *Miss Julie*, with three characters, a table and two chairs, and no sunrise![99] [-]


To Joseph Seligmann (1836–1904), publisher. In 1878, he founded the firm of Seligmann & Co. and a year later he brought out *The Red Room*, S's breakthrough as a writer. Upon receiving the manuscript of *Miss Julie*, Seligmann immediately accepted it for publication on the condition that he could make a number of cuts and amendments. S agreed and the play appeared in bowdlerized form. The uncensored text, based on S's rediscovered manuscript, was not published until 1984.

Lyngby, August 22, 1888. [-] It has been nearly ten years since Sweden's first naturalistic novel[100] was published by your firm, with the consequences of which we are now aware.

Today I am sending for your perusal the first Swedish naturalistic drama [*Miss Julie*], written as I believe it should be, for reasons I have given in the preface.

It is not very likely that the play will be performed in Scandinavia for some time, but a letter yesterday from the director of the naturalists' theatre in Paris, M. Antoine, has given me hope that I shall see one of my plays staged there, for he says that *The Father* would in all probability have already been put on this season if *Ghosts* had not already been in rehearsal.

So far as naturalism as a literary movement is concerned, it may be going through a temporary depression in Sweden but as we know, it is already making its entry into the Academy in France, and it can no more be superseded than Darwinism, the philosophy of the future, of which it is the logical consequence. [-]


To Joseph Seligmann.

Holte, September 29, 1888. [-] The enclosed tragedy [*Creditors*], written for the Théâtre Libre at the same time as *Miss Julie,* was never intended for publication in Swedish because my enemies always try to injure me with their comments on my works.

However, having seen from the enclosed advertisement[101] how revealingly one may write, I am sending for your perusal a drama which is better than *Miss Julie,* and where the new formula is taken still further, to hear if you would be willing to publish it in one volume, together with the other drama.

The plot is exciting, as a psychic murder can be, the analysis and motivation are exhaustive, the point of view impartial and determinist. The author judges no one, he simply explains and forgives, and although he has made even the polygamous woman likeable, this doesn't mean he is advocating polygamy; in fact, he specifically says that this is unprofitable, because of its unpleasant consequences. [-]


To Edvard Brandes.

Circa September 29, 1888. [-] Thanks for reading *Julie.*[102] [-]

It is most plausible that the daughter of a count kills herself after having committed bestiality and burglary!

And if she doesn't do it immediately, she becomes a waitress at Hasselbacken,[103] just like the real Julie did! [-]


To Edvard Brandes.

Holte, October 4, 1888. [-] So that your misapprehensions about *Miss Julie* may not take root, I will show you right away that you are wrong on all counts.

1. The monologue has already been cut with one stroke of the pen!
2. The ballet remains, since with the fall of a curtain, the bourgeois snobs would snigger over a glass of Swedish brandy at Jean's sexual mounting of Julie, wondering if *he* will re-enter in the second act with his trousers unbuttoned.
3. Miss Julie is new: a half-woman born of a half-woman.
4. The ending is not romantic, on the contrary, it is quite modern with *waking* hypnotism (the battle of the brains).

A combination of motives is not as old as dramatic art. The reason for Oedipus's incest is only *one* [-]: ανανχη!¹⁰⁴

The reason for Othello's jealousy: *one* [-] = jealousy

The reason for Harpagon's avarice = 0 (not stated at all!)

So you see how damned modern I am!

And how right I am! [-]

Like me, Nietzsche[105] does not believe in plot in a dramatic work! Only in events! He is right! [-]


To Joseph Seligmann.

Holte, October 16, 1888. [-] A French version of *Creditors* is now ready and will go off to Paris today. I asked you to return the one you have. However, if you want to dwell on it a little longer, do so by all means! It is my great favorite, and I read it over and over again, continually discovering new subtleties. [-]

*Miss Julie* is still a compromise of romanticism and *coulisses* (even though I deliberately left out the ringing of the church bells, which [Frans] Hedberg would have seized on without fail), but *Creditors* is thoroughly modern, humane, charming, and all three of its characters likeable, interesting from beginning to end. [-]


To *Politiken*, November 17, 1888.

Holte, November 15, 1888. As it is my intention to establish in the near future an experimental theatre after the Parisian Théâtre Libre model, I hereby announce that I will accept all kinds of theatre pieces for perusal but prefer producing those that take place in the present, are not too long, and do not require complicated machinery or a large staff. [-]


To Carl Price (1839–1909), actor at the Royal Theatre in Copenhagen.

November 26, 1888. [-] I hear that like myself you are founding a theatre, but I believe mine is the more secure undertaking [-].

If you want to hear about my program, acquaint yourself with my repertoire and see if we could work together – albeit with different ideas – then pop around to Holte! [-]

Preliminary: I intend the plays to be in Danish and Swedish, but only *one language* in one and the same play. I already have a brilliant part for you!

Would also want you as a director!

We would open fire with two new pieces by myself, one in Danish, the other in Swedish, and then go on tour to ten or twenty cities in Scandinavia! (A staff of only six people!) [-]


To Gustaf af Geijerstam (1858–1909), novelist and dramatist. He was active as an impresario for a group of writers in the 1880s who called themselves Young Sweden. At the end of the 1890s, as the literary editor for the publisher Gernandts, he also basically became S's agent, responsible for the publication of, among others, *To Damascus* and several of the history plays.

Holte, December 1, 1888. [-] The reason the siskin[106] isn't released depends on quite an acute piece of observation: people of the subtler kind never release their animals or give them away when they are forced to part from them. They don't wish them to suffer, nor do they wish that deposits of their owner's soul should fall into other people's hands. They often kill their creatures themselves because other people aren't allowed to lay their hands on the owner's substitute! [-]

An Experimental Theatre in Scandinavia can only exist on an itinerant basis, because the elite is so negligible and has to be sought in the capital cities, the university towns, and the major centers of trade and learning! [-]

Moreover, I don't want to be at the mercy of on one type of audience! There'll be opposition to overcome here, believe you me! [-]


To Georg Brandes (1842–1927), Danish literary critic and biographer. With his large and influential oeuvre, Brandes was the central figure of the Scandinavian radical intelligentsia. He was instrumental in introducing Nietzsche to Scandinavian writers in 1888. The realism of the prose version of *Master Olof* owes much to Brandes's essay on Hotspur in *Critics and Portraits* (1870). Brandes wrote appreciatively of several of S's works, especially of *The Father*.

Holte, December 4, 1888. [-] I regard Christianity as a regression, [-] because it is quite contrary to our evolution, which seeks to protect the strong against the weak, and the current pressure from women seems to me a symptom of the regression of the race and a consequence of Christianity. To me, therefore, Nietzsche is the modern spirit who dares to preach the right of the strong and the wise against the stupid and small (the democrats), and I can imagine the suffering of this great spirit under the sway of the petty host which dominates this feminized and stupid age. And I hail him as the liberator, ending my letters to my literary friends like his catechumen with: Read Nietzsche!

And so to *Miss Julie*! "The deadly hatred of the sexes"[107] which Nietzsche sees in *The Father,* is found there too, but with the addition of a conscious aversion in the weak species to reproduce itself (cf. Schopenhauer on pederasty), the weakness of its will to live, the dream of falling from the pillar, her mother's aversion to intercourse, her male upbringing, etc. The suicide is properly motivated: her dislike of life, the longing to let the family die out in its last defective individual, the aristocratic shame regarding sodomy with a lower species; more immediately: the suggestions from the blood of the bird, the presence of the razor, the fear of the theft's discovery, and the command by the stronger will (primarily the servant, more remotely the Count's bell). Note that, left to herself, Miss Julie would have lacked the strength, but now she is both driven and encouraged by numerous motives.[108] [-]


To *Politiken.*

Holte, January 24, 1889. *The Stronger,* a so-called *quart d'heure*, since it only lasts for fifteen minutes. In it only two ladies appear, of whom the heroine does not say a single word.


To Nathalia Larsen (1855-1925), Danish writer and actress. At Strindberg's request, she translated *Sir Bengt's Wife, Miss Julie, Creditors* and *The Stronger* into Danish. She also played the part of Tekla at the premiere of *Creditors* in Copenhagen on March 9, 1889.

Holte, February 26, 1889. [-] Having rested after my trip to town,[109] I thought it might interest you to hear in more detail about your qualifications as an actress, such as I could perceive them in the poor light, which at times distorted your features.

Your figure is truly beautiful, but you should perhaps not walk with your legs splayed and your feet turned out. The first scene with Gustaf was very good and your gestures highly tasteful when you stood behind the sofa. Your face, which can't be considered beautiful, is excellent on stage, because you have large features that stand out and merge at a distance. Your eyes are expressive, and you understood very well how to direct them at the audience as often as possible – something you should never forget – but never higher than just under the dress circle [-].

Your voice is strong and ringing, revealing an intelligent and attractive person. You speak all your lines well; you possess all vocal shades, from the serious to the playful. Your laughter is superb and your face lights up when you smile – also, and especially, when you show your teeth a little.

In the more powerful and agitated moments you should perhaps not look quite so ferocious, for it is unbecoming; at least keep your eyes on the audience; expressions of sorrow or anger easily look like nausea.

Try to vary how you hold your arms; don't let them hang straight down too long. [-]

I don't know whether you are drawn toward tragedy (the old kind) or comedy. Possibly we're all being drawn toward comedy – tragedy included – and then you're with us! [-]


To Siri von Essen (1850–1912), S's first wife. She came from an aristocratic Finland-Swedish family and was, when she first met S, married to Baron Carl Gustaf Wrangel. Her relationship to S – they married in 1877 and had four children – colors many of his works. The plays include especially *Sir Bengt's Wife*, *Miss Julie*, *The Stronger* and *The Bond*, the first three having been written as vehicles for Siri as an actress. S's writings during the 1880s are profoundly affected by their life together, particularly his views on the Woman Question.

Circa March 6, 1889. [-] So you read *The Stronger*! I don't have the part [of Mrs. X] here but play it like this:

1. She is an actress, that is, not an ordinary proper housewife.
2. She is the stronger, that is, the more pliant. For what is hard and inflexible breaks, what can adapt bends aside – and rises again.
3. She is elegantly dressed. Use your dress from *Miss Julie*, or a new one.
4. If you choose a new coat, beware of plain surfaces and plain pleats and buy a new hat! Some kind of fur capote (*pas à l'Anglaise*).
5. Study the part with extreme care but then play it with simplicity! That is, not in a simple manner. Add 50% of the charlatan to it [-] and suggest depths that don't exist.
6. Change any phrase that doesn't sit well and see that your exit gets an ap-

plause but without grimacing too much.

7.  Speak with a chest voice without squeaking or ranting.

8.  Play it so that Pontoppidan[110] and Mrs. Nansen[111] get cystitis.

9.  Build a corner of props on stage, a crypt or alcove (as in the Dagmar Café). Hang prospectuses, travel brochures and theatre posters on the walls, so that it looks like a café without the counter showing, put up an umbrella stand, a coat stand, etc. Add something 'new' in the stage design and the piece will be a success.

10. Don't present it first, for it is too short to withstand its stronger enemies.

11. Therefore, begin with *Creditors*. Then Wied will be good too![112] [-] You can be pleased with the role of having directed the theatre of the future! And you can say to yourself: *Hier liege ich und mache Litteraturge-schichte!*[113]

"On Modern Drama and Modern Theatre,"[114] *Ny Jord*, no. 3, March 1889.

February–March, 1889. [-] Current crises in the theatre have led people to conclude, on the one hand, that the theatre is a dying art form, on the other, that this art form has merely fallen behind and needs to be modernized in accordance with the demands of the age, so that it may once again assume its fairly unpretentious place as an instrument of culture. It cannot be denied that there is something archaic about the theatre in its present form, as huge as a circus, opening out on to a stage with a Greco-Roman triumphal arch, decorated with emblems and grotesque masks reminiscent of the centuries before Christ. The red drapes, the brilliant curtain, the place of the orchestra retained since antiquity, the traps leading down to Charon,[115] the elaborate machinery by which gods descend to close the final act, all take one's memory back to prehistoric times when the theatre was the site of religious and national festivals. The masses still go to the theatre expecting to see an episode from world history, or at least scenes from the annals of their own country, which revive grand memories of important events. [-]

This hardy popular conception of the theatre as first and foremost a place of festivity, an arena where gaudily clad soldiers, princes and women galore display themselves and where secret, preferably inexplicable events unfold in castle halls, wild forests or trenches is so deeply ingrained that a successful piece must usually be in that style. [-]

What could be of prime importance in Shakespeare when there was no decor, namely the psychological course of events, was perforce neglected by the romantics, when so much time was spent on intermissions and on operating the stage machinery. It was, therefore, necessary to create interest through the plot, which the characters had to declaim until they became hollow.

The romantic drama or large-scale play also made it necessary to maintain a big company of actors, with all its risks: the emergence of a theatrical proletariat, given that these pieces only required three or four actors of rank while the other twenty were condemned to second- and third-rate roles, possibly for life, not to mention the generation of incalculable expenses on costumes and sets, and the ensuing deficit. [-]

With Molière, French drama has embarked upon a stage where all scenery was abandoned, and the mental changes in a character have become so central that the wonderful vivisection of Tartuffe takes place on a bare floor with two stools. The size of the cast has already diminished, and the principal interest is concentrated firmly upon a couple of central figures.

With this, the style of modern comedy is established. It proceeds with minor variations by way of Diderot and Beaumarchais, is rejuvenated by Scribe and Augier and rises to the grand style in the unjustly forgotten Ponsard, only to descend into insignificance with the decadent Sardou.[116]

Sardou represents the imperial comedy in decline, the end of an era, and as such suffers by comparison when a new age dawns. [-] Every trace of human life has disappeared from Sardou's plays, in which people talk as if they had been born the editor of a comic paper, and where the principal question is always the one that people ask themselves when they read a cheap serial: What happens next? [-]

Some people wish to date the new drama from the Goncourt brothers' *Henriette Maréchal*, performed at the Comédie Française as early as 1865, when it was booed off the stage. But the reasons for this dating are not well founded, since the Goncourts represent a Christian physiological movement from an earlier period and in their play structure merely use a few bold devices, which every previous realistic movement has also utilized.

It is more likely that Zola's *Thérèse Raquin*[117] will be considered the first milestone of naturalist drama, thus linking it to the year 1873. [-]

When Zola [-] approaches the theatre to make a serious attempt at trying out new methods, he is immediately attracted by a great and powerful motif, in this case a murder of one spouse so that the other may gain the freedom to make another choice. But he does not proceed like Dumas or Augier, partly excusing the murder because of the prevailing legal system, which did not permit divorce. He neither excuses nor accuses, for he has abandoned such concepts, but restricts himself to portraying the course of events, indicating the motivation for the act and showing its consequences. And in the pangs of conscience of the criminals, he sees merely a manifestation of disrupted social harmony, the results of habit and inherited ideas.

*Thérèse Raquin* is a new departure, but since it is adapted from a novel it is still not perfect in form. The author has, however, felt that a greater unity of place would provide his audience with a stronger sense of illusion, thus enabling the action to impress its main features more forcefully upon the spectators, who would be haunted by their memories of the preceding act at every curtain rise, and hence be captivated by the action through the impact of the recurring milieu. But because of the difficulty of determining the before and after of the crime, he commits the error of letting a year elapse between the first and second act. Presumably he did not dare to offend against the prevailing law concerning a year's widowhood, otherwise a day between the acts would have been enough, and the play would have seemed more unified. [-]

With *Thérèse Raquin* the great style, the deep probing of the human soul, had attracted attention for a while, but no successors seem to venture forth. Even so, since 1882 there has been a tendency to regard Henry Becque's *Corbeaux*[118] as a pioneering work. To me this seems to be a misunderstanding. If art is to be, as has been said, a piece of nature seen through a temperament,[119] then there is certainly a piece of nature in Becque's *Crows*, but the temperament is missing. [-]

This is photography, which includes everything, even the speck of dust on the camera lens. This is realism, a working method elevated to art, or diminutive art, which does not see the forest for the trees. This is the misconceived naturalism which believes that art simply consists in copying a piece of nature in a natural way, but not the great naturalism which seeks out those points where the big battles take place, which loves to see what one doesn't see every day, which delights in the struggle between natural forces, whether these forces are called love or hate, the spirit of revolt or social instincts, which do not care whether something is beautiful or ugly as long as it is great. [-]

The theatre, especially the Parisian, has long been a kind of industrial concern, with a capitalist as the prime mover. A staff of popular actors was assembled and then writers were asked to produce roles for star performers, resulting in a star theatre, with Dumas and Pailleron at the head.[120]

This was a back-to-front method of creating theatre and drama [-]. [-]

But every time a writer has had a theatre at his disposal real drama has arisen, from Shakespeare and Molière onwards; and along with the repertoire actors have developed, which is the right way of going about it, putting first things first.

When M. Antoine opened his performances for subscribers in a room at the Place Pigalle in Paris, he did not have the capital, the actors or the theatre, and he was neither a writer nor an actor himself. But he did have a repertoire and knew that plays would come in without his needing to advertise for them [-].

[-] Antoine [-] was alert to the fact that the new repertoire could not be played by old actors, and therefore he began from the beginning. But he also realized that the new psychological drama, which he guessed would come, and of which he already had some examples, could not be performed on the large stage designed for tournaments. He thus established his enterprise in a room and with amateurs, with the result that after six months the Théâtre Libre was hailed as a pioneering undertaking when *Sœur Philomène* by the long-decried, abused and persecuted Goncourt brothers moved from the novel to the stage. [-]

A repertoire had rapidly arisen, so that about twenty plays a year were performed, and naturalism, which had been declared impossible on the stage by critics and other timid persons, now enjoyed a triumphant breakthrough there. One already sees signs of a search for a form which seems to take the new drama in a somewhat different direction from the first attempts in *Thérèse Raquin*, and which breaks completely with Zola's adaptations of *L'Assommoir* and *Germinal*, with their large-scale effects and elaborate theatrical apparatus.

Hardly a full-length play is to be seen, and Zola himself makes his debut with a one-act. Where three-act plays do occur, a strong predilection for the unities of time and place is noticeable. At the same time, all attempts at creating a plot seem to have been abandoned and the main interest is placed on the psychological course of events. All this suggests that the falseness of intrigue drama had been discovered by some.

In ancient Greek, the word for drama seems to have meant event, not action, or what we call conscious intrigue. For life does not unfold as regularly as a constructed drama, and conscious spinners of intrigue get so few opportunities to carry out their plans in detail that we have stopped believing in these cunning plotters who without hindrance are allowed to control other people's destinies, so that nowadays the villain in his conscious deception merely arouses our ridicule as not being true to life.

In the new naturalistic drama, a striving to look for the significant motif was at once apparent. Therefore, the action usually focused upon life's two poles, life and death, the act of birth and the act of death, the competition for a spouse, for the means of subsistence, for honor, all these struggles, with their battlefields, cries of woe, wounded and dead, during which one heard the new view of life seemed like a fresh southerly breeze. These were tragedies of a hitherto unknown kind. But the young authors of a generation that had hitherto been schooled in suffering [-], severe intellectual oppression, stunted growth, even such cruel forms as persecution with imprisonment and starvation, seemed themselves reluctant to impose their suffering on others any more than was absolutely necessary. Therefore, they made the suffering as brief as possible, letting the pain pour forth in one act, sometimes in a single scene. One such small masterpiece, for example, was *Entre frères* by Guiches and Lavedan. The play is so short that it is performed in fifteen minutes, and the genre was immediately called a *quart d'heure*. [-]

This is drama reduced to a single scene, and why not also have that? Anyone who has had the task of reading plays that have been submitted to a theatre manager soon observes that every play seems to have been written for the sake of a single scene, and that all the author's creative joy was about this scene, which had sustained him during the terrible pains which exposition, presentation, complications, unraveling, peripeteia, and catastrophe had caused him.

For the satisfaction of having written a full-length play, he torments his audience by arousing its curiosity about matters it already knows. He inflicts upon the theatre manager the need to maintain a large company. He makes life miserable for those unlucky actors who will play the secondary roles – messengers, confidants and raisonneurs – without whom no intrigue or full-length play can emerge, and to whom he must go through the trouble of giving character.

Therefore, well-constructed five-act plays are extremely rare and one has to put up with a lot of stuff and nonsense to get to the gist of the matter. Having recently read some twenty-five plays, including one of four hundred pages and with seventeen characters, certain suspicions of mine about the reason for the lack of good drama have been confirmed. Every beginner seems to me to be able to write one good act; in that he is true to life, every word is accurate and the action is honest. As soon as he embarks upon longer plays, everything becomes labored, contrived, affected and false. The two-act plays form a genre of their own, but not a very happy one. It has a head and a tail, but no body. It is before and after the catastrophe, usually with a year in between. The second act frequently contains the moral [-] : This is what happens if you do this and that in the first act. The most beautifully constructed are those three-act plays which observe the unities of time and space when, that is, the subject is a significant one, as for example in Ibsen's *Ghosts* which should be compared with *Rosmersholm* that proved to be far too long. The taste of the period, this headlong, hectic period, seems to move toward the brief and expressive [-].

In the *proverbe* one got the heart of the matter, the whole unraveling, the battle of the souls, sometimes approaching tragedy in Musset, without having to be bothered by the din of weapons or processions of extras. With the help of a table and two chairs one could present the most powerful conflicts life has to offer. And in this type of art, all the discoveries of modern psychology could, for the first time, be applied in popular form. [-]

I do not mean to say that this is the only approach, and the Théâtre Libre did not begin its activities by prescribing a program, never promulgated an aesthetic, never sought to form a school. [-]

May we [-] establish such a theatre where one can shudder at the most horrible things, smile at the most ridiculous matters, and play with toys; where one can see everything and is not offended if one gets to see what has so far been hidden behind theological and aesthetic veils, even if this means breaking with the old established conventions. May we establish a free theatre where one has freedom for everything, except the freedom to lack talent and to be a hypocrite or a simpleton! [-]

# 1891-1899

To Richard Bergh (1858-1919), Swedish painter. A leading force among the artists who seceded from the Royal Academy of Fine Arts in 1885, Bergh was an outstanding portraitist of contemporaries and friends. He described S as "the most interesting model I have ever had. I read in his face, with its many lines of fate, as in a marvelous book."

> Djursholm, September 27, 1991. [-] In light of the assured success, our intention would be to try, in due time, either to found a company for a Strindberg *Bühne* or persuade Egnell, the restaurant's creditor to build a theatre out here [-].

To Fredrik Vult von Steijern (1851–1919), journalist, editor of the daily *Dagens Nyheter*, and a benefactor of S.

> Dalarö, May 2, 1892. [-] The unfortunate thing about my plays in book form is that they are meant for the stage, and hence make no impact when read. *Creditors* was recently performed in Uppsala and seems to have made an enormous impression [-]. It was ridiculed when it first appeared in print! [-]

To Adolf Paul (1863–1943), Finland-Swedish writer, acquainted with S in the period 1892–94 when S lived in Berlin and Austria. During this period, Paul was often cast in the role of S's literary amanuensis and errand boy.

> London, June 12, 1893. [-] A theatre in Berlin! [-]
> I have two actresses, beautiful, cultured, and well dressed.
> However, I don't think we should rent some notorious pub premises.
> Do you still feel for it? Then put out some feelers ahead of time when you go down to Berlin.
> The name shall be The Strindberg Theatre, if we obtain a permit? That is the first question. Furthermore, we have to begin with something that won't run into trouble with the censors! [-]

To Richard Bergh.

July 9, 1894. [-] Should anything else be done for me, nothing seems more suitable or honorable to our country than this: Give me a theatre!

Sweden lacked a drama; I created one, and one which will soon be the best in the world. [-]

In order to write plays there must be some prospect of having them performed. The theatre should be small and simple, a converted courtyard or large room. Not a new building but a rented one.

Lindberg, the Engelbrechts and some others could be assembled, with Lindberg as director of the "Strindberg Theatre"; that's what it will be called, and only Strindberg will be performed there. [-] Only Strindberg because Sg isn't performed anywhere else; and because the "others" are performed elsewhere, especially if they write shit; their circumstances are splendid! [-]

"Césarine: On Alexandre Dumas fils' Drama *La Femme de Claude*,"[121] *Le Figaro littéraire*, September 30, 1893.

No feeling compares in intensity with that of the dramatic author at work. He creates people, sometimes from nothing, sometimes from a lump of clay. He controls their fates according to his whims. He punishes and rewards. He rules over life and death in bringing his world to a happy or unhappy end. And people take his creations as if they were real, love or detest them, discuss them at least, and criticize the creator just as they judge the Great Unknown, each after his own heart. [-]

M. Dumas seems to have done himself an injustice with the preface to his admirable drama. The artist works unconsciously, and like nature, creates at random, with an astounding lavishness, but the moment he, *post festum*, tries to reflect on his work and analyze it, he awakens from his half-slumber, and falls to the ground like a sleepwalker.

Consider Césarine in this play. What a character! At once varied, complex, attractive and abominable, altogether woman! In the preface the writer pares her down, reduces her to a paragraph in the penal code, imputes intentions to her that she does not have in the play. [-]

"Character a Role?" *L'Écho de Paris*, January 2, 1895.

[-] It would appear that character is not as stable a thing as people would like to believe. That is why I do not undertake to classify characters; people cannot be classified. Every time I choose to study a man, I find I end up thinking the object of my studies is mentally deranged. The way people think and act is so incoherent if one follows closely the restless movements of their souls. Record their daily expressions of opinion, their fixed ideas or their passing fancies, and one discovers a hotchpotch that does not merit the term character. Everything has the appearance of inconsequential improvisations, with man himself being the greatest liar in the world, continually at odds with himself. The simplest bourgeois will emerge as the most complex of individuals; after a while you will be obsessed with him, and in the end you will be convinced that this man is concealing something, and that he is making fun of you and your interests. [-]

To Torsten Hedlund (1855–1935), publisher. Printing manager and later managing editor of the daily *Göteborgs Handels- och Sjöfartstidning*. An avid theosophist.

Paris, November 10, 1895. [-] I don't read a newspaper of any kind. Don't look at posters. Never go to the theatre. And no longer give permission for performances of my plays. I've been played here three times but haven't been to see a play, not even to the theatre. [-]

To Gustaf af Geijerstam.

Paris, March 17, 1898. [-] Just received your letter about the play [ *To Damascus I* ]! You were the first to read it, and your opinion delights me!

Yes, it is certainly fiction but with a terrifying half-reality behind it. The art lies in the composition which symbolizes "The Repetition" Kierkegaard speaks of:[122] the action unrolls forwards to the Asylum; there it kicks against the pricks and rebounds back through the pilgrimage, the relearning, the eating of one's words, until it begins anew at the same spot where the action had stopped, and where it began.

You may not have noticed how the settings unravel backwards from the

Asylum, which is the spine of the book that shuts upon itself and encloses the action. Or like a snake that bites its own tail.[123]

I suggest the following alterations: The Lady hasn't cursed him, but by reading his book, she has eaten of the tree of knowledge. She begins to reflect, loses her *Unbewusste* [unconsciousness], discovers the difference between right and wrong, is filled with discord, and thus loses her charm for him. I intend to separate them voluntarily in the final scene which will be extended. Shall I separate them? Yes! For the relationship is foul, but as instruments of torture for each other, they may continue being attracted to one another. I also want to arrange some details. Her knitting must be finished. The line "Shall we talk about you now?" is taken up again when she wakes to say: "Now we ought to talk a little about me, perhaps." His conversion to a religious awareness after the terrible blow at the Doctor's, when he discovers he has been in a lunatic asylum, must be apparent through intense contrition in the last scene. [-]

To Gustaf af Geijerstam.

Lund, October 17, 1898. [-] After reading through *Damascus* again, it seems to me that the two parts with cuts are short enough to be premiered on the same evening between 7 and 11. If this proves to be a success, the play could then be split up. [-]

And tell [Harald] Molander that of the scenery only the kitchen, the doctor's courtyard and the rose room really matter. The rest can be patched up. The movement from summer to winter can be done with set pieces, with the tree in the foreground, and for the rest by lighting if the scenery is kept in an abstract, shadow-like, colorless tone, which is in keeping with the play. [-]

To Gustaf af Geijerstam.

Lund, October 23, 1898. [-] One thing: Would you please send Ibsen[124] a copy of *Damascus*, and simply say: Strindberg is ashamed that as a prominent Swedish writer, he did not join in the tribute to the Master, from whom he learned much. But he was feeling depressed and did not believe his tribute could honor or delight anyone anywhere. [-]

To Gustaf af Geijerstam.

Lund, January 3, 1899. [-] Why *Advent*? Well, as you can see, I adopted a purely Christian, childlike point of view and conjured up the child Jesus [-] as the peace offering, the only one who can undo all of our evil, which we cannot do ourselves, however great our penitence and remorse [-].

I've stressed this in the child Jesus's line "Blame me!" Advent is also the arrival of the happy news that the Evil One was compelled, through Christ's descent into hell, to serve the Good, and that the Evil One (who is everywhere) is only an *Esprit correcteur* (Swedenborg's idea!), not an evil principle. In this way, the dualism of Good and Evil is abolished. In the last Christmas Eve scene in hell, Advent is explained as "the hope or tidings that punishments are not eternal."

The Judge and his wife are great criminals who think they can buy the "kingdom of heaven" and display man's infinite power of imagination by fooling himself into believing he is righteous. This illusion is a form of punishment (according to Swedenborg) by means of which man is kept in a state of impenitence in order to suffer the lack of blessedness. [-]

Interview in the Swedish daily *Svenska Dagbladet*, January 21, 1899.

For my new plays I don't want to use the usual stage scenery. All of those stereotypically painted theatre rags have to go. I only want one painted backdrop of a room, a forest or whatever. Or perhaps the backdrop could be brought about by a sciopticon image drawn on glass and projected onto a white canvas.

Furthermore, we'll have only one raised stage on which the actors perform, similar to Shakespeare's stage. It has to go, all this theatrical kitsch that floods the stage nowadays, weighing down the play itself, the lines, the content, which is what should captivate the audience and create illusion.

To Gustaf af Geijerstam.

Lund, February 24, 1899. [-] Hereby a new play, the value of which I [-] cannot judge, except that "it is theatre" and psychology! This time I wanted to deal with the problem of evil will, the responsibility of evil thoughts and the individual's right to punish himself.

I therefore have several titles in mind and I ask you to choose but choose wisely!

"At Higher Court" or "Crimes and Crimes."

But isn't it wiser to hide the threads and let the play pass for what it is: an event that is not the work of human hands? Especially perhaps since several problems cross each other in the play? [-]


To Leopold Littmansson (1847–1908), one of S's oldest friends. The son of a cantor in Stockholm, he married a wealthy Frenchwoman and lived in Versailles, where he devoted himself mainly to music as an enthusiastic amateur.

Lund, March 21, 1899. [-] Please specify in the parenthesis about Beethoven's Sonata in D minor that it is particularly bars 96-107 of the Finale that should be executed.[125] These notes always act like a center bit drill upon my conscience. It should sound as if the player was practicing these bars, that is, repeating and repeating them, with pauses in between. And so over and over again! (Did you notice that my play is based upon this sonata, fugal?) In the Prostitution scene, please choose moderately coarse words: *fille, drôlesse, ces dames*, etc.[126] [-]

# 1900-1906

"An Effective Drama." Undated note.[127]

> An effective drama should make use of intimations, contain a secret made
> known to the spectator either at the beginning or toward the end. If the
> spectators know the secret but not the actors, the spectators get to enjoy
> their game of blind man's buff. If the spectator does not know the secret,
> his curiosity is increased and he remains interested;
> an outburst of emotion, rage, indignation; [-]
> a discovery;
> a punishment (nemesis), a humiliation;
> a careful resolution, either with or without a reconciliation;
> a *quid pro quo*;[128]
> a parallellism;
> a reversal (*revirement*), a rebuff, a well-prepared surprise.

To Nils Personne (1850–1928), actor and stage director. Was engaged at the Royal Dramatic Theatre from 1876 and became its leader in 1898.

> November 17, 1900. [-] Just a word about the girl's (Eleonora's) part.[129] You
> know my weakness for Miss Bosse. I miss in her colleagues the fund of poetry
> and seriousness which she possesses; and her childlike figure is well suited for
> a girl with a pigtail down her back .
> The role of her brother is no bravura part, but Palme would no doubt take
> it and give it a breath of his irresistible poetry.
> If you, *mon Directeur*, would honor me by playing Lindqvist and give that
> terrible creature a touch of humor, I would be eternally grateful!
> I believe it requires a girl (but with short hair) as Benjamin, for young rascals of that age are extremely unpoetic. [-]

To Harriet Bosse (1878–1961), actress. Born in Norway, of Danish and German ancestry. Having charmed S as Puck in *A Midsummer Night's Dream*, she was chosen to play the Lady at the premiere of *To Damascus I*. She and S were married on May 6, 1901, and had a daughter, Anne-Marie, born the year after. Even after their divorce in 1904, they remained lovers until 1907. Harriet played a central role in S's life and he wrote several parts with her in mind: Indra's Daughter in *A Dream Play*, the title roles in *Kristina* and *Swanwhite*, Emerentia Polhem in *Carl XII*.

Stockholm, February 8, 1901. [-] A family tragedy has brought Eleonora [in *Easter*] to a state of mind – some would call it an illness – which has forced her into a (telepathic) rapport with her relatives, with mankind as a whole, and with the lower forms of creation, so that she suffers with all living things, or realizes the idea of Christ in Man. She is thus related to Balzac's Séraphita [-].[130]

However, with regard to the basic mood of the role: seriousness, of course. But Eleonora must be kind and tender, and should prattle and babble with Benjamin, like a child playing a mother. Never hard or even severe, for she pretends she is so would-be-wise, and one never knows what her faith is, though she has a cheerful, childlike trust.

To show she has brought an angel of peace with her, as her mother says, you must keep her bright, gentle, and above all not be harsh or preach like our pietists. And, note as well, when Benjamin asks if she's a pietist, and she answers yes, she does so merely to cut short an indiscreet question, not to profess a faith. For our pietists can't smile but Eleonora can, because she believes in a good God who can forgive, even though he delights in frightening children. You know, it may sound strange, but here as in *Damascus,* I think I'd like "a little of Puck" [in *A Midsummer Night's Dream*], roguishness! Sad, by all means, but not severe! [-]

And then this: I beg you to read the enclosed play [*The Crown Bride*] and see whether your role there might attract you. The piece has been submitted to the Opera, but observe: it hasn't yet been accepted.

It's an attempt on my part to enter Maeterlinck's wonderful world of beauty, leaving analyses, questions and opinions behind, and seeking only beauty in color and mood. I know I've only stopped at the gates. I must burn the rubbish in my soul before I am worthy of entering.

Please read the directions carefully and play the melodies, the ancient tones of Swedish folk music. Kersti[131] is not so incurably wicked that you need fear the contact. [-]

Another time, soon, I hope to hear your impression of *La Princesse Maleine,*[132] and after you have read *The Crown Bride,* I shall introduce you to Judith, the splendid girl in *The Dance of Death.* [-]

To Emil Schering (1873–1951), German writer and translator. During the first decade of the twentieth century he functioned as S's factotum in Germany. He is responsible for the 48-volume German edition of S's works (1910–24). His translations, though often criticized, helped make possible the great wave of S productions in Germany during the period 1915–26.

April 30, 1901. [-] Concerning *The Crown Bride*, yes, let me have lists with questions to answer. As for the style, it's Icelandic. [-]

If you want to understand my upcoming work, I ask you to read Maeterlinck's *Le Trésor des Humbles*, the greatest book I've ever read and which I've anticipated in *Easter*, *Midsummer* et al. The task is basically finding a likable aspect in an otherwise unlikable everyday person.


To Emil Grandinson (1863–1915), stage director. Apart from August Falck, Grandinson was the most responsive contemporary Swedish director to the demands of S's late dramas. According to S, his *To Damascus I* in 1900 was "a masterpiece of direction." Grandinson, who had earlier that year directed *Crimes and Crimes*, later staged *Easter* in 1901, *Carl XII* in 1902, *The Last Knight* in 1909 and *The Black Glove* in 1911.

Hellebæk, Hornbæk, July 6, 1901. [-] You have received *Damascus,* Part II. I have nothing against having it staged, but I ask that my wife be spared the part of the Lady, just as she herself, if there ever was a revival, asks that she be spared having to play the same role in Part I. [-]

As for your remarks about *Swanwhite*, I will only briefly state my intentions. [-]

To introduce the young King goes against the simple style of the ballad because two rivals about one person, or a *ménage à trois*, is French comedy and requires a thick Brussels carpet.

The flower test is from the ballad. The rose trees bend over the lovers' bier or tomb. The linden trees wind their leaves over church roofs. The lilies sprout from the dead woman's pure heart, through the burial mound.

The bursting of the troll in the sun[133] can be indicated by having her billowing clothes fall apart and drop like the shell of the chrysalis when the butterfly crawls out into light and liberation.

Otherwise, the piece hangs together well, nailed to the structural framework "the Duke goes to war – the Duke comes home."

The *ritardando* = The putting away of the horn.

The peripety = When they find each other, the Prince has drowned.

The denouement = The Prince is brought back to life because of Swan-white's compassion (= Love), because the Stepmother moves the Eternal One to annul an imposed sentence, and because the Stepmother herself is touched by this love (Caritas) [-].


*The Occult Diary*, as facsimile, in 1977.


November 18, 1901. Am reading about the teachings of Indian religion.

The whole world is but a semblance (= Rubbish or relative nothingness). The Divine Primary Power (Maham-Atma, Tad, Aum, Brama), allowed itself to be seduced by Maya, or the Procreative Instinct.

Hereby the Divine Primary Element sinned against itself. (Love is sin; therefore the pangs of love are the greatest hell.)

The world has thus come into existence only through a sin – if indeed it exists at all – for it is really only a mirage (consequently my *Dream Play* is an image of life), a phantom, and it is the task of asceticism to destroy it. But this task comes in conflict with the love instinct, and the sum total of it all is a ceaseless wavering between sensual orgies and anguished penitence.

This seems to be the answer to the riddle of the world!

I came across the above in the *History of Literature*,[134] just as I was about to finish my dream play "The Growing Castle",[135] on the morning of the 18th. The same morning I saw the Castle (= The Horseguards' Barracks) illuminated, as it were, by the rising Sun.

Now Indian religion showed me the meaning of my *Dream Play*, and the significance of Indra's Daughter. The Secret of the Door = Nothingness.

Read Buddhism all day.


Author's Note to *A Dream Play*, published together with the play circa June 1, 1902. [see further p. 109]


Circa November 20, 1901. In this dream play, the author has, as in his former dream play, *To Damascus*, attempted to imitate the disconnected but seemingly logical form of a dream. Everything can happen, everything is possible and probable. Time and place do not exist; on an insignificant basis of reality the imagination spins and weaves new patterns into a blend of memories, experiences, free fantasies, absurdities, and improvisations.

The characters split, double, multiply, evaporate, condense, disperse, converge. But one consciousness holds sway over them all, that of the dreamer; for him there are no secrets, no incongruities, no scruples, no law. He neither acquits nor condemns, merely relates, and, just as a dream is mostly painful, less often happy, so a tone of melancholy and pity for all living things runs through the swaying tale. Sleep, the liberator, often seems painful, but when the pain is at its worst, the sufferer awakes and is reconciled with reality which, however painful, at this moment is an instant of bliss after the tormenting dream.

To Emil Schering.

May 13, 1902. [-] Understand *The Dream Play*? Indra's daughter has come down to earth in order to find out how mankind is doing, and then she gets to see how hard life is. The hardest thing of all: hurting others, which one is forced to do if one wants to live.

The form is motivated in the "Author's Note," the jumble of the dream in which there is, nevertheless, a certain logic! Everything improbable becomes probable. People flit past and are sketched with a few traits; the sketches merge. One character dissolves into several who merge into one again. Time and space do not exist; a minute is like many years; no seasons; the snow covers the summer scenery, the lime tree turns yellow and then green again, etc. [-]

After having read *Götz*[136] recently, I couldn't take *Florian Geyer*;[137] struggled through it. It is worked out but the spirit is lacking! It is so meticulously studied that one wishes it were less so. A work of art should be a little careless, imperfect like something in nature, where not a crystal is without a flaw and not a plant without a miscarried leaf. Like Shakespeare. Serious play, but no labor and no scholarship in art! [-]

To Emil Schering.

September 10, 1902. [-] Thus "Intoxication,"[138] in Berlin! But this time I as the author would ask to be obeyed for once, for I know its dangers.

The greatest of these, and where we went wrong before, is the preaching or moralizing, despite the play's obviously liberating tendency.

(1)  Mrs. Eysoldt must appear psychically seductive; the vampire who drinks souls and needs nobody. [-] Unconscious of good and evil: "everything is permitted." But as she doesn't take into account that deeds have consequences, she is at first surprised and enraged; then she discovers that everything isn't permitted – but makes the discovery with an elegant resignation, without remorse, but with a certain sadness! Besides, the role is drawn in great detail, and Mrs. Eysoldt should take careful note of what the others say about her when she is off stage.

(2)  Maurice's role is clear.

(3)  Mrs. Cathérine is good-natured and tolerant; smiles at their weaknesses and [-] never punishes!

(4)  The Abbé is the most difficult. He should be [-] exactly like Mrs. Cathérine but without being scurrilous! With humor then, and spirit. In the final scene particularly, roguish, tolerant, childishly surprised by the enormous lack of scruples that has appeared here. [-]


To Emil Schering.

August 24, 1905. [-] Now I want *The Dream Play.* Tell me that it can be performed without all this scenery. Just with an arch of poppies as in *Damascus* and the Castle in the back. The rest are set pieces or screens or nothing; one simply pretends that it is this or that. [-]


To Harriet Bosse.

September 17, 1905. [-] If you were here, I would write monodramas for you. Or turn *Macbeth* and Schiller's *Maria Stuart* et al. into monodramas. But I'm afraid to truncate. With three people I will set up a theatre and play with screens and an arch. [-]


STRINDBERG ON DRAMA AND THEATRE

To Harriet Bosse.

September 26, 1905. [-] Your monodrama is already planned in five acts, only one character. I dare not write a play just now, because our plan this time has to be independent of other plans.

If everything fails, we can drive all around the country with Thespis's cart,[139] you, me, and Anne-Marie.

I'm trying hard to do something fine; perhaps there will only be one of them; this is difficult and new, therefore enjoy it. We'll have to have a dresser and a director and they can say the odd line off stage from a book. [-]

However, with two characters I could create a little world, and with three move it!

To Harriet Bosse.

April 14, 1906. [-] The novel tempts me the most. I loathe the theatre. Pose! Superficiality, calculation.

Read Shakespeare's [*The Taming of the*] *Shrew*. It was awful. Circus; false, clumsy, untrue. Just try to imagine how the audience permits its vision to be distorted. [-] Most people evidently go around like dozy dolts, and can be made to believe anything. [-]

"A Religious Theatre," September 12, 1907, in *A Blue Book I*.

June 23–November 20, 1906. The Teacher spoke: People don't seem to think very highly of themselves, for when they watch a really vicious satire in the theatre, they enjoy it without taking it personally. After all, it only applies to others. In my youth, there was a playwright who, after being a satirist, finally began feeling pity for people. Since he had mellowed after a good and relatively happy life, he saw people in a more favorable light. He wrote a play with only noble characters, full of sentiment and a tender heart. What happened? The audience thought at first it was a piece of irony, but in the second act they discovered the treachery. A voice roared from the stalls: Hell, but it's serious! And the performance proceeded under mounting disgust. The spectators felt ashamed of one another as well as on behalf of the author.

Some ran out while those remaining behind laughed; laughed at the goodness, the sacrifice, the privation, the forgiveness. They didn't recognize themselves and considered the depiction unnatural. This was not how it was in reality. People were not angels. Hence, it is dangerous at times to speak well of people. But it must be noted that religious people do not frequent the theatre, since the theatre is godless. Greek tragedy began with sacrifices to the gods, and all their tragedies deal with man's impotence in his struggle against the gods. Why don't our religious people set up a theatre where we can get to see how evil is ridiculed and unmasked?

Program for Strindberg's Scandinavian Experimental Theatre at the Dagmar Theatre in Copenhagen, March 1888. Three Strindberg plays are listed: *The Stronger, Creditors, Miss Julie.*

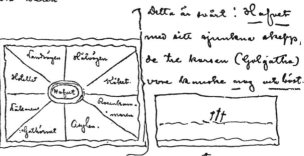

Strindberg's comments on the scene procedure and attributes in *To Damascus I*.

Jag hade mig tänkt att göra kompromiss och uttaga t. ex.
3 af Gunnarshus fonder till Damaskus I . Men börjas man
ändra dekoration, så än man inne i cirkulationen och då
begäres alla . Vilket är mig bäst ! Eller Landsvägen ?
Röda rummet går icke bra till denna !

Sg.

P.S. Fonden till de två blädsarne kunde kanske vara alldeles
slät; förställa ingenting; en verklig duk med Pinard-
skepen midt i en oköld : Detta som synes på Katolsk
grafver är :

Korset.
Törnekronan.
Lansen.
Gisslet.
(svampen) på en
stång; som höll
ättikan

De fyra spikarne, nederst .

Derunder: Veronicas Svetteduk med
Christus. Ansigtet, mycket svagt.

Detta vore kanske aldra bäst . Men då måste piano-redskapen af-
bildas precis efter Katolsk tradition (präga en Katolsk; Katolska
Franska skolan!. Fröken Falkner!)
Dermed vore allt sagdt, och inga dekorationer begäres.

Scene procedure and attributes in *To Damascus I* (continued).

Harriet Bosse, Strindberg's third wife, as Indra's Daughter in *A Dream Play* at the world premiere in 1907 at the Swedish Theatre in Stockholm.

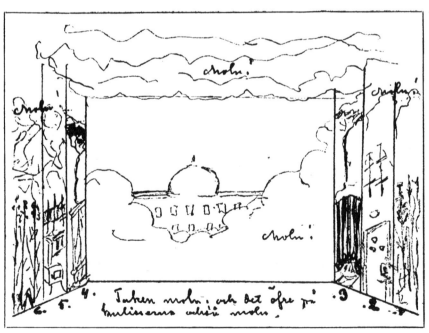

Strindberg's sketch for the scene procedure of *A Dream Play*. The growing castle in the background, symbol of life, forms a permanent setting. The text below reads: "The roofs clouds; and the upper parts of the wings also clouds."

The stage of the Intimate Theatre in Stockholm, led by August Falck and Strindberg 1907-10. On either side of the proscenium copies by Carl Kylberg of Arnold Böcklin's paintings the Isle of the Living (left) and the Isle of the Dead (right).

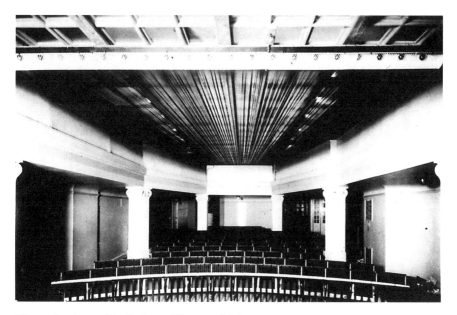

The auditorium of the Intimate Theatre with its 161 seats.

August Falck beside the bust of Strindberg by Max Levi in the foyer of the Intimate
Theatre.

STRINDBERG ON DRAMA AND THEATRE

Strindberg at the dress rehearsal of *The Burned Site* at the Intimate Theatre. Drawing by Gunnar Widholm in *Stockholms Dagblad*, December 6, 1907.

The original edition of Strindberg's *Memorandum to the Members of the Intimate Theatre* (1908).

The original edition of Strindberg's *Open Letters to the Intimate Theatre* (1909).

The end of *The Father* at the Intimate Theatre in 1908. The Captain, in straitjacket on the couch, has suffered a fatal stroke.

Strindberg at his writing desk in 1911 in his last domicile, Drottninggatan 85 in Stockholm, referred to by him as the Blue Tower.

STRINDBERG ON DRAMA AND THEATRE

# 1907-1912

To Adolf Paul.

Stockholm, January 6, 1907. [-] If you write anything new, then get in touch, but seek the intimate in form, a restricted subject treated in depth, few characters, large points of view, free imagination, but based on observation, experience, carefully studied; simple, but not too simple; no great apparatus, no superfluous minor roles, no regular five-acters [-], no long drawn-out evenings.

Here *Miss Julie* (without an intermission) has stood the test of fire[140] and proved to be the form demanded by today's impatient people. Thorough but brief. [-]

To Emil Schering.

March 27, 1907. [-] By today's post I am sending you a second chamber play (Opus III), called *A Ghost Sonata* (with the subtitle *Kama Loka*,[141] which should not be included). It is *schauderhaft* [dreadful], as in life when the scales fall from our eyes and we see *Das Ding an Sich*.[142]

It has form and content, the wisdom that comes with the years when our knowledge of life has accumulated and we have acquired the ability to survey. That is how the World Weaver weaves men's destinies. Secrets like these exist in *every* home. People are too proud to admit it; most of them boast about their imaginary happiness, and generally hide their misery. The Colonel plays his auto-comedy to the end; illusion (*Maya*)[143] has become reality to him; the Mummy wakes up first, but cannot awaken others [-]

I have suffered as though in *Kama Loka* (*Scheol*)[144] while writing it, and my hands have bled (literally).[145]
What has saved my soul from darkness during this work is my Religion (= *Anschluss mit Jenseits*).[146] The hope of a better life to come, and the firm conviction that we live in a world of folly and delusion (illusion), out of which we must struggle to free ourselves.

For me, however, things have grown brighter, and I have been writing with the feeling that these are my 'last sonatas.'

When you've given me your impression of *The Ghost Sonata,* I'll send you Opus I of the chamber plays [*Thunder in the Air*], which is total (lower) reality or an excellent piece for philistines, which might 'work.' [-]

To Emil Schering.

April 1, 1907. [-] It was a great and novel joy for me in my Easter suffering to find you so quickly taken by "The *Gespenster*[147] Sonata" (that's what it should be called after Beethoven's Ghost Sonata in D minor and his Ghost Trio,[148] thus not *Spuk.*[149] And you are the first to read it! I hardly recognized myself what I had done, but sensed it was something sublime, which made me shudder, the same overwhelming feeling as when one weeps with joy or [-] witnesses a noble deed in one's old age. [-]

*The Dream Play* opens in eight days! If you could get here, it would help you greatly in ascertaining its stageworthiness.

I have written a Prologue in verse [for *A Dream Play*]; among the clouds Indra's Daughter talks with her invisible father about descending in order to sense what life is like for mankind. The music for this is from Beethoven's Pastoral Symphony, the *Gewitter und Sturm*[150] movement.

Opus IV of the Chamber Plays is in progress; it is more horrifying than the others! I throw it aside, but it pursues me; and with bleeding hands I lay bare the misery, sacrificing myself for my work, burning up consideration, shame, gratitude, every human feeling. I suffer, but regret nothing; I must drink the cup [-].[151] How cruel life is, more cruel than we! [-]

To Emil Schering.

April 2, 1907. [-] No, that task was too heavy, and today I burned Opus IV, called "The Bleeding Hand."

Now I beg you, read my new dramas only as that; they are mosaics as usual, from my own and other people's lives, but please don't take them as autobiography or confessions. Whatever doesn't correspond with the facts is fiction, not lies. [-]

The burned Opus IV was a self-defense, that's why it was burned. [-]

I'm now probably entering upon something new. I long for the light, have always done so, yet have never found it.

STRINDBERG ON DRAMA AND THEATRE

Is it the end that is approaching? I don't know, but I have that feeling. Life is squeezing me out, as it were, or pestering me to leave, and I have long since rested my hopes on 'the other side,' with which I am in contact (like Swedenborg).

A feeling has also come over me that I have completed my task, and have no more to say. My whole life often seems to me as if it has been staged for me, to make me both suffer and depict it. [-]


To Emil Schering.

April 7, 1907. [-] Don't you think the following could be inserted into the final scene of *The Ghost Sonata*, or made visible in the letters of fire above *Toten-Insel*:[152]

"And God shall wipe away all tears from their eyes; and there shall be no more death, neither sorrow, nor crying, neither shall there be any more pain [-]: for the former things are passed away" (Rev. 21: 4).

*The Dream Play* will be performed this coming week!

Mind that you don't forget the Soya bottle,[153] the Soya bottle with its colored liquid which I've endured for thirty days; I have eaten colored water! [-]


Addition to "Author's Note" to *A Dream Play.*

April 1907 (?).[154] Until recently, the notion that life is a dream seemed to us only a poetic figure of Calderón's.[155] But when Shakespeare in *The Tempest* has Prospero say that "we are such stuff as dreams are made on" and when the wise Brit on another occasion has Macbeth characterize life as "a tale told by an idiot," we ought surely to give the matter some further thought.

Whoever accompanies the author during these brief hours along his sleep-walking path will possibly discover a certain similarity between the apparent medley of the dream and the motley canvas of disorderly life, woven by The World Weaver who sets up the warp of human destinies and then makes the weft out of our conflicting interests and changing passions.

He who sees the similarity will be justified in saying to himself: "Maybe it is like that."

As far as the loose, disconnected form of the play is concerned, that, too, is only apparent. For on closer inspection, the composition is found to be quite coherent – a symphony, polyphonic, fugued here and there, with the main theme constantly recurring, repeated and varied by the thirty odd voices in every key.

No solos with accompaniments, that is, no bravura roles, no characters, or rather, no caricatures, no intrigues, no curtain lines that invite applause. The voice arrangement is strictly applied, and in the sacrificial scene of the finale, everything that has happened passes in review, with the motives repeated once more, just as life in all its detail is said to do at the moment of death – hence another similarity!

Let us now see – and hear; with a little goodwill, half the battle is won. That is all we ask! [-]


*The Occult Diary.*

April 15, 1907. [-] Today, at 12 o'clock [-],the dress rehearsal for *The Dream Play* takes place. The odd thing is that this play was written after forty days of suffering (August–September 1901), after Harriet, carrying our unborn child, had left me. Now, when it is about to be performed, I have suffered for forty days both from a depressed (black) inferno mood and from domestic misery. [-]

A kind of calm, resigned feeling of uncertainty prevails within me. I wonder if a catastrophe will perhaps stop the play from being performed, which in fact should not be performed. True, I have talked nicely to mankind, but wanting to influence the World Ruler is presumptuous, perhaps blasphemous. That I have revealed the relative nothingness of life (Buddhism), its insane contradictions, its wickedness and unruliness, may be praiseworthy, if it makes people resigned; and also because I have demonstrated humanity's relative guiltlessness in this life, which of itself entails guilt, is surely not an evil thing ... But ...

Just now a telephone call from Harriet: "How this will end is in the hands of God." "I quite agree," I answered, "and I wonder whether the play will be allowed to be performed." (I believe High Powers have already made up their minds about that and about the outcome of the premiere as well – if there is to be one.)

It feels like Sunday at this moment. I can see the white figure on the balcony of the Growing Castle. During these past days, my thoughts have been much occupied with death and the life to come. Yesterday I read Plato's

*Timaeus* and *Phaedo.* Am I going to die now, or soon, I wonder? At present I'm writing *Toten-Insel,* in which I describe the awakening after death and what follows it, but I hesitate and dread to lay bare the abysmal misery of life. I recently burnt a play that was so honest that it made me shudder. This is what I never understand: Should one conceal what is vile and flatter humanity? I wish to write brightly and beautifully, but I may not, cannot; regard it as my dreadful duty to be truthful, and life is indescribably ugly. [-]

Evening, 8 o'clock. I went to the rehearsal of *The Dream Play* and suffered intensely; had the impression that this ought not to be performed. [-] It is presumptuous, probably blasphemous (?) [-]! Am out of harmony and frightened (unblessed). [-]


## The Occult Diary

April 17, 1907. *The Dream Play* is being performed today. Snow fell gently this morning. Read the last chapters of the Book of Job where God punishes Job for his presumption in daring to find fault with His works. Job begs for forgiveness and is forgiven. Quiet and gray until 3 o'clock. Then Greta[156] came with the news that I had been nominated to receive an Honorary Doctorate in Uppsala at the Linnean Celebrations in May, and that the dress rehearsal of *The Dream Play* had been favorably reviewed. Alone at home in the evening. On the stroke of 8 the doorbell rang and a girl entered with a laurel wreath and three roses, sent anonymously and inscribed: "Truth, Light, Liberation." I immediately took it to the head of Beethoven on the stove, as there is so much I have to thank him for. [-]

At 11 o'clock this evening, Harriet, Castegren, and Ranft[157] telephoned to say that *The Dream Play* had succeeded. Thanks be to God!


## To Emil Schering.

April 24, 1907. [-] As you can see from my chamber plays, after having read *Clavigo, Stella,*[158] etc. I have gone back to the *long* speeches and monologues. The French form of dialogue has degenerated into catechist questioning and precludes profundity and exhaustive treatment.

The incomplete (abortive) intentions should be retained, because they give a naturalness to the portrayal of life, since life is full of stranded plans, whims, projects which serve to fill out conversations, yet still constitute sources of energy. The Bishop's funeral [in *The Burned Site*] just sets the scene, contributing atmosphere and may mean something I no longer remember; maybe an undeserved nimbus, hinting at the nothingness of everything, and the glorification of nothingness! [-]


To Emil Schering.


April 26, 1907. [-] I began a major chamber play with *Toten-Insel* (Böcklin's) as a setting. The beginning was good (*Kama Loka*) but I lost interest, as I have lost interest in life, and have a presentiment of the end. For ten years I have been preparing myself for death and have lived, as it were, 'on the other side.' [-]

N.B. In the chamber plays one doesn't ask your kind of question! Discretion – *s'il vous plaît*!

There one lives in the world of intimations, where you speak in muted half-tones, because you are ashamed of being a human being! [-]


To Emil Schering.


May 6, 1907. [-] Yes, that is the secret of all my short stories, novellas and fairy tales – they are dramas. During those long periods when [-] the theatres were closed to me, I hit upon the idea of writing my plays in epic form – for future use. [-] Now I believe that with a more modern, informal notion of drama, it might be possible to take the stories *exactly as they are*! That would be novel! There would be many scene changes, but that is after all a remnant of Shakespeare's ubiquity; the author's reflections would become monologues. Or one could introduce a new character (corresponding to the Greek chorus) who would be the prompter, half-visible, reading the descriptions (of landscapes, etc.), and narrating or reflecting on events while the scenery was changed (in so far as one need employ any). A permanent arch and the Shakespeare *Bühne* from Munich[159] would solve everything. [-]

To Emil Schering.

May 16, 1907.[160] [-] You must compose the dialogue in my manner; the long speeches must be cut short by brief replies. However, we mustn't turn it into an oldfashioned 'machine' with a lot of unnecessary minor characters, crowd scenes, etc., but achieve a compromise that has the concentration of the chamber play. [-]

The first rule of writing is: Don't be impatient! It mustn't go quickly! Four weeks for four acts! Never write *invita Minerva*[161] but plan carefully. However, *nulla dies sine linea*,[162] a little every day, otherwise one loses the thread! [-]

And in drama: Stick to the subject! Don't forget the leitmotif! Weave people's fates together, the warp and the weft! Make the dialogue exhaustive, not too cropped (short); prepare the entrances well, round out the exits! Don't disclose all your secrets in the first act. Hold back, reveal piecemeal! A scene = an electrical discharge! But charge first, long and hard ! [-]


To August Falck.

Circa June 27, 1907. P.M.
    No bar service on the premises.
    No Sunday matinées.
    Short Performances: 8-10 p.m.
    Short or no intermissions. No calls during the performance.
    Only 160 seats in the auditorium. No danger of fire since smoking is not allowed. Central heating and electric heat sources in the dressing rooms.
    Air circulation according to the system xxx.
    No prompter.
    No orchestra, only music on stage.
    The text is to be sold in the box office and the lobby.
    Summer performances.
    The premises, location, etc. = The Nobel Library.[163]
    The repertoire: *The Nightingale in Wittenberg* and *Damascus* to be performed with simultaneous sets or Munich's Shakespeare stage = arch and drapery.

To Emil Schering.

July 24, 1907. [-] You are welcome to add lines, but it is better to have the actor fill out entrances and exits by repeating the last words slowly, with *ritardandos*, with small filler words and such [-]; even with little improvisations or pantomimes, so-called cadences in music. [-]


To Emil Schering.

August 25, 1907. [-] Falck begins in October with *The Pelican,* called 'Sleep-walkers' in order not to unmask motherly love again. He has already rehearsed all four chamber plays over the past fourteen days. Places 'Sleepwalkers' at the top!

He is the perfect man for the enterprise! As a manager, director, actor! [-]


To Axel B. Svensson (1879–1967), preacher in the Evangelical-Lutheran Missionary Society of Stockholm. In 1908, he became editor of a religious magazine entitled *Nya väktaren* (The New Guardian).

September 28, 1907. [-] Give me a piece of advice, just on intuition: What should I write now? My earthly calling is to be a playwright and I have ten beautiful plans, but I don't know if I am allowed to think about theatre. [-]

Sometimes I want to write biblical dramas, especially Easter plays, to be staged in or outside churches, in cemeteries, though I would not want to see Christ represented unless Christian young men wanted to perform.

I am a layman and feel it is my duty to cultivate the dramatic gift I have received. Isn't that right? Especially since I want to put it in the service of religion, building and planting on the sites I have torn down and cleared. [-]


To August Falck.

November 14, 1907. [-] After this morning's visit, I am convinced that if we open the theatre with this set and this play [*The Pelican*], our enterprise is doomed! [-]

I admit: A writer cannot bear to see the products of his imagination made real, for they never come true. That goes even more for the acting! I don't think I dare watch you! I might perhaps leave even if you acted well, and thus dishearten you! [-]

*The Burned Site* is a more attractive piece with which to open, easier to present, has greater breadth and perspective! [-]


To Axel Strindberg (1845-1927), S's eldest brother. One of the participants in the musical circle that met regularly in S's apartment. Composed incidental music for *Gustav Adolf* and *The Last Knight.*


November 29, 1907. [-] I have written this play [*The Pelican*] against my will; thought of burning it during the writing; threw it aside; but it returned, pursued me!

I have also suffered from its being played. I suffer every evening, but have still not come to regret it, or to wish it undone. It is as if the departed[164] demanded this satisfaction of me, or insisted that I *also* saw him from that side, where he was innocent and had merit.

No harm can come of it, for it's really a good thing if people who walk in their sleep out on the roof gutter are awakened. [-]


To August Falck.


January 29, 1908. [-] As a result of our discussion yesterday morning: You must have an intermission in *The Bond,* or you will tire, Miss Flygare[165] will tire, the audience will tire! But with an intermission you and Miss Flygare can speak more slowly, the audience will follow better, and the play will gain by it. [-]

And tell all the jurors that there is no humor at the district court, where people's fates are decided; it is all terribly serious, which is also clear from the text. Their make-up mustn't evoke the South Theatre;[166] they are all "trustworthy and honorable men."[167] [-]

When you speak to her, your posture (with your arms) should be more relaxed, intimate; one hand in your vest pocket, on your lapel, behind your back. When you speak to the judge alone, your arms can hang at your side, signifying respect for authority.

The final scene should be taken *ritardando* – a slower tempo with pauses.

The last phrase should be said after a pause, with deep feeling, accentuated, almost with emphasis. And both partners should leave the stage inspiring fear (for Fate) and arousing compassion. [-]

And Alexandersson must arouse compassion; not a trace of humor; when one's hopes are in ruins, one isn't a humorist.

Tell the whole cast: This is a *tragedy,* even if it is set in the present!


To Svea Åhman (1876–1937), actress. Engaged at the Intimate Theatre 1907-08, where she played the Daughter-in-law in *Playing with Fire*, the Mother in *The Pelican* and the Mummy in *The Ghost Sonata.*

January 31, 1908. [-] It [*Playing with Fire*] is a comedy, not a farce, a very serious comedy where people hide their tragedies beneath a certain cynicism. And the young wife is both well-bred and familiar with the ways of the world. To arouse the love of the serious man, she must be modest and yet possess a feminine charm. Remember how he (Ljungqvist)[168] portrays her. And use that to make the role plausible! At present one is amazed that this simple coquette of yours has been able to charm him, and the play doesn't make sense.

If you want to save your role and yourself, observe the following:

move as little as possible on stage, rather sit still;

don't accompany every word with grimaces or gestures;

restrict your voice to one register, and don't run up and down the scale; above all, don't squeak;

speak more slowly, monotonously like educated people, almost as if it were an off-book rehearsal, without any nuances;

be extremely reserved, like a young wife from a good family who conceals her emotions; [-]

actually have a reserved character in mind who by consorting with artists has fallen into a jargon that is foreign to her nature [-].

What I saw of you today was oldfashioned and out-of-date!

And, after all, we met here to try and renew things.

These are harsh words, but they must be said. [-]

To Svea Åhman.

February 2, 1908. [-] For the future and for the sake of your talent:

Don't *act* so much! Our small stage cannot bear that and doesn't need it.

Never burst into laughter! A sensitive person smiles but a nasty one roars with laughter!

Be simple but not to the point of vulgarity.

Be sparing of gestures and grimaces!

Speak slowly but with an inner feeling, so that the word is alive and has time to make an impact.

Avoid *staccato*, snapping and a strident voice!

The spoken word is everything on stage, almost everything!

Settle into your role but also into the predominant mood of the scene you are in. Therefore, it's good to anticipate your line from the wings, listen to the tone of voice of the actors on stage, grasp the mood and the tone and then make your entrance, rather than directly from the chatter of the dressing room! [-]


To Helge Wahlgren (1883–1958), actor and stage director. Engaged at the Intimate Theatre 1907–10.

February 2, 1908. [-] I found nothing to criticize in your role as the Judge in *The Bond*; he was excellent, and you have my thanks, encouragement and congratulations.

But in *The Ghost Sonata*, you didn't play my part: the dashing Student, the new, skeptical young man, who doesn't speak of eternal love. Therefore, I could do nothing to change it. [-] But I told the director to pay attention to the gravity and profundity of the play. [-]

I don't really know what I can teach you. But next time in *The Ghost Sonata*, please speak to the girl; it is with thoughts and words that he enters her soul.

And stress the poisonous effect of the flowers, which drives him mad like his father, and motivates his eruption.

In the final scene, try gently to bring her back to life or at least, by taking her hand, to find out if she is dead!

The tableau would be more beautiful if you went down on your knees, not before the Madonna but before death. [-]

To Anna Flygare (1880–1968), actress. Engaged at the Intimate Theatre 1907–10. Appeared as the Baroness in *The Bond*, as Eleonora in *Easter* – the most successful production in the short history of this theatre – and as Alice in *The Dance of Death I*.

February 3, 1908. [-] The art of acting today for today's tired and reserved but overly intelligent people will undoubtedly be the spoken word as the chief thing, assuming you speak clearly enough for every word to be heard. This can only occur if you keep the phrase together (*legato*), and not *staccato*. But no disturbing emphases, which the audience might find offensive. [-]

Even if the line is vehement, don't sneer, don't bite. Even if the Baroness is angry, she must appear charming in order to motivate the Baron's love for her and to retain the audience's good will.

Some say that you shouldn't reveal your profile so frequently but face the audience. This may or may not be based on the role, but I think that a full face with the gaze out toward the audience is more winning and puts the actress in touch with those she is addressing.

To Ivar Nilsson (1877–1929), actor. Played Gustav Vasa in the premieres of *The Last Knight* and *The Regent*, and the title role of *Master Olof* in the revival of 1908.

Circa February 9, 1908. [-] The historical Master Olof is in a few words: A hot-tempered and pushy fellow who trusted neither princes nor the lower classes. An anarchist in his youth, accused of having known about murderous plots against the King. [-]

If you read my drama *The Nightingale in Wittenberg* (Luther), it will clarify the role of Master Olof to you. It's the same type! And the weak moments in Master Olof are only due to his temporary fatigue and not part of his character. Therefore, his soft side should be played down. If you've received other instructions, then throw them out. I alone am competent to interpret the role! And don't forget to play the *historical* Master Olof! On the other hand, forget the one that has been concocted by all that talk and has crept into my text! [-]

I won't get to see you, for I cannot expose myself! I was born that way. Don't think I'm uninterested or ungrateful because of this, and tell your fellow actors the same thing. I was invited to the dress rehearsal on Sunday evening, with no fanfare, I thought. Now I hear there will be a full house! Then I cannot come! But I'm with you from afar! [-]

To August Falck.

February 11, 1908. [-] Don't choose a red beard and wig in *Pariah*; it stands out too strongly for this character (= provincial). Villains are seldom red-haired. Choose rather a washed-out blond one. And make a little more of the role. Use your hands, which seemed somewhat embarrassed; hold on to the cigar butt, thumbing it, chewing on it [-] etc.

You are on stage too much, which leads to your being careless![169] Keep a few starring roles but stress being primarily a theatre manager and a director, or the theatre will go to the dogs, and so will your art. Keep the actors occupied or they will become despondent; give all of them a chance; they have more time than you! [-]


To Ivar Nilsson.

February 16, 1908. [-] Once again: play the role [of Master Olof] as I have written it, and you will succeed! He is no elegiac Hamlet, but "an angry man." It says so in the text. "The pale cleric," sharp in logic; thinks a lot, etc. [-]

A man of iron, then, with an immense amount of self-assurance, who isn't likeable and doesn't care to be. Most actors have made the mistake of playing him with warmth instead of fire, and, paying little heed to the author's characterization; they have insisted on being likeable or flirting with the audience, showing him as torn and pathetic. This way of interpreting a role subjectively has the drawback of making everything false. For when the performance of the part doesn't agree with the characterization given by the other figures, the role clashes with the author's description of it [-].

Everything he says is arrogant, no matter who he is addressing, whether peasant, bishop or king! [-]

Strength, almost brutality; fire, but no so-called warmth; even at his mother's death, he is hard, but is overwhelmed by sleep and weariness, as he himself says. [-]


To August Falck.

February 28, 1908. [-] The reason I've cut "Kerstin" and "Little"[170] is because the role was written for Bosse, for whom the diminutives were fitting. But as the more regal Mrs. Björling is to play Kristina, these changes are necessary. [-]

Tell Mrs. Björling the role in two words: The amazon who fights for her legitimate freedom but is finally conquered in battle when she encounters a love "stronger than death." Tott[171] was Kristina's only love! The rest was simply mischief and a desire for power! At first she merely playacts, arousing Tott's love, then it overwhelms her. She falls in love herself, and suffers.

And don't forget, she is more Queen than coquette! The Queen first and last! She sometimes makes herself small when she wants to obtain something, but this is only hypocrisy! "A Cat"! She must never *be* considered small. Remember what I told you about her make-up. Big eyes, unusually big, eyebrows, high above like eagle's wings, [-] a clear forehead, strong nose, the corners of her mouth curved, her lower lip thicker, dark hair as in the portraits of her.

The costume for the final act, Pandora[172] ad lib, but preferably a Greek chiton,[173] hair *à la grec,* a becoming dress. [-]


To August Falck.


March 26, 1908. [-] Kristina must not neglect the big scene in the Treasury, where every word is a knife; and she should pay attention to where it strikes. The stabs are to be carefully distributed. Oxenstierna and De la Gardie exchange glances throughout the scene. [-]

Because *Kristina* is now produced with one standing set, these costume changes become superfluous and seem disquieting, disturbing. Since the setting is not changed, the costumes must not be changed (except Pandora). If the actor retains the same costume, the audience gets a better grasp of him, does not lose track of him, and the character becomes more unified; also, the actor begins to 'find his feet'! It is easy to confuse the characters in costume plays. Therefore, don't change costumes in costume plays! [-]


To August Falck.


March 28, 1908. [-] A table and two chairs! The ideal! The biggest scenes in *Kristina* were performed with a table and two chairs.

The table offers so much support; and such rich opportunities for beautiful, lively gestures; it becomes a hyphen between the two speakers, keeps the dialogue together, separates but joins. Like the duet in an opera!

I now think of Ebba Brahe and Ebba Sparre[174] as silent roles that should have been cut! They don't keep the promise they present in the first act. Cut them! It's also hard on the actresses! [-]


To August Falck.


April 1, 1908. [-] The drapery scene in *The Father* will lift the play out of its everyday sphere and turn it into high tragedy. The people become sublime, ennobled and seem to be from another world. (Same as in *Easter*!) In *The Father* the Captain's interrogation [of Nöjd] could be cut.

We've lapsed back into what was called the Molander style or realism, naturalism, which is all passé! It's the Michaelson style these days![175] This is my fault, for sometimes I get tired and backtrack!

We have to take a firm hold of ourselves and pull ourselves together.
Use the Molière stage in *Kristina*! We pretend the space is wherever we want, and it will work! Try it! Then we have liberated the stage, the actor – and our conscience, for anything else is a crime! [-]

In *Miss Julie*, in Copenhagen, everything was painted on the wall, shelves and kitchen gadgets, chairs and other pieces of furniture.

The Molière stage is from 1600, Kristina's time. *Gustav III* can be performed on a rococo stage (Molière). [-]


To August Falck.


April 18, 1908. [-] Now, I beg you, in the future and at once, to delete every insult to religion or what is holy, beginning with *The Father*! [-] It will free me from this sense of being at odds with myself, since I'm responsible down there[176] for the preaching of false doctrines, which I now preach against and no longer profess! Only then can I pray for a blessing upon the little temple at Bantorget! and then the blessing will come!

To Uno Stadius (1871–1936), Finland-Swedish advocate of temperance and folk education. Lived for many years in Sweden.

April 18, 1908. [-] I am a Christian and am convinced that people should not be raised with theatre and paintings but with work and the fear of God. Instead of the surrogate of art, they possess the original, God's wonderful natural world! [-]

To August Falck.

April 23, 1908. [-] *The Father* must be played as a tragedy! Big broad gestures, raised voices!

Alexandersson should be the lioness that did not come out in *Easter*.[177] She should be a tragedienne but at the same time modern, of our time; not tame, not a comedienne; not afraid of outbursts and wild passions, great hatred, power-hungry like a woman from hell.

And you! That's what you have to figure out! But you must absorb your part this time and not come half-prepared! For then the success of *Easter* is wiped out!

Release your passions, your outbursts, but don't get hoarse, let all hell break loose! [-]

To August Falck.

April 26, 1908. [-] Once more: pay attention to the exits. Someone who shuffles out takes with him some of the ambience of the scene; but he should leave something of his role behind. And when he is offstage, he should not cut off the thread by talking or doing something else. If he plays the lead, he must not lose touch while he is offstage. His thoughts should remain on stage and engage in the action; his soul should be present though his body has left. Those remaining on stage will feel this and when they mention him, the audience should imagine his presence. [-]

Furthermore, when a role takes complete possession of a person, it lives in every muscle, nerve and sinew. With the word, the gesture will follow of its own accord; not a muscle is lifeless. In the opposite case, arms and hands hang as if dead, like objects. But if the words come from the heart, the hands will follow the movements of the mouth, without giving it any thought. I have at last discovered that one achieves the most convincing illusion by not thinking about the audience but rather about the scene itself. That is what Kjellgren did as Benjamin and Falck as Lindqvist [in *Easter*]. Flygare sometimes had to speak with her eyes on the audience since her words were not enough, and she did that well. For a while, Rydell made it a special feature of her part to dedicate her words to the stalls; it sounded oldfashioned and placed her outside of the frame. De Verdier was just right. It's possible to turn one's face to the audience without 'talking to the people.' De Verdier did that; he directed himself to the audience but kept himself inside the curtain; that's the trick!

Alexandersson on the other hand cut herself off at times; she might very well direct her gaze outwards but above the heads of the audience. She avoided catching their eye, which is always disagreeable; and she did so through a circular movement of her head, so that she looked down toward the floor rather than letting her eyes be seen. Let her show her eyes at times, but not the whites by looking up too high. The whites of the eye can indicate a plea to the heavens, but it can also look like madness. (I mean, the whites *under* the pupil.)

For entrances, the same applies as with exits. Don't rush in and disrupt! Glide into the situation, and don't introduce an alien tone; instead, stand in the wings and follow the lead of those on stage! Those who have already warmed up may be thrown off by someone rushing in who has left his newspaper or cigar in the dressing room; they may fall out of character, as when an outsider interrupts a conversation [-]; they should confront him with their mood and genuine tone of voice and impose these on him. [-]

Preach to the pupils and others that announcer roles are very important. If one doesn't hear the name of the person announced, it will be a stranger who enters and it will remain a stranger until the curtain falls and the audience can look at the program. Tell them that I know of actors who have been discovered in announcer roles and gone on to success. "There was a correct intonation; there appeared a gesture that was true!" What usually goes wrong is that the announcer despises his small part, doesn't find out what it means and so doesn't understand what he is saying, stumbles into an unfamiliar situation and seems phony, thus making the others seem phony, too. He often hides his bruised vanity under a feigned shyness or an assumed impudence and throws away his part, suggesting that he (the pupil) is too good for it and showing that "underneath this coat" there is more than just the hide of a servant![178] [-]

To Anna Flygare.

May 5, 1908. [-] Now I am waiting for the memory of the *Easter* girl to come back before we turn to *Swanwhite*.

Only two words ahead of time about this new mental image. Eros is not the main motif; the image represents only Caritas, the great Love that endures all, survives all and forgives, hopes, believes even when it is betrayed by everything! It is expressed better in the Stepmother's change of character – and best in the final scene: Love is stronger than death! [-]


To August Falck.

May 9, 1908. [-] By keeping the staging simple, one gains calm on the stage, and a little comfort and ease behind the wings, which the poor actors need. [-]

By keeping the scenery simple, what matters emerges: character, role, speech, mimicry, gesture. It is often a waste of effort to reset the stage for a short scene; the spectator doesn't have time to take it all in, for he is fully occupied with listening to and making sense of the spoken word!

"In the beginning was the word!" [John I:1] Yes, the spoken word is everything!


To Fanny Falkner (1891–1963), painter and actress. Though she and S were twice engaged, marriage was never a serious proposition.

May 30, 1908. [-] I will now give you my impressions of your reading today, and what you can learn from it.

It was beautiful, sensible, and sounded good.

But [-] it was the kind of conversation used in a small room; in a larger space, like the theatre, everything must be proportionately enlarged, without the voice needing to be amplified to any great extent.
1. Speak slowly, *legato*, every word in the phrase linked; the punctuation marks must not create a *staccato* effect, one glides over them with a minor sound, which I shall teach you.
2. Speak naturally, but don't chatter! [-]

To August Falck.

June 2, 1908. [-] At all other theatres it is the custom at least to ask the author about the assignment of roles in his plays. But you don't ask me, you only hand out the parts and not even with good judgment!

I have now tested Fanny Falkner here at home, where she did the first scene in *Easter* with Kjellgren; quite excellent! Though soft spoken. But she is a born actress! [-]

Now I wish to see her and Kjellgren in *Swanwhite*, and she is now going to read for Mrs. Engelbrecht[179] at my expense.

I have also recommended Falkner to Ranft as Swanwhite, for I believe in her lovely childlike temperament and stage talent!

You can alternate with Mrs. Björling and Flygare who may also be successful, but as an author and co-owner I demand to have a say in a matter where common sense and good taste are on my side! [-]


To Tor Aulin (1866–1914), violonist, conductor, and composer. He founded the Aulin String Quartet, was for many years first violin at the Royal Opera House and took part in S's Beethoven evenings.

July 6, 1908. [-] *The Ghost Sonata* was only supposed to show you the form I am seeking for the new music drama; starting with chamber music, condensed, concentrated, with only a few voices. [-]

But *The Ghost Sonata* has another side! To extract atmosphere (poetry!) out of contemporary everyday reality without turning to the Orient or medievalism or the fairy-tale play. [-]


*Memorandum to the Members of the Intimate Theatre from the Director*, August 20-26, 1908.

July 14-21, 1908. [-] *The Concept of Intimate Theatre.* When anyone in the 1860s and 1870s submitted a full-length play to the Royal Theatre, he had to observe the following requirements if to get it performed. The play should preferably have five acts, each act about twenty-four pages long or, in total, 5 x 24 = 120 folio pages. The division into tableaux or *changements* was not appreciated and was considered a weakness. Every act was supposed to have a beginning, a middle, and an end. The end of an act should be the place for applause, which was brought about by an oratorical figure; if the play was in blank verse the last two lines should rhyme. There were 'numbers' within the plays for the actor, called 'scenes.' The soliloquy was often the show piece. A longer emotional outburst, a chastisement or an unmasking was almost a necessity. You could also relate something: a dream, an anecdote, an event. But roles were also required, rewarding roles for the theatre's stars.

These prescribed poetics for a drama included of course much that was justified and attractive. They stemmed ultimately from Victor Hugo and, in the 1830s, were a reaction against the antiquated abstractions of Racine and Corneille. But this form of art degenerated like all others when it had run its course. Every kind of motif, even the insignificant [-] anecdote was crammed into the five-act play. Practical considerations such as not letting any of the theatre's important personnel be unoccupied forced one to create minor characters to be played by actors rather than extras. The matter of roles was confused with the depiction of character, and we have recently even heard that the practical Bjørnson[180] is the great creator of roles.

The fear of a dominant motif was accompanied by the stretching out of trifles, so that managers were ultimately forced to suggest the deletion of long uninspired passages.

Around 1870, when I had written "Sven the Sacrificer" in five poor acts of verse and tried to read it aloud to fellow poets in Uppsala, I found the entire play boring. So I burned it [-]. Out of the ashes rose the one-act *The Outlaw*, which along with its great weaknesses has the merits of sticking to the subject and of being brief but complete. Here I was undoubtedly influenced by Bjørnson's splendid one-act *Between the Blows* which I found exemplary.

The tempo of the times had picked up. People demanded quick results and had become impatient.

In my first version of *Master Olof*, I tried a compromise. I substituted prose for verse, and instead of the opera-like blank verse drama with solos and special numbers, I polyphonically composed a symphony in which all the voices were interwoven, major and minor characters were treated equally, and no one accompanied the soloist. The attempt succeeded, but since then, the play has been cut, for it proved to be too long for contemporary people. But in the 1880s, a new era began extending its demands for reform even to the theatre. Zola attacked the French comedy with its Brussels carpets, lacquered shoes and lacquered motifs, and a dialogue reminiscent of the questions and answers of the catechism. In 1887, Antoine opened the Théâtre Libre in Paris, and *Thérèse Raquin,* although only an adaptation of the novel, became the model. The strong motif and the concentrated form were new, although the unity of time was still not observed and the lowering of the curtain remained. It was then that I wrote *Miss Julie, The Father,* and *Creditors.* [-]

A certain silence then ensued, and the drama resumed its semi-old tracks until Reinhardt opened his Kleines Theater at the beginning of the new century. I was in on that from the beginning with the long one-acter *The Bond,* plus *Miss Julie* [-], and *Crimes and Crimes.*

Last year Reinhardt took this even farther by opening the Kammerspiel-Haus, which by its very name reveals its secret program: the concept of chamber music transferred to drama. The intimate action, the significant motif, the sophisticated treatment. Last autumn, the Hebbel Theatre [in Berlin] opened in almost the same spirit, and throughout Germany, theatres with the name Intimate Theatre have sprung up.

In the last days of November 1907, August Falck opened the Intimate Theatre in Stockholm, and I had the opportunity to follow the stage activity in all its details more closely. Memories from my forty-year career as a dramatist were awakened, older observations were checked, old experiments were repeated, and my newly awakened interest gave me the idea of writing this memorandum.

If anyone asks what an intimate theatre seeks to achieve and what is meant by chamber plays, I can respond by saying: In drama we seek the strong, significant motif, but with limitations. In the treatment we try to avoid all frivolity, all calculated effects, places for applause, star roles, solo numbers. No predetermined form is to limit the author, because the motif determines the form. Consequently, freedom in treatment which is limited only by the unity of the concept and the feeling for style.

When Director Falck avoided the long performances which end near midnight, he also broke with the classic tradition of serving liquor in the theatre. That was courageous, for the sale of liquor usually pays at least half the rent for the large theatres. But the combination of theatre art and alcohol was accompanied by long intermissions, their length determined by the restaurant keeper and their observation controlled by the director.

The drawbacks of letting the audience out to imbibe strong drinks in the middle of the drama are well known. The mood is destroyed by talk, the enraptured spirit is hardened and becomes conscious of what should remain unconscious. The illusion the drama sought to convey cannot be sustained, and the half-hypnotized theatre goer is awakened to banal reflections. Or he reads the evening paper, talks about other things with acquaintances he meets in the bar. He is distracted, the threads in the play are cut, the development of the action is forgotten, and in a completely different mood the spectator returns to his seat to try in vain to pick up where he had left off.

That system degenerated to the point where many people reserved tables before the play started and treated the play as an interlude; yes, there were those who missed an act because the shag sofa was so soft and difficult to get out of.

The finances of the Intimate Theatre suffered from this break with tradition but it gained in another way. The attention in the auditorium was focused more on the stage, and after the performance the audience was compensated by being able to go to supper and discuss comfortably what they had heard and seen.

We looked for a *small* house, because we wanted the voices to be heard in every corner without forcing the actors to shout. For there are theatres so large that the actors must strain their voices so that every intonation becomes false, and where a declaration of love has to be shouted; a confidence revealed as if it were a military order; the secret in one's heart whispered with a full voice; and where it sounds as if everyone on the stage is angry or in a hurry to leave. [-]

The art of acting is the hardest and the easiest of all the arts. But, like beauty, it is almost impossible to define. It is not the art of pretense, for the great artist does not pretend but is honest, true, and natural, while the low comedian does everything to pretend through make-up and costume. It is not imitation, because poor actors most frequently have a fiendish ability to imitate well-known people, while the genuine artist lacks that skill. The actor is not the author's medium except in a certain way and with reservations. In aesthetics, the art of acting is not considered one of the independent arts but rather a dependent one. It cannot exist, of course, without the author's text. The actor cannot do without the author, but, if necessary, the author can do without the actor. I have never seen Goethe's *Faust,* Part II, Schiller's *Don Carlos,* or Shakespeare's *The Tempest,* but I have seen them all the same when I have read them, and there are good plays that should not be performed, that cannot hold up to being seen. But there are poor plays that must be performed to come alive; they must be filled out, ennobled, by the art of acting. The dramatist usually knows what he must thank the actor for, and he is usually grateful. So is the superior actor toward his author, and I would prefer to see them thank each other, since the obligations are mutual, but they would be on the best of terms if that unjustified question were never raised. Yet it is often raised by conceited fools and by stars, when they happen to perform a play that deserves obliteration; and then the author is a necessary evil as someone who writes the text for their roles since there has to be a text. I have never heard this question considered at the Intimate Theatre and I hope I never shall. There I have seen roles which were better and more attractive than my originals, and I have frankly admitted that.

The art of acting seems to be the easiest of all the arts since in everyday life every person can talk, walk, stand, gesture, and make facial expressions. But then he is playing himself, and that is clearly something else again. For if he gets a role to learn and perform, and is let out on the stage, one soon notices that the wisest, most profound, and strongest person is lost there, whereas a rather simple person can at once play the part. Some people show that they are born with the gift of recreating; others don't have it. But it is always hard to judge the beginner, because the gift can be there without being immediately revealed, and great talents have sometimes had very miserable starts. Therefore the manager and director[181] has to be careful in his judgment when the fate of a young person rests in his hands. He has to test and observe, have patience, and postpone his judgment into the future.

What makes a person an actor and what qualities are required is very hard to say, but I shall try to list a few. First of all, he must be able to attend to the role, to concentrate all his thoughts on it, and not let himself be distracted. [-] The second requirement is, I guess, having [-] the gift of imagining the character and the situation so vividly that they take shape.

I assume that the artist falls into a trance, forgets himself, and finally *becomes* the figure he is going to play. It is like sleepwalking but not quite the same. If he is disturbed in this state or awakened to full consciousness, he becomes confused and is lost. That is why I have always hesitated to interrupt a scene during rehearsal. I have seen how the actor is tortured by being awakened; he stands there dazed and needs time in which to get into the trance again, to recover both mood and intonation.

No form of art is as dependent as the actor's. He cannot isolate his artistic creation, display it, and say: It is mine. Because if he receives no response or support from his fellow player, then he is distracted, lured into false notes. Even if he makes the best of his own role, it does not jell. Actors are at each other's mercy, and unusually selfish actors have been known to play down their rival, efface him in order to let themselves be seen.

For that reason the spirit at a theatre or a good relationship is of the greatest importance if the play is to have its full effect [-]. Above all else, the actors must work together, fit into a unit. That is asking a lot of people, especially in a field where a justified ambition drives everyone to be seen, to win recognition, and accept well-earned praise.

Once the actor has a truly vivid concept of the character and the scene in which he will play, the next thing he must do is memorize the role. It begins with the spoken word, and that I believe is the main thing in the art of acting. If the actor has a strong imagination and if his tone of voice is right, gestures, facial expressions, bearing, and positioning follow naturally. If he lacks that, we see his arms and hands dangling like lifeless things, his body seems dead, and all one can see is a speaking head on a lifeless body. The beginner usually has this difficulty. The spoken word has not had the power to penetrate the body and make all the joints function in unison. [-]

I am inclined to consider the spoken word of the highest importance. You can present a scene in the dark and enjoy it, provided it is effectively spoken! [-]

The first requirement, therefore, is to speak slowly. The beginner hasn't the slightest notion how exceedingly slowly he can and ought to speak on the stage. [-]

Speaking so that it "sounds like theatre" is something [-] to be avoided. These intonations do not belong to the role; they go alongside like loose horses that do not pull; one sees the blue script in the air; that is, the role has merely been memorized; it sounds memorized, and this means that the artist is not *in* the role but outside it. [-]

*Studying the role.* There are perhaps several ways, but the surest is probably this: First, read the script carefully; this used to be done at the initial group reading of the play which I consider essential. For I have seen with horror how great artists pick out *their* roles like grains from the sand and leave the rest to its fate as if it did not interest them. I have also seen the results of this; they have misunderstood their roles or portrayed their characters falsely. Since they don't know what people say about them when they're offstage, they don't know who they are. It often happens in a play that people characterize someone who is absent, who can be a self-deceiver who doesn't know his value. [-]

Analyzing and studying a role can also be carried too far so that you end up seeing the intentions which a frivolous artist can turn into tricks. A play can also be rehearsed too long so that it loses its freshness. [-]

The character actor [-] forgets himself, steals into the role completely, and becomes the character he is playing. I have seen genuine magicians of that kind, and I have admired them. But the character actor can easily be tempted to create types and to transform them into caricatures. Character is, of course, the essence of a person's *inner* life, his inclinations, his passions, his weaknesses. If the character actor emphasizes the nonessential externals or tries to express the uniquely individual qualities of the role by means of strong external means, the interpretation can easily become a caricature, and instead of creating a character he creates a funnyman. [-]

*Listening on stage and silent acting.* The actor not speaking but listening to what someone else is saying must really listen. He mustn't look bored even if he has heard what is being said by the other a hundred times; he must not look as if he is merely waiting to speak or as if he were impatiently waiting for the other to finish so that he himself may talk. There are listeners who lower their eyes and look as if they were memorizing their next speech, which they are already chewing to have it ready. [-] Others *try* to look interested by raising a glowing face but instead only look hypocritical, drumming their hands and moving their lips as if they were listening to every word being said.

The one who listens should not fall out of his role, but his face must reflect what the other is saying, and the audience must be able to see the impression it is making [-]. I have [-] seen masterpieces in the art of listening and silent acting. I have seen Jean listen to Miss Julie's long autobiography as if he were hearing it for the first time although he had heard it a hundred and fifty times. In the same play, I have seen the cook listen to Miss Julie's death fantasies about an imagined happy future in such a way that I had to applaud her. [-]

It is as a listener that the selfish, mean actor takes the opportunity to nullify or play down his rival. Through a carefully calculated absentmindedness, by making himself hard, turning his back on his rival, looking skeptically impatient, he can avert interest from the speaker, cancel his words and personality, and direct attention toward himself. But the speaker must not lose his self-control, not become angry, but apply the same tactics, adapt his acting to the tricks of the other, anticipate if necessary and with a calculated silent contempt unmask him. Then the audience will get the impression that this is part of the play, and the situation is saved. [-]

*Positions.* [-] The big scenes are generally played near the footlights so that the actors will be plainly heard and seen, but sometimes the opposite has a greater effect. Explanations and settling of accounts are done face to face. Longer explanations and speeches I usually situate at a table with two chairs. The table divides and unites the antagonists; it also provides for natural, easy gestures, is restful, supports arms and hands. The chairs must not be too low, because the body then is cramped and the actor has a hard time talking. [-]

Even in our little theatre, the actor must always remember that he is not acting for himself alone up on the crowded stage and that some 150 people are sitting in the auditorium who have the right to *see* and *hear*. So it won't do to mouth the role; it must be spoken outward in a magnified way – like the public speaker [-] who must raise his voice and phrase what he has to say so that he will be heard and understood.

Even the most intimate scene must be performed with the audience in mind, without the actor playing *for* or *with* the audience. He must not direct his eyes or his speeches to the audience but to his fellow actor on stage, though not as if the two were alone in the room. Every attempt to direct a phrase toward the auditorium or to make a confidant out of a member of the audience, to play up to or to try to gain the favor of the audience should be banned. [-]

Turning one's back to the audience is permissible if the role calls for it, but should not be misused in major conflicts or disclosures where one wants to see the actors' facial expressions. [-]

Like the orchestra conductor, the director is not a particularly popular person, since he is only there to criticize. He has to admonish even the mature artists and often gets tit for tat. Experience has taught me that the artist can be right without the director being wrong, for in questionable cases a matter *can* be resolved in various ways. It's better then for the sake of harmony to accept the director's interpretation since some decision has to be reached. And the director is usually the only one who knows the whole play: the development of the plot, all the intrigues, all the roles; [-] and for that reason he ought to have the final say. Even if he is not an actor himself and is not able to perform the part, he can still discern how it should be performed.

The artist may certainly present his ideas to the director, but he must not ill-naturedly challenge or try to browbeat him, for this causes a tense relationship and can lead to animosity, from which come uneasiness and strained feelings, making the entire project suffer.

As the author who attends dress rehearsals, I have often seen an actor render another character than the one I had intended. If his interpretation has proved to be thorough and not harmful to the play, I do not change it and allow him to have his way. Far better that he should realize his characterization as he has conceived it than that I should tear to pieces his creation which, after all, is something whole and coherent. The author is, of course, the one who ought to know his play best and know what he has intended. But he may have been away from it for such a long time that he has forgotten the details and he

STRINDBERG ON DRAMA AND THEATRE

may therefore be wrong compared to the actor who has the whole play fresh in his mind. Then the author must admit that he is wrong. As an author, I have seen actors who have made a neglected character greater and better than I could have ever dreamt of. Even after a dress rehearsal I've had had to admit: This is certainly not my work, but it is just as good, in some places better, in others worse.

Here I must come to the conclusion: Give the actor as much freedom in his work as possible; otherwise, he will remain a pupil all his life. For I have seen subjective directors who have drilled and thrashed a play to pieces, and I have seen those who have wanted to force upon all of the artists – young and old, men and women – their own gestures, their own intonations, their own fragile voices, their mannerisms, yes, even taught them tricks. We don't engage in that sort of thing.

With regard to make-up and costume, the actor usually understands these matters best, and he ought to have a measure of freedom in this, but if an obvious mistake has been made, the director must have the right to insist on a change, or require it when necessary.

In delicate pieces, particularly in costume plays, the director alone must select the colors to make them fit and work in the ensemble, but he should be willing to consult the major actors and will certainly accept their views when they are valid. [-]

Reading a play is almost like reading a score. It is a difficult art, and I don't know many people who can do it although many say they can. The very arrangement of the text, where the eyes have to wander from the name of the speaker to his speech, demands close attention. The seemingly uninteresting exposition has to be struggled through and carefully recorded in one's memory, since it contains the warp by which the weft is set up. The action noted within the stage directions also delays and distracts one. Even to this day when I read Shakespeare, I have to pencil in notes to keep the characters and particularly the numerous minor characters straight, and I have to go back constantly to the list of characters and return to the first act to see what the characters said there. You have to read a play at least twice to have it clearly in mind, and in order to be able to assign the roles you have to grind away at it several times. The author (or the translator) and the director are usually the only ones who know the play thoroughly; therefore they are the most competent in assigning the roles. [-] The person who knows the cast, every artist's disposition, ability, and limitations, sees right away, while reading the play, who is suitable for a given part. [-]

Authors are often amazed when a really good play is returned to them. But it may be because the same subject has just been playing at this or other theatres so that it is worn out and no longer desired. The play may be boring in spite of its superb technique, or painful, or impossible to cast, or too expensive to produce. [-]

Following the public's taste can be risky, because taste is forever changing and often can change quite suddenly. [-]

A drama does not become superb because the author has a great name or has been dead for a long time. Goethe was a theatre manager and an actor, but his sense of form failed him when he tried to construct a drama. [-]

*The beginner* must begin at the beginning; so he gets the minor roles, especially the announcement roles. I want to add immediately that the author does not create these roles without intention. Maybe an important person needs to be introduced; his entrance has to be prepared in order to be effective; and the author wants to focus the spectator's attention on this character. It is thus very important [-] that the announcement is made clearly and distinctly [-]. If it is not, the entire scene may be lost since the spectator will be annoyed at not hearing the presentation of the character he has just had the honor of meeting. Consequently the beginner must not despise the announcement role, and he must also know whom he is announcing, the latter's significance in the play, and be aware of the upcoming situation, whether it is calm or violent, decisive or not; all of this should be heard in the announcer's tone of voice and tempo. [-]

On the other hand, the pupil should not do too much, not elbow his way ahead as a minor character, not fix unnecessary attention onto himself; yet he must not consider himself superior to his role and look at it contemptuously. I have been a pupil. It is not fun to hang about in the wings and wait for three hours to make an entrance in the fifth act. But the time can be spent usefully and relatively pleasantly if you follow what is happening on stage, listen and see, see and hear, how different the actors are every night, observe how different the audience is, how differently it reacts to the performers. *There* is a school and a place for studying, especially if the pupil has the opportunity of seeing how roles are doubled, so that he can compare different interpretations of the same role by different artists.

I advise against reading too many books about the art of acting. Your studies should be pursued in daily life by observing living people, in rehearsals and at performances. [-]

To Manda Björling (1876–1960), actress. Came to prominence under August Falck in 1906 as the first professional Swedish Miss Julie. Together with Falck, whom she married in 1909, she appeared in numerous productions at the Intimate Theatre.

July 16, 1908. [-] Since your gestures, pose, facial expression and appearance were perfect and your positioning was admirable, your diction should also be superior. If you ordinarily spoke as you did during the performances, I would think you had been careless in your articulation from the start. Your speech was too fast and slurred, as in a comedy – but this [*Miss Julie*] is a tragedy! [-] I had difficulty hearing you at times, for it was *staccato* or careless. You should put on airs a little, be proud, declaim as if in verse, for there is a secret rhythm in this prose where every word counts. Her story to Jean about her family situation was good, varied, well paused, accompanied by all shades of facial expression. But then the tempo increased and the words got jumbled. [-]

Make your exit in the final scene like a sleepwalker, slowly, with your arms stretched out in front of you, gliding out as if seeking support in the air to avoid falling on stones or something like that; drawn irresistibly toward the final great darkness.

To August Falck.

July 24, 1908. [-] I must reiterate what I told you before. You perform too much, you absorb your roles carelessly and don't take time to reflect on them. Jean, too, was handled carelessly. The whole thing went too fast, monotonously, without nuances or pauses, and often in a tone that was alien to the role and the situation. Your business tasks are distracting you. [-]

Give Mrs. B. *Crimes and Crimes* at once, so she will have a brilliant leading role to mull over.[182] The Lady in *Damaskus* is a hopeless task! Believe me! [-]

To Karin Alexandersson (1878–1948), actress. Engaged at the Intimate Theatre 1908–10. She played Laura in *The Father*, Kristin in *Miss Julie*, Mme Cathérine in *Crimes and Crimes*, and the Mother in *To Damascus*.

July 30, 1908 [-] What the Captain, her Brother, and the Nurse [in *The Father*] say about her [Laura] when she is offstage contributes to her characterization, of course. You ought to know what she was like as a child, as a sister to the Pastor, what she is like as a wife, a mother, a matron (to the Nurse). Listen to what they say about you from the wings, when you are offstage. They can always be lying, or embroidering, or exaggerating, but that's not what we are to believe is the case here. Her brother speaks of her morbid stubbornness and craving for power, etc. That is surely the leitmotif which you ought to stress. But we mustn't turn her into a monster, and you haven't. Yet, by illuminating a figure from many sides, it easily becomes shallow, unfocussed, flat. Perhaps a one-sided light is best on stage; the shadows, it is true, then emerge as blacker, and the light as brighter, and the figure stands out in relief. I think you showed a little too much human feeling in the role, but I'm not certain about that. And if you've created a vivid image of Laura, then keep it, I won't tear it apart. [-]

The role has always been played strikingly, and has never failed. When regarded as easy and transparent, it has perhaps been done too simply. [-]

To August Falck.

July 30, 1908. [-] No stoves [in the production of *The Father*] (unless the play specifically prescribes them).

No windows (unless, etc.). Windows are always improbable unless they can be solidly constructed. And masking set pieces behind are always ridiculous, since the silhouette is too sharp, and with their false perspective they are always false.

Large wall surfaces with restful corners are the most beautiful [-].

Too many doors on a small set break things up; and the set should be lower, wider and the doors lower. A high and narrow backdrop seems unpleasant; a low and wide one suggests coziness. [-]

To August Falck.

August 18, 1908. Note to *The Father*.
1. Add my changes; the coarseness in the first scene is obsolete.
2. I cannot make changes when you are still on-book and will return to this when you know it by heart.
3. Your conception in the third act of the husband as shattered will do and

adds subtlety. But retain your tone of voice. Let the whole act proceed at a raging speed, except for the end, where it gradually slows down. [-]

Don't do too much; the role plays itself. Hunderup created it throughout like a sane person who is murdered and explodes solely from rage![183]

Don't use different tones of voice but do as Ljungqvist did, stick to your bass, the words themselves will provide the nuances!

The role is an easy one if you avoid analyzing it too much. Just learn it by heart and it will work out fine. [-]


To August Falck.

Summer-October, 1908. [-] *To Damascus I* (with a drapery stage,[184] or standing set). Since the main thing is to avoid set changes, it's not necessary to use the red drapery from *Kristina*. Instead, we could very easily choose what is needed from Gunnarson's backdrops.[185] Hence, I suggest playing *Damascus I* with

1. The barriers, which should be repainted since they are cheap, dull.
2. Gunnarson's two standing sets: The Grove with the Altar and the Hill with the three trees.
3. As a standing backdrop for the whole evening: either the Sea since you don't see what it is; or the Highway, which allegorizes the Pilgrimage.
4. A fourth possibility might be to dream up a new backdrop, which would introduce motifs from the entire first Part, as in a weaving ( = The Lady's embroidery) [-].

I had thought of making a compromise by, for instance, selecting three of Gunnarsson's backdrops for *Damascus I*. But once you start changing one set, you are in the midst of a run-around and have to change them all. The Sea is probably the best! Or the Highway! [-]

P.S. The backdrop for the two standing sets could perhaps be completely plain, representing nothing; a folded cloth with the torture instruments in the middle of a shield. What is seen on Catholic tombs is: the cross, the crown of thorns, the lance, the scourge on a pole, the sponge that held the vinegar, the four nails, furthest down.

Underneath: Veronica's veil with Christ's Face, very faint.

Perhaps this would ultimately be the best. But then the torture instruments must be drawn exactly according to Catholic tradition [-]. [-]

To August Falck.

Summer 1908–Summer 1910 (?). *To Damascus* (with the drapery stage).
The Street Corner. The barrier:[186] Flower pots with Christmas roses.
At the Doctor's: Two beehives on the barrier.
The Hotel Room: Two flower pots with Christmas roses.
By the Sea: Two big seashells.
The Highway: Two crucifixes.
The Ravine: The same.
The Kitchen: Mary icons.
The Rose Chamber: On one side, roses; on the other, thistles.
The Asylum: Two skulls.


To Emil Grandinson.

September 6, 1908. [-] Since you value my play and wish me well, I must tell you I don't understand your choice for the part of Sture, since you both have good sense and much experience![187]
The last person I imagined!
This is so terrible and so bitter that under such circumstances I would rather my drama were read by a few hundred people than seen by a few thousand! [-]


To Emil Grandinson.

September 9, 1908. [-] A crazy idea has haunted me for a few days! That Sture would be performed by – Julia Håkansson![188]
Her fifty years are equal to the man's twenty. She has a pleasant voice, beautiful features and a good figure to look at! Is it as crazy as it seems? [-]


To Helge Wahlgren.

September 20, 1908 [-] Don't *use* technique but 'grind' yourself into your role [as the Prince in *Swanwhite*], so that your gesture is born with the word. Enter into rapport with the girl, perform toward *her*, see only her and don't make a monologue out of the dialogue. Don't ponder the role, don't analyze it but learn it by heart and it will come by itself. Your concepts of 'stylization' have misled you a little. As you see, my prose is refined and rhythmic, sometimes versified. So let our Swedish language ring! And take care not to talk! Speak! [-]


To Karl Börjesson (1877–1941), publisher and bookseller. Börjesson brought out, among others, S's provocative novel *Black Banners* (1907). This was followed by *The Blue Books, Open Letters to the Intimate Theatre* and S's last three history plays.

September 23, 1908. [-] Part II of the trilogy, named *The Regent*, is ready and you will receive it first [-], because it belongs with *The [Last] Knight*; it is the sequel and the two must be published together. It is better than *The Knight* and composed in a very strict form, like *Damascus I*. Same sets as in *The Knight* but in reverse order (counterpoint treatment). [-]


To August Falck.

End of September 1908. [-] When you have only one set [in *Abu Casem's Slippers*], it should be typical and schematic (contain and express the main thing.)
The Orient = Palm trees, cupola, minaret seen against the sky.
Cypresses and plane trees can be found in the Orient, but they are also characteristic of Italy and Greece. [-]


To Victor Castegren (1861–1914), actor, director and theatre manager. Directed the unsuccessful premiere of *A Dream Play* at the Swedish Theatre in Stockholm in 1907.

October 22, 1908. [-] I expected to get to hear your impression of *The Ghost Sonata* which you must realize is 'theatre,' and that it is impressive and hangs together; is a drama of catastrophe and settling of accounts, with both plot and characters. On our small stage it does not work as well as it ought to.
What I intended to present is a fairy-tale and fantasy piece in the present

with modern houses, and this I feel I have achieved successfully as I already have disciples here and in Germany. [-]

*Hamlet. A Memorial on November 26, Our Anniversary, Dedicated to the Intimate Theatre*, November 19–25, 1908.

October 20–November 10, 1908. [-] At the end of the century I resumed my studies at the university[189] which included Shakespeare. My enjoyment was not unmixed, but I was determined to study how he constructed a drama. I noticed then that Shakespeare is both formless and at the same time pedantically formal. All his plays have the same cut: five acts, with four or five scenes, but one cannot really see how this is done. He begins at a certain point; then the play develops in a straight line toward the end. The technique doesn't show, no effect is calculated, the great battles are there after a well-accomplished deployment, and then comes the peaceful denouement with drums and trumpets. Someone once noted that it all seems like nature itself, and I agree.

What we call a scene, according to the French (Sardou) concept, is the result of a calculated strategy and refined tactics. We younger dramatists have to work with foreshadowing and hints, piecemeal revelation of secrets, reversals, peripety, stratagems, counter-stratagems, and parallels (that is my strength!). [-]

[-] *Hamlet* can be presented uncut. But to enjoy this powerful tragedy in its entirety you have to prepare for it as if you were about to listen to an opera. You should read the text in advance, try to interest yourself in the action and its background. And so as not to be distracted by small talk during intermissions, the play should be produced with only a couple of curtain calls; and to make time for all twenty scenes which should follow closely upon each other, the Shakespeare stage that was constructed in Munich in the 1890s should be used consistently. This is an absolute must: no scenery! A permanent abstract architectonic frame that can represent a room but also a street or square, when the curtain is closed; when it is pulled open, one is suddenly out in the countryside. [-]

If furnishings – tables and chairs – are needed, these can be brought in; if properties are used, they can be procured. Otherwise not. The spoken word is the main thing; and if Shakespeare's sophisticated contemporaries were able to do without scenery, we too should be able to imagine walls and trees. We can *read* the text silently and enjoy it, imagining we hear the voices and see the changing scenery; and when the actors pretend to be kings and queens, we can certainly pretend it is a room in a castle or a forest we have in front of us. Everything is pretense on stage.

I think the experiment Director Falck undertook without my assistance in staging *Kristina* at the Intimate Theatre was very successful. As the author of the play, I am the expert. I certainly know best what I want. Besides, I am a veteran in this profession, since I have been writing plays and have had them produced for forty [-] years now. [-] Act I of *Kristina* in the printed text is set in the Riddarholm Church [in Stockholm]; but when we cut all references to this church, the setting became only a room in which people gather; and I did not miss anything. The Treasury in Act II was represented by two shelves with accounting books. It was enough for me; and the set was among the most beautiful I have seen in a theatre. The last two acts were just as superb, and the whole production was a delightful surprise, a successful experiment and innovation which will be recorded in Swedish theatre history. Since I did not have anything to do with the production, I have not been praising myself, but simply given recognition to the one who deserves it. As no scene was set outdoors, no background curtain to conceal the landscape was needed.

Falck's drapery stage had several advantages. Since it was not necessary to drag scenery in and out, calm and reverence were sustained on the stage, which is extremely important for the actor for whom the stage is the study where he realizes his art. The open wings, three on each side, provided depth and nuances of light and shadow, and made it unnecessary to open and close the doors. Entrances and exits were made without disturbance of any kind. With a soft carpet added, the artists at the Intimate Theatre lived in a carefree, pleasant milieu, in which they felt at home and could play their roles undisturbed by the noise of the theatre and the bustle of the stagehands which otherwise is part of the experience. [-]

Notice how many shots must be taken in sequence by the cinematograph to reproduce a single movement, and even then the image is still shaky. There is a missing transition in every vibration. Where a thousand shots are needed for one movement of an arm, how many would not be needed to depict the movement of a soul? The writer's depiction of human beings is consequently only contractions, contour sketches, all of them imperfect and all semi-false.

A genuine depiction of a character is therefore difficult, almost impossible, and, if someone tried to make it completely truthful, no one would believe it. Ultimately one can only suggest. [-]

I have always had the bad taste of liking good actors but have been unable to tolerate great ones. The good actor always plays his role, is adequate without going too far, and fulfills his duty of rendering the text. But human frivolity is so great that the good actor never becomes a big name, never gets the flowers, and is treated as if he were just an average person and is referred to as useful in a derogatory sense. [-]

The extra something that an actor has the right to give is his outstanding or winning personality, if he has any; but this shines through of its own accord and is not feigned. As soon as one *sees* the technique or notices that the actor is puffing himself up, shouting, or brandishing his arms, the whole matter is infected. His intention is clearly something other than rendering the role, and the audience instead gets to witness an actor who is strutting about and playing to the crowd. [-]

When one of my plays has been performed without my noticing the actors, it has been a sign that it has been well acted. I once saw my painful tragedy *The Bond* mounted; when the performance was over, I had had a deep experience. I couldn't find any faults. Falck, Flygare, and Wahlgren were all authentic. A judge among my friends and a friend of the theatre declared afterward: "All criticism is silenced; this is not acting; it is something else; it is absolute reality." I agree! And if you ask me why, I think the answer would be: Because this is honest, unaffected art, created by young, uncorrupted people, who have gone through difficult years at school, who are not spoiled, who have not learned tricks, who are not arrogant, who don't try to either play down the drama or each other. They have just the right amount of unselfishness to be more interested in the play itself than in their own personal success. [-]


*Julius Caesar. Shakespeare's Historical Drama. Together with Some Remarks about Criticism and the Art of Acting and an Addendum about the Theatre Crisis and the Theatre Muddle. Dedicated to the Intimate Theatre,* December 17–21, 1908.

November 10–23, 1908. [-] Shakespeare's manner of depicting historical persons – even heroes – at home, intimately, in *Julius Caesar* became the decisive pattern for my first big historical drama, *Master Olof,* and, with certain reservations, even for those written after 1899. [-]

I have always found it difficult to arrive at a fixed final judgment of a stage production. The art of acting is the child of a series of moments, sciopticon

STRINDBERG ON DRAMA AND THEATRE

images that disappear when the footlights are turned down, something half real that one cannot quite grasp. I was a theatre critic for a daily newspaper for a few months,[190] and I didn't find it pleasant to sit down at my desk after the performance and put down on paper my improvised judgments that upon closer scrutiny could be expressed just as well in another way. When I wanted to postpone my judgment and sleep on it, the editor explained that the type-setters and printers were waiting and that I had to write my review right away. When I remained hesitant, he advised me to give the performance the benefit of the doubt instead of condemning it. I envied the people who could go to a café to talk about the evening's performance, and I wondered why my judg-ment had to be typeset and published when I, at the age of twenty-some-thing, had seen so little of the art of acting. When I go to enjoy art, I am in an unreflective, receptive, positive mood, ready to receive something. If some-thing displeases me, I usually ignore it and continue on without coming up with a reason. If something pleases me, I just enjoy it but do not want to dis-turb my own enjoyment by having to reflect upon it. But the critic proceeds in a contrary fashion. He steels himself to make judgements, to determine why this pleases and that displeases, and that is why he so rarely enjoys any-thing. Since the theatre is there to create illusion, there is nothing easier than making oneself unreceptive to the deception. One resists it and so the illusion does not come, and consequently, the purpose of going to the theatre is inval-idated, and the critic might just as well have stayed home if he was not open to the delightful illusion that the performance was a slice of life on stage. If I go to see a traveling magician, I am paying to be pleasantly duped. But if some critically inclined person in the audience gets up to declare that the goldfish did not come directly out of the hat but had been hidden in the magician's coat pocket, I would not be grateful for the information. He would have spoiled my pleasure.

That is why people in theatre circles often ask what the point of criticism is since the director, the theatre manager, and their comrades understand the matter best, and their judgment is constructive. The audience understands fairly well whether the characters in the play resemble real people, and whether the actors can stir the emotions or merely entertain. An artist knows whether he has acted well or not; if it didn't go well this time, then better luck next time.

If the theatre critic has any claims to being a judge, he should know the rules and be impartial. If the critic serves as a teacher, he should have studied for the profession and he should pursue his calling with a sense of responsibility. Nowadays a newspaper hires someone as a theatre critic because he can write or has an agreeable style. He is not asked if he has been backstage, attended rehearsals, or himself written a play. He does not even need to be interested in theatre and can come from a totally different profession. Since the job does not always imply having talent, one often reads the most preposterous opinions that most theatre people would laugh at, if their bread and reputation were not at stake.

A blind person is not eager to judge colors, but if he permits himself to do so at an art exhibit, he has to put up with being reminded of his blindness even if it is considered cruel to point out that someone has a handicap. If an intoxicated or deaf person attends the theatre to write a review of the play after *one* performance, I as the accused should have the right to challenge the witness or the judge by declaring: "But he's drunk! He's deaf! Get rid of him!" [-]

At least one reviewer, if not more, felt that the Riddarholm Church in *Kristina* did not look enough like a real church. Either the reviewer wasn't at the performance or he failed to notice that the Riddarholm Church had actually been eliminated. "Drunk or deaf! Get rid of him!"

There is a special breed of theatre critic who chooses this career out of mischief or a lust for power in the false belief that the audience actually reads reviews. A professional journal should be edited by experts in the field and offer the reader a survey of everything of importance in the foreign and domestic theatre world, including facts, notes, and realities that could benefit theatre people, and not only present bouquets to friends of the house and throw stones at personal enemies.

People with totally different callings and practices are frequently seized by the inclination to express themselves in print on the theatre; and often, like executioners, take great pleasure in the decapitation without running the risk of revenge.

The actor's profession involves his personal presence. He stands there body and soul, defenseless, a target, fair game for everyone. He encounters evil glances, little contemptuous laughs, remarks about his eyes, nose, and mouth. Don't you pity him? He is put together just like the rest of us, with feelings and passions, and he does his best, because he doesn't dare do anything else. He may not have been good tonight, no, but he may have been ill and afraid to say so; he may be grieving, which he would be even less inclined to mention!

People have organized societies for the protection of ferocious animals.

Can't public opinion also begin to protect the actor, not from the published review but from the audience's undeserved insults? [-]

As I have said, I was a theatre critic for a few months. It was no pleasure; and I can comfort the actors with this: when my opinion conflicted with that of my colleagues, it was like a wasp's nest. I lost friends, was no longer greeted, and, when the editor began to worry about me and suggested that I praise what I did not approve of, I had to give up the post.

The job is not an enviable one, but it can basically be eliminated as superfluous since directors, managers, and actors understand theatre much better. The director, who may have seen some thirty rehearsals, knows the play especially well; the way something should be said has been considered and discussed for thirty days, the stage positions have been tested, and the nuances have been thought through. The audience, which knows as much as the critic, wants to make its own assessments and experience its own pleasures, and if a theatre goer reads a review, he does so to have his judgment confirmed, not to have it set straight.

When an actor has complained to me about the injustices, errors, and deliberate distortions found in the newspapers, I have merely responded by saying: "Don't read the stuff!"

Criticism can never be totally objective or universal as long as there are kinships and friendships, sympathies and antipathies, coteries and special interests. A couple of years ago, there was an organized protest against my *Dream Play*. A year ago, warnings about my chamber plays were issued. Half a year later, the public was being urged to see a potpourri of all these and a little more, now labeled a masterpiece by the plagiarist. This is not criticism; it is poor taste based on the principle of personality; it is the blindness of hatred or self-inflicted stupidity! [-]

*Being* your character intensely means acting well, but not so intensely that you forget punctuation; whereupon your acting becomes as flat as a musical composition without nuances, without piano and forte, without crescendo and diminuendo, *accelerando*, and *ritardando*. (The actor should know these musical terms and always keep them in mind, because they say almost everything that is necessary.)

But there are fine, modest people whose acting can easily seem colorless because they forget the enhancements that the stage requires. If they see the scenery and note how coarsely it is painted, they will realize that the acting, too, must be somewhat embellished and not on a small scale. A work that is too refined does not stand out enough against the background; it is like a painting on ivory, which you don't mind picking up in your hand but do not consider hanging on the wall.

The superb actor reveals himself the minute he makes his entrance. When he comes on stage, he immediately impresses and elevates. He transmits energy. He attracts interest without forcing it. A strong personality has indescribable assets: intelligence, worldly wisdom, culture, and humor.

The great actor is often unpredictable. He acts from an inner self, but if he does not find that inner energy, he can end up being quite wretched, flat, nothing. This is called acting by inspiration, but I think the word should be disposition. [-] It is not enough to simply leave the exhilarated company at a dinner and then hurriedly change into one's costume and dash on stage to play Hamlet. [-]

There is a type of tendentious actor and actress who cannot create a role or enjoy creating it without being able to declare their own ideas. These are the political actors and the suffragette actresses. They are wretched when the role does not call for a sermon, either about socialism or about the woman question. Lugné-Poë was a poor actor who became interesting when he began preaching, preferably regarding women's issues but also about platonic anarchism.

A good actor is one who considers himself an artist, regards his art as art and does not brood about universal suffrage or emancipation; who does not speculate about world problems and zoology. His art will benefit the most if he manages to live unreflectively, naively, a little carelessly, and does not read too much but instead interacts with people, not to study them but just to live with them and enjoy himself. Studies and reflection lead to calculated thinking, which becomes speculative and premeditated. There is no need for him to read solely dramas; novels are just as good, sometimes better. I think Dickens would be a good teacher, both because his characterizations are more thorough than those of the dramatist and because he provides endless motivations. And he offers something else for the actor: He supplements every character's appearance with a wealth of incredibly fine physical expressions and gestures. I have recently reread *David Copperfield,* and my admiration for the teacher from my youth goes beyond words. In only a few words he manages to call forth the same illusion one expects in the theatre with its large apparatus or, better yet, he creates for me the hallucination of actual experience.

When I, as the author, have ever been satisfied with the performance of a play of mine, I have never understood how any reviewer could be dissatisfied. But when I see how one reviewer was delighted while another attacked the same performance, I understood how purely subjective their criticism was. While one actor's personality may appeal to me, somebody else may find him unattractive. Furthermore, the spectator may be indisposed as the play's content and the intention go against his grain. This may lead to his transferring his animosity to the innocent or indisposed actor [-] who meanwhile transmits his low spirits to the spectator; or the actor may have been assigned a role that does not fit his disposition, and therefore he does not become credible.

There may be a spectator in the audience who came to the theatre quite reluctantly and may have such a strong personality that he can actually have a profound impact on a certain actor to the point that the actor actually feels the spectator's hatred, awakens from his trance, and ends up performing poorly. One older actor has told me that he can feel when an enemy is in the audience even before he has seen him; when he locates the source of his discomfort, he dedicates the role to him and usually 'plays him down' but does not always succeed in pinning him down. If a coterie in a hostile mood arrives shortly after a sumptuous dinner, they can ruin the entire evening for both the audience and the actors. It is, of course, a touchy and delicate matter to practice art, and all artists seek some solitude behind closed doors. However, the actor, unlike other artists, has to work with the curtain raised, publicly, and for that reason, people should show some mercy toward him. [-]

But there are also purely personal motives for treating an actor unjustly. I know an actor who is always on. He always plays his role effectively, doesn't ruin anything, always makes an effort to become his character, and succeeds. But when he is excellent, people say nothing; when he is merely competent, he is booed and jeered. People pick on him, although he irritates no one by being arrogant. I do not fully understand the reasons for all this. He is admittedly a lone wolf and does not belong to any coterie; he is also independent and does not need to kowtow to anyone. I believe he has to bear the burden of hatred for having the same name as a notorious and despised relative. Even his colleagues nag him, but, when I meet with them and discuss him and ask, "But isn't he a good actor?" they always respond in unison: "Yes, of course, he's good!" Yet he never receives any recognition or acceptance. I know another actor who is always excellent, is recognized by everyone, but he has never achieved the reputation he deserves. We experts are amazed by this fact and we can find no real reason for it.

To receive recognition requires, I suppose, a little extra personal goodwill from a group of friends interested in ensuring that one of their own becomes famous, thereby casting reflected glory on those around him.

During my many years of association with actors, directors, and theatre managers, I have received miscellaneous bits of information about the following simple fact. I asked one theatre employee who was forced to see the same play sixty times running whether my actors always acted in similar manner evening after evening. He responded: "No, they're never the same any two evenings!" Other experts have asserted quite the contrary: that the actor's acting reality is quite consistent. I have not had the chance to research this very thoroughly, but when I recently saw one of my plays anew at a dress rehearsal, I found the same flaws had gone uncorrected that I had commented on six months earlier. When I asked the manager why the otherwise willing and cooperative actor had not corrected the flaws, he answered: "He can't – although he would love to. They're stuck in his body."

I had tracked down a routine. The actor usually has a lot of ideas that cannot be gotten rid of. For example, as soon as an actor in a Protestant country puts on a monk's cape and the monk catches sight of a woman, the actor immediately thinks it is a question of Tartuffe or some other swindler. If I tell him that in this case it has nothing to do with Tartuffe, it does not help. That is routine and conceit.

When my *Saga of the Folkungs* was about to be produced, I found the actor playing the main part decked out as Christ. I explained to him that Magnus Eriksson,[191] who indeed was called Magnus the Good in Norway, was not a Christ figure, and I requested that the actor not carry the cross on his back like the Savior on His way to Golgotha. But he seemed to know better, for in his youth he had seen Uhde's[192] paintings [-]. So that was that.

In the final scene of *Gustav Vasa* in which the Dalecarlian Engelbrekt comes in drunk, I asked the actor to refrain from staggering. He staggered anyway. I pointed to a passage where it says, "*merrily drunk, but steady in his movements.*" He still insisted on staggering! I explained that a merrily drunk person is capable of becoming quite sober at an important moment – as before a king – and that a drunk person above all tries to stand straight as he attempts to act sober. This didn't help, although the entire play was in danger because of this prank.

I have heard that Norway's greatest dramatist [Henrik Ibsen] used to hand slips of paper with instructions to the actors after a dress rehearsal, but not one of his recommendations was ever followed.

Is acting so mechanized after so many rehearsals that it cannot be altered? This is possible, but I believe that, quite literally, an actor does not understand what a director is saying because his acting is so unconscious, so much like a sleepwalker. Whenever I have made a polite suggestion, the response has often been a perplexed smile as if I had said something silly. But sometimes an actor also acquires the little professional weakness of falsely believing that he has written the role himself and that the playwright is just some unauthorized intruder, who should be grateful for what he has done and not be so critical.

When the author shows up at a dress rehearsal and makes some critical remarks, the response is usually: "It's too late!" But whenever I have made similar remarks at an earlier rehearsal, the answer has mostly been: "It isn't ready yet! It's too early to criticize!" So I have concluded: Let them do as they wish as long as they don't do anything absolutely crazy that distorts the meaning of the play. Freedom in the free arts!

And I think that method has been successful at the Intimate Theatre, where the director does not tear a play to pieces. A few days ago, I met a forty-year-old poet whose plays have been performed before. He had seen my latest play, and when I asked him what he thought about the acting, he responded: "I didn't notice the acting; it was so honest and unaffected that it wasn't noticeable." Furthermore, he could not remember the name of a single actor. This made me wonder aloud in a meeting with the actors [-] how they would feel if their names were not listed on the playbill. After some hesitation, they pointed out that the public would eventually find out the names anyway! Had I inquired further whether they preferred a quiet incognito to the scaffold, I don't believe they would have been able to respond. After all, every premiere is a test, and it can get quite tiresome to be a pupil your entire life; but it creates suspense and keeps up one's interest so that one doesn't have time to grow old. On the contrary, life is rejuvenated with every new assignment! If theatre people could choose, I think they would choose the present, with all of its annoyances and advantages.

It is impossible to establish valid rules for the theatrical arts, but they ought to be abreast of the times in order to arouse us who are now alive. I mean, if the times are as skeptical, insensitive and democratic as ours are, there is no point in employing grand airs or sentimentality. It is in these times that some light skepticism and a certain insensibility reigns in the theatre, however much this may look like coarseness to many. In this kind of period, people are less likely to weep over Axel and Valborg;[193] Lear seems unmanageable; and Timon[194] does not arouse pity when he is deserted by paid flatterers. Even tragedy itself turns to a light conversational tone and leaves the *cothurnus*[195] for the low *soccus*;[196] verse gives way to prose, the styles blend, and kings dare not walk on stilts any more than "the wild mob"; all of them speak a similar language, and blunt words can be used anywhere. The acting in this kind of repertoire is fairly obvious. Following the text leads to a search for reality or nature, truth, and words that have been misinterpreted but whose meanings need no explanation. I saw the very opposite of this type of art at the Théâtre Français toward the end of the 1870s. There everything was stilted in the tragedies. The play *Rome vaincue*[197] was in verse and contained general observations, *loci communes*, which had become mere phrases and effusive rhetoric. The acting was not much better.[-]

"Beauty first, then truth." This was, strangely enough, Goethe's primary ideal as a theatre leader in Weimar. But I didn't find it beautiful, possibly because I was not French, because, as we know, no other art is so closely associated with what is national as acting. But when Goethe survived the reactions against crude German naturalism, his beauty hardened into a fatal formalism, which eliminated the individuality of the actor and was actually caricatured in Goethe's own *Rules for the Art of the Stage*.[198] This is where we have inherited the pathetically excessive, exaggerated manners, the artificiality, and extravagance, all of which are now considered "provincial."

The requirements of our time are not those of the near future. If we finally are approaching a period when people become more sensitive and acquire an alternative view of the world that succeeds the zoological viewpoint,[199] a different repertoire will certainly be necessary, and will require a new kind of acting. So there is no use drawing up rules that will only be quickly discarded. The wise will listen to the voices of the present era, but they will slowly be silenced by the voices of the dawning age, and to be his own contemporary is the task of the ever-evolving artist. [-]

Weimar-Goethe went too far in establishing rules when he forbade the actors from performing in profile or with their backs to the audience, ordered stars to occupy the right side as the more distinguished side of the stage, to walk on stage only diagonally, never straight across [-]. Goethe's attempts at reform were correct in his opposition to a vulgar conversational tone, which later degenerated into chatter that could scarcely be understood, and which has reduced the actor to being a reporter of the play's content. Goethe demanded that the audience hear and see, and he remedied the sad state of affairs through the employment of excesses, some of which survive to this very day.

Whenever I have reacted at the Intimate Theatre against rapid enunciation that approaches chatter, I have also warned against the opposite, speaking so slowly as to put the audience to sleep. In music there is a slow tempo, an inner movement (*mouvement*), indicated by an *agitato,* for example, which does not increase the speed, but strengthens the delivery, tightens from within, makes the speech vibrate and pulsate. This is what makes the slow tempo bearable.

I have also pointed out the lack of nuances which comes from speaking too rapidly. If one hears a long speech uttered in one tone, in one and the same allegro, without punctuation, without pauses, without *ritardando* or *accelerando*, then one soon grows weary and bored. This is more like reporting on the play than actually acting it. If the actor were to make his observations of daily life and observe how a conversation takes its course, a conversation in which the participants take the time to think before they speak, he would soon notice the difference between that and the memorized lessons so often heard on the stage.

The actor speaks too rapidly for several natural reasons. He thinks the audience will grow impatient, whereas the opposite is actually the case; for if it moves along too quickly, it becomes too exhausting to grasp the meaning of the many words. A certain fear of losing one's train of thought also prevents him from pausing; the memorization during rehearsals lingers, and learning one's lesson, the major task during rehearsal, lingers like a bad habit during the performances. For that reason, learning the lines and mastering the role should occur at one and the same time. Hearing only the lesson ends up being a disaster. The actor's art begins where the lesson ends and that is why one expert has observed that a production is never ready on opening night and isn't really ready until about the fifth performance. Thus, I have asked the actors to use every performance as a rehearsal, to develop, modify, invent, fill in, and to prevent their acting from becoming mechanical. Experience has brought me to the point where I would rather hear flaws in memorization than a lesson that is too well memorized; and I think that the prompter's presence adds a feeling of security that is necessary to prevent the anxiety of a failing memory from hastening the actor's recital.

People are generally too quick to criticize the actor [-]; the critic is proud when he discovers small lapses in the actor's memory. A slight faltering doesn't bother me, as long as someone does not skip an important passage, to which the dialogue later refers. Once I heard a famous actor deliver a speech in a play that was several pages long. He forgot his lines a few times. I went backstage and found the actor beside himself. I comforted him by pointing out that we, the audience, did not notice any of this and that his speech actually sounded more natural, because "Who can deliver such a long speech without stumbling?"

I have experienced excellent actors who have never fully memorized their lines and have always depended on the prompter. But at least they were acting! And I dare say that lessons can actually kill acting.

I know a superb actor who never reads his lines at home and instead uses the rehearsals to learn his part. He claims that reading his lines at home without any rejoinders can never amount to anything.

I have also said to my actors: "Tamper with your speeches if you can get them to flow better; stretch them a bit, if you want to, but make sure that your speeches are tit for tat."

People are generally too demanding of the poor actors; they can even be quite petty. Thereby robbing them of their necessary self-confidence and frightening them. There probably is too much rehearsing; the play is thrashed to pieces. "Treat them like artists, and not like laborers or schoolboys!" They learn more from one performance than from thirty rehearsals, and no play can develop in an empty theatre with a director and a prompter, least of all if the director keeps interrupting the mood that the artist has suffered an inner agony to summon up. [-]

When the Intimate Theatre was getting by without a special director until this fall and everything was going fine, even with such difficult plays as *The Ghost Sonata, The Bond,* and *Kristina*, I immediately felt that I was almost superfluous as the regular director. At the rehearsals, the actors explored, adjusted each other's acting under the director's guidance, and achieved good results with *The Father* and *Swanwhite* without my assistance. If I here add the fact that I cannot bear to hear my own words from the past drummed into my ears day after day and if I confess that it was my writing that fascinated me, I have stated the principal reasons for my withdrawal as a regular director although I remain so nominally.

Since I wrote the preface to *Miss Julie* in 1888, I have now and then speculated about the theatre. I have asked myself whether the theatre and the drama have not clung to old forms for too long without renewing or adapting them to the needs of our times and the demands of today's audiences. Is it reasonable to expect that people who have worked hard all day and who keep old bedtime habits will come out of their homes to engage in intellectual toil until midnight? A tired person demands entertainment or rest. He is happy to relax in a neutral place (a tavern or his own home) among kindred spirits to reflect quietly on the labors of the day. But to dress up to appear at a public gathering, to expose oneself to intellectual activity and mental excitement, that means to work anew. Around 1880 I saw *Faust* at the Swedish Theatre; it began at seven and ended at midnight. That was ghastly! In Shakespeare's and Goethe's time, I understand, the performance started at five-thirty and ended at bedtime, or around nine. That was acceptable! Today one has combined the tavern and the theatre to maintain people's energy, but that has not improved the situation. The Intimate Theatre tried to be up to date and cut the strain, from eight to ten, and this seems to agree with the taste of today. Another issue is that the theatre is not a theatre of the people. It is aristocratic in its oldfashioned seating arrangements based on social importance or the amount of income tax paid, so that the 'better' people get the best seats and those of lesser means occupy the balconies where they can neither see nor hear. This is how it is throughout life, but in the theatre it is all *too* obvious. In a church, courtroom, or parliament one does not notice it but here you see everything even without opera glasses. People have told me that in the old Dramatic Theatre people in the third balcony never saw a backdrop. Making people pay for what they cannot see is not nice.

The result has been that balcony audiences were the first to abandon the theatre for the movies. The modern institution called the movie house reflects the spirit of the age and it has made terrific headway. It is democratic: all the seats are equally good, are priced the same, and there is no charge for the cloakroom. For a very low price, a minor distraction is available at one's convenience, a bit of contemporary news or some pure entertainment. Since we can learn from anything, the Intimate Theatre has borrowed two principles from the movie house: all seats are equally good, and performances are at a civilized time long before bedtime.

The movie house is the first nail in the theatre's coffin, and the high prices are its second; the third are the late hours, late even for those who don't go to bed early; and the fourth are the long plays which the French call *machines*. [-]

The biggest competitor of the theatre probably remains the operetta. I was brought up in the golden age of the operetta when the arch-demon Offenbach almost drove humanity mad. [-]

The operetta focuses on whatever is banal in a tired person; he who is exhausted is literally ambushed, pursued and disturbed by these evil musical thoughts that interfere with his serious or even devotional mood.

Since Offenbach, the operetta composer and his fellow criminals have become veritable professional thieves, pursuing basically only one motif: to ridicule what even the biggest skeptic would consider somewhat sacred [-].

You do not hear an operetta unpunished, for it is as suggestive as it is evil; and you become a medium for the unknown composer, feeling the dance steps in your body as he pulls the strings. You literally become contaminated; and whoever wants to remain free, independent, and untouched is on his guard for this virus, especially if he has any open wounds. The operetta is not innocent because it is covered up by expensive costumes and polished instrumentation. It is not witty, because it is plainly idiotic to laugh at what one takes seriously, perhaps tragically, in daily life. Even a movie or an innocent circus with its handsome horses and hilarious clowns is preferable if the goal is harmless entertainment! [-]

*Shakespeare's Macbeth, Othello, Romeo and Juliet, The Tempest, King Lear, Henry VIII and A Midsummer Night's Dream,* January 21–27, 1909.

November 23–December 23, 1908. [-] Malcolm gives the amazing information that Macbeth is bloodthirsty, voluptuous, avaricious, false, deceitful, fierce, and cunning. With this kind of description without any counterpart in the person described, one ends up somewhat lost [-]. I have made the same comment about Horatio, who Hamlet says has "a merry spirit" but who never reveals it during the course of the play. Casca, in *Julius Caesar*, is also given long characterizations that do not fit the man. Are these unpremeditated slip ups or plain carelessness, or has Shakespeare had a profound desire to depict man both as he is and as he is believed to be, viewed differently by friend and enemy? Or are these escapades what I would call abortive intentions [-]?

An example from my own experience opened my eyes to this sort of conceptual ellipsis. The German translator of *Easter* asked me whether it was a mistake or had a special significance that Benjamin, having just failed in Latin, is asked by Eleonora who his Latin teacher is. He answers: "Dr Algren!" Eleonora responds: "I'll remember that." Later she recalls the name, and I believe the author had intended to let Algren appear as Providence later on. I say "I believe," for the process of literary creation is just as mysterious to me now as it was forty years ago, whether it has to do with fully conscious calculation or not. Well, I told the translator that it was probably an oversight. When he then suggested eliminating it, I was unable to. I had the feeling that I should keep it, and then I began to wonder why it should remain and what it actually signified. I found myself missing it when it was no longer included. I also found that it lent an appearance of reality to the whole play because it recalled the common human way of tossing out a thousand projects of which only a few are actually carried out. I let it remain and called it an abortive intention. [-]


To August Falck.

December, 1908. [-] When *A Dream Play* is performed with drapes that elevate the piece to a higher level, the rest of the play should also be rescued from physical reality.

Fantasy costumes should be introduced, perhaps according to Craig or in the art deco style. Agnes can surely wear a white tunic; the poet a Roman toga with accessories (lyre or something like that); the Lawyer a 1700s wig as English lawyers do to this very day; or the Bailiff's headgear from *Sir Bengt's Wife*, but better and more beautiful! The Billposter: a seventeenth-century burgher, etc. The Officer as a knight (*Swanwhite*). [-]

There are three ballet scenes for Flygare and Falkner:

In the corridor below the opera; the dismissed dancer and the newly appointed one.

At the promotion ceremony where the two ballerinas deliver the laurel wreath but end up fighting in a pantomime about whether the Lawyer should receive it or not.

At Fairhaven where Flygare, dancing Bach's Fugue, overcomes Falkner's Waldteufel Waltz.

But this is something the ladies themselves should figure out and compose in grand style (Duncan!).[200]

Let us use the existing costumes! One can imagine a masquerade or something else (in the dream), as long as it is beautiful. [-]

As for the barrier emblems, one should be careful not to lapse back into reality and the grotesque! [-]


To August Falck.

December, 1908 *The Dream Play.* Barrier emblems.
Poppies, red, with pods = Sleep and Dream.
A blue monk's hood = The treacherous hope.
A green scoop net = Even the fulfillment of one's wishes is unsatisfying.

The Lawyer: Bulletin boards with public notices and resolutions.

The bulletin boards become hymn boards[201] in church, laurel wreaths hanging from them (the promotion ceremony).

Statues: One white = Fairhaven. One Black = Foulstrand.

Flags = Signal [-].

The Mediterranean = palm trees or dracaenas.

Fingal's Cave: large shells = closeness to the sea.

The shawl, the roses, the scoop net, the diamond, the protocol, a black mask (The Moor), posters (The Billposter's).

The End = When She walks into the castle that has been set aflame, the back drapery can be opened, showing a burning castle, [-] or let her walk into a sea of fire.


To August Falck.

December, 1908. Music for *The Dream Play*.

P. 206 called Kyrie: From Beethoven's *Fidelio*, Act II, No. 12 Duet, the first thirteen bars.

P. 207 A sound ensemble of waves and wind: From Mendelsohn's *Ouverture to The Hebrides*, only the first bars with the main motif repeated.

P. 222-23 "music and dance up on the hill": a Boston waltz.

P. 228 "a dissonant chord."

P. 229 Bach's D minor toccata and a Boston waltz.

P. 247 "Complaint of the Winds": Beethoven's Lied 32, "An die Hoffnung" [To Hope], only the accompaniment from the first movement.

P. 248 = Ditto.

P. 249 The Song of the Waves: From Beethoven's "Adelaïde," bars 39-70, but only the accompaniment.

P. 252 "Why Art Thou Born in Pain," Beethoven's Lied 5, "Vom Tode" [From Death] only the accompaniment.

P. 274 "Our Parting is Near": From Beethoven's *Fidelio*, Act II, grave, as long as needed [-]. [-]

The pagination is according to the separate edition (Gernandt's) "*The Crown Bride, Swanwhite, The Dream Play*" [-].

To August Falck.

December 1908–August 1909. *The Dream Play*: One single set design.
*The backdrop*: Veils of clouds: The Castle is visible only with backlighting.
Page 1. Hollyhocks.
Page 2. The door. Above are the masts of the ship's boy brig.
Page 3. Fingal's Cave or the Music Organ. Above it a pine = Italy.
Page 4. A piece of furniture from the Lawyer's room. (cypress, pine).
Page 5. An iron stove = Foulstrand (quarantine) or the Lawyer's home. Above it a railing [-]. Mast tops.
Page 6. Hollyhocks.
If the set designer reads the play he can figure out several things himself: The blue monk's hood, the sound buoy, figure heads, wrecked anchor, promotion props, laurel wreaths, school desk, teacher's desk. [-]

This might work well! As the Castle opens and closes the play, the sides are placed in the shade and only the backdrop is lit (from behind). [-]


"August Strindberg about himself," in *Bonniers månadshäften*, January 1909.

*How did you choose to become a dramatist?*
[-] I found it easiest to write plays; people and events took shape, wove themselves together, and this work gave me so much pleasure that I found life sheer bliss as long as I kept on writing and I still do. Only then am I truly alive! [-]

*Which of your plays do you consider have been produced most successfully, and by whom?*
My first good period was [-] with Ludvig Josephson, who dug me out of the sandpit of oblivion.[202] The second was with Ranft under whom *Gustav Vasa, Erik XIV, The Saga of the Folkungs, The Crown Bride* and *A Dream Play* were beautifully done. But I also had some good days with Personne, with *Crimes and Crimes, Damascus, Easter* and *Carl XII.* Falck I won't mention, because I am prejudiced regarding his case.

*How do you write?*
I wish I knew! It begins with a kind of fermentation, a sort of pleasurable fever, which turns into ecstasy or intoxication. Sometimes it is like a seed, which grows, attracts interest to itself, consumes everything I have experienced,

though in a selective way that requires some discarding. Sometimes I think I am some sort of medium, for it comes so easily, half unconsciously, hardly calculated at all! But it usually lasts no more than three hours (usually from 9 in the morning to 12 noon). And when it's over, everything is as boring as ever, until the next time. But it doesn't come upon demand, and seldom when *I* want it to. It comes when *it* pleases. But most often after big catastrophes! [-]

*Open Letters to the Intimate Theatre*, October 14–20, 1909.

January–September 1909. [-] *Master Olof,* written in 1871–72, came into being under the influence of Shakespeare's *Julius Caesar* in particular. Very early on I was amazed by Shakespeare's manner of depicting in his play one of the greatest men in the world: a hero, conqueror, statesman, legislator, scholar, historian, and a poet. Caesar was just a human being to Shakespeare, and as such, he is almost a minor character in that bit of world history which has been given the title *Julius Caesar.* [-]

In 1870, I discovered in my youthful ignorance that Shakespeare's *Julius Caesar,* with its positive and negative aspects, its great and small elements, put me on the right track despite my doubts about the hero's weaknesses and the looseness of the dramatic structure. My inborn desire to go beyond what I had learned, to develop and perfect, turned me into an examiner and a critic. I said to myself that for our skeptical and questioning age, with our ideas of human rights and human dignity, it would not be appropriate to make external distinctions between 'higher' and 'lower' people and let princes, courtiers, and their equals be eloquent in verse, while common people spoke plain language and were ridiculed in comic situations. As a result, I cut down the heels on my high-ranking characters and raised them a bit on the lower-ranking ones. That is how the script of *Master Olof* was prepared.

When I returned to historical drama twenty-five years later, I could ignore the scruples I had had back in 1872 when I wanted to depict historical men and women, so I went back to my dramatic techniques from the first version of *Master Olof.* Like my teacher Shakespeare, my purpose was to depict human beings both in their greatness and in their triviality; not to shun the proper words; to let history be the background; and to compress historical periods to fit the demands of the theatre of our time by avoiding the non-dramatic form of the chronicle or the epic. [-]

My goal with *The Saga of the Folkungs* was to summarize in the life of one person the bloody saga of the Folkungs,[203] which very much resembles England's War of the Roses. Magnus Eriksson, the last reigning Folkung, who in my schooldays still had an ugly nickname,[204] has been vindicated by more recent historical research.[-] According to what I learned from history, Magnus was in fact a good man who had learned to bear his fate with humility and therefore was despised by evil people in an evil age. It was easy for the author to consider him a vicarious sacrifice atoning for the guilt of others, which meant placing the question on a classical and Christian foundation. With this, I discovered the basic idea of the tragedy. The indispensable Birgitta[205] belonged to Magnus Eriksson's court. She has recently become a sort of Lutheran saint in Sweden, and succeeded in arranging matters so that there are definite accounts of her works and deeds. She was an ambitious woman, eager to rule, who consciously strove for canonization and for domination over the opposite sex. [-]

In accordance with the historical records I made this disagreeable woman the unmanageable fool in the drama, although I allowed her to redeem herself by letting her wake up to a clear understanding of her foolishness and pride. Since today's historians seem incapable of labeling Queen Blanche a poisoner, I carefully allowed the question to remain unresolved. Likewise, the accusation that she was guilty of adultery has never been established; and thus I also had to keep that point ambiguous. [-]

The Swedish language is currently undergoing a revitalization through our dialects and I do not consider it inappropriate to use strong words that are contemporary and well known to everyone in the spoken language. [-]

Engelbrekt[206] is one of Sweden's most memorable historical figures, and I felt I should keep his character as high and pure as Schiller kept his Wilhelm Tell.[207] [-]   Since I begin constructing a drama with the last act, I proceeded from the murder of Engelbrekt, which is a fact. History does not make the motive for the murder clear. Engelbrekt had had a quarrel with the murderer's father but reconciled their differences. Since no one knows what the quarrel was about, I had the right to let Engelbrekt undergo the misfortune of getting in the way of the envious Måns Bengtsson [Engelbrekt's murderer]. While it is certainly true that ingratitude is often [-] the reward of the world, I did not feel I had the right to toss out any prejudiced and comfortless half-truth about Engelbrekt but tried to give the great man some semblance of tragic guilt. In the wake of the Greek tragedians, I took the liberty of foisting upon him the very human sin that quite regularly follows great success: arrogance, *hubris,* which the gods hate most of all. [-]

The destiny of Gustav Vasa begins like a legend or a miracle story, develops into an epic, and is impossible to survey completely. To fit this gigantic saga into a dramatic play [*Gustav Vasa*] is inconceivable, of course. So the only possibility was to find its most rewarding episode. This occurs during the Dacke feud.[208] The king was then in his second marriage with children by two wives, and at the height of his power. But Providence wanted to test and temper the man to whom the building of the realm was entrusted, and so I had him stricken with all the misfortunes of Job. Such a period of despair provides the best opportunity to depict the great human being Gustav Vasa with all of his human weaknesses. [-]

[-] A characterization of a characterless person, that is indeed my Erik XIV.[209] [-] Göran Persson's[210] history has been written by his enemies. I had to accept him as a man of principles, and I have not concealed the evil man's minor good qualities, which is an author's duty when he is writing a drama as opposed to a lampoon or a memorial address.

That the Stures[211] were not completely blameless in their relationship with the Vasas has been proven. Therefore, I have suggested their relative guilt, manifesting itself in their sympathy for the traitor Johan,[212] the king's enemy. He who insists on chronological order in the construction of a historical drama has no idea what a drama is and therefore ought not to express himself with any claims to being heard. Someone can learn something about theatrical time in Hagberg's notes on Shakespeare.[213] Fifteen minutes on stage can be experienced as a whole forenoon, for example, and an intermission with a dropped curtain can be imagined as the passage of many years, depending on the author's skill at concealing dates, which can be done most simply by not mentioning them. That is what I have done.

*Gustav Adolf.* A Lutheran saint who has almost become a textbook legend was not attractive to me in the least. But then came the 1894 tercentennial with its various memorial ceremonies. In an unpretentious little booklet, I happened to read that Gustav Adolf, who had started his career by torturing Catholics [-], eventually went too far when he began hanging his own men for disturbing a Catholic service in Augsburg [-]. Then I immediately saw his entire character and the complete drama, and I called it my *Nathan the Wise.*[214]

The blond man with the gentle spirit who was always ready with a joke even in the darkest of moments, was very much a statesman and a bit of a musketeer, but also a dreamer who dreamt of a universal kingdom [-]. He was sufficiently sinful to be a human being as he encounters inner conflicts that make a drama so rich and interesting. Supplied by Cardinal Richelieu with

400,000 a year on condition that he not disturb the Catholic League,[215] he eventually participates in the Thirty Years' War against the House of Hapsburg. As a dramatic character he gets involved in the resolvable difficulties of distinguishing a friend from an enemy; and only his death on the battlefield can restore the harmony and cut the tangled threads.

*Kristina.* [-] Kristina was such a genuine woman that she was a woman hater. In her memoirs she states quite categorically that women should never be permitted to govern. The fact that she had no desire to get married I find natural. The fact that she tinkered with love and got caught in her own net is, of course, highly dramatic.

*Gustav III.* The enlightened despot who carries out his own French Revolution at home in Sweden, that is to say, crushes the aristocrats with the help of the third estate – this is a paradox that is hard to depict.

And as a character he is full of contradictions, a tragedian who plays comedy in life, a hero and a dancing master, a despotic friend of liberty, a humanitarian, a disciple of Frederick the Great [-] and Voltaire. He is almost likeable, as the Revolutionary who falls into the hands of the Revolutionaries. For Anckarström[216] was a man of the Revolution [-].

*Carl XII.* The man who ruined Sweden, the great criminal, the warrior, the idol of the ruffians, and the counterfeiter, this was the king I was going to present on stage to my countrymen. Well, everyone has his own motives for his actions and every criminal has the right to defend himself, so I decided on a classical tragedy of fate and catastrophe. The end of a life that was one big mistake. A strong will that struggles against historical development, pardonable if only because he was so unwise. [-] The issue of who fired the bullet at Fredrikshald[217] has thus far not been resolved. I let it come from up "above," which Swedenborg, Carl XII's last friend, interprets in his own elevated fashion, while general opinion believes it came from the fortress. [-]

My *Carl XII* is a drama of character and catastrophe, the last acts in a long story, also in the sense that it follows to some extent the classic tragedies, in which everything has already happened. And it also resembles the admired Dovre dramas [by Ibsen], which involve nothing more than the unraveling of what has already taken place. In my *Carl XII* I begin with his return,[218] I depict in vivid images the miserable condition of the realm and present the half-insane despot who refuses to utter a word and to receive the representatives of the four estates. In the second act, he is in Lund doing nothing; is ashamed to return to Stockholm; looks for a war anywhere in order to regain his lost honor or – die. [-]

In Act III, you see the consequences of the despot's reckless behavior. [-]

In Act IV, the suspense is sustained through waiting. [-]

In Act V, the bullet (fired at Fredrikshald) is foreshadowed. The suspense is sustained here, as well, through waiting, waiting for the storming of the castle or "the bullet."

When I began to plan and ponder the subject of Earl Birger[219] about ten years ago, I soon discovered that the material was unwieldy. [-] As I went ahead, I noticed that the strongest motifs were found at the end of his career, while the motif of Jutta and Mechtild[220] comprised his entire lifetime and extended even beyond his grave. People usually remember 1266 as the year when the Earl died, while the date of the Jutta incident is seldom remembered; so I took the liberty of antedating this motif and combining it with Valdemar's pilgrimage of penance to Rome and Magnus's regency.[221] [-]

As usual in my historical dramas, I have placed Swedish history within the framework of world history; therefore the fool's listing of the foreign guests and ambassadors is not insignificant and must not be omitted. The fool is a voluntary slave who glorifies the Earl's humanity as a lawgiver, but he is also the *raisonneur*, as found in Shakespeare, who bluntly states what the rest are thinking; he also represents the people (*vox populi*), or the Greek chorus, which reflects on the action of the drama, by forewarning and advising. [-]

I admit that even in the theatre it is fun to look at pictures, to have one's eye periodically refreshed by a new set every time the curtain rises. But that sort of thing is not always relevant and if pleasure is to be provided at the expense of the drama, then forget about the scenery.

Until 1880, when open wings were still in use, changing scenery was quite easy. But when people began to build sets on the stage, then the carpenter's shop moved in and the long intermissions became a nuisance which scared the audience away from the theatres. These intermissions, however, became closely linked to the increased sale of liquor. A practical age had discovered that the restaurant keeper could pay his entire rent for the theatre if he could be guaranteed that the intermissions were long enough. The director managed these liquor breaks and when there were no intermissions in the drama, he simply inserted them. It went so far that plays actually got amputated and certain types of plays were more readily performed. Yes, people began to detect [-] a new kind of drama, called refreshment drama. The strong temperance movement made its silent counterattack, and those who did not want to imbibe [-] stayed away from the theatres. [-]

Even if beautiful scenery is fun to look at, it is a wasted effort considering the short period of time it is on view. And to listen to the lines and observe the mimicry of the actors is so taxing that no one really has time to look at pictures. For example: It just so happened that I didn't get to see the production of my *Crown Bride.* I asked several people who had attended the premiere, and also later performances, whether the church rose from the lake in the final act. They all responded: "I didn't notice!" I had expected a beautiful effect at the end of the play with the church rising out of the lake on Easter morning with its gilded church rooster appearing first. And no one had noticed it! In Helsinki, the stage machinery failed to work and the church did not appear at all, but no one missed it, although the play had already been published and read. [-] The audience, it is said, wants scenery and will not come if it does not get it. People demand it in an opera or an operetta, but they actually do not insist upon it in a stage play. [-]

Grandinson's production of *To Damascus* was beautiful. The play could never have been performed if we had not opted for simplification. Composed in strict contrapuntal form, the first part – the one that was actually produced – consists of seventeen tableaux. Allegorizing the pilgrimage, the drama proceeds until the ninth tableau, which is set in the Asylum; then the exiled couple retrace their steps and they have to struggle back. The scenery is reversed to make the drama end at the very street corner where it had started. In order to do this quickly, a smaller stage was constructed inside the ordinary one and placed within an unusually attractive arch painted by Grabow.[222] Sides were not needed; we played against backdrops which, hung up one behind the other, were raised by a silent pulley. Instead of unnecessary curtain falls the stage was darkened. [-].

After theatre director Castegren had succeeded in getting the play accepted at the Swedish Theatre, we began discussing the means for converting the dream into visual images without actualizing it too much. Here the sciopticon was successfully utilized for the first time. We had already tried it in *To Damascus* at the Dramatic Theatre. Sven Scholander[223] projected a backdrop sufficiently large and distinct, but since it had to be dark in front of the backdrop in order to be seen, the actors became less visible. Another disadvantage was that the electric light showed through the fabric, but this could be corrected by placing the light below the level of the stage floor. However, we were in a hurry and got fed up. But based on my own experiments, I believe that if one uses various light sources, the sciopticon backdrop can be used. For example, if one has [-] violet-colored light behind the backdrop, and illuminates the figures in front of it by means of a red incandescent light or a white

Auerburner, it should be possible to illuminate the figures and keep the drop visible.

As for *A Dream Play*, I had stated in the text that it should be played with standing sides of *"stylized wall paintings, functioning at the same time as rooms, architecture, and landscape."* I assumed that meant changing the backdrop when necessary. Castegren went to Dresden, where they had recently used the sciopticon for *Faust*, to buy the apparatus. But tests here at home (which I never got to see, however) showed that it did not measure up to its promise. [-] Castegren, who had ruined himself in Gothenburg because of his good taste and exclusive repertoire, now used all of his inventiveness and energy to get *A Dream Play* produced, resisting certain currents that are against everything new. I have thanked him, but I have also told him that the staging was not successful since it was all too concrete to successfully evoke dream images. Grabow had also not made much of an effort and had been careless. And a certain justified fear of reproducing the same lighting effects "as were used in variety shows" prevented the director from using exactly those resources we needed. [-] Rebuilding the scenery disturbed the actors' concentration and called for endless intermissions. Furthermore, the entire performance became a more materialized phenomenon than the intended dematerialization. We now intend to make another attempt at producing *A Dream Play* at the Intimate Theatre, and we are going at it with no holds barred. But instead of painted sets, which in *this case* cannot reproduce unfixed and fluid mirages, we intend to go solely for the color effect because we discovered that red plush drapes can create many nuances of color, from azure blue [-] to purple, simply by applying varied lights. And instead of using contemporary colorless costumes, we have decided to introduce colorful costumes from many different ages, as long as they are beautiful, because in the dream there is no question of reality; in this way we can fully justify our preferences for *Schönheit* over *Wahrheit*.[224] On the railing that we have borrowed from the Molière stage, we intend to set up allegorical attributes, indicating [-] the place where the scene is meant to take place. For example, a couple of large sea shells indicate the proximity of the sea; a couple of cypresses take us to Italy; two signal flags in red and blue indicate Foulstrand; a couple of statuettes represent Fairhaven; a hymn board with psalm numbers suggests the Church and the laurel wreaths signify the promotion ceremony and a blackboard with eraser is the School, etc. [-]

We can say that since the Intimate Theatre began with Falck's successful production of *Miss Julie* [-] three years ago, it is understandable that the young manager is influenced by the preface [-]. But this was twenty years ago, and, if I do not exactly need to criticize myself on this point, all that scribbling about properties and attributes was quite unnecessary. The play itself, which in its day was considered a piece of villainy in Sweden, has now had time to become accepted, and August Palme,[225] who resurrected it, noticed that it was a *Figaro*,[226] which means it was more than just some unusual seduction story. It includes the radical renewal of society, the struggle between race and class, between the patrician and the plebeian, woman's foolish attempt to free herself from nature, the raging revolt of modern life against tradition, custom, and common sense.

Falck, who remained faithful to these themes, came up with a kitchen complete in all of its details, which I didn't get to see until later, however. Everything was as it should be!

The first production I saw at the Intimate Theatre was *The Pelican*. I was amazed by the *art nouveau*-style room with furniture in kind. It was both fitting and beautiful, but there was something else in that room; there was atmosphere, a white fragrance of a sickroom and a nursery, with something green on a bureau as if it had been placed there by an invisible hand. "I'd like to live in that room," I said, though one could sense the tragedy that was about to be played there in the last act with the presentation of the most horrible motif of classical tragedy: innocent children suffering, and their humbug mother, Medea.

It was a beautiful production in which modern art was brought on stage, and it seems consequently to have been roundly denounced by the enlightened critics.

Afterward I saw *The Burned Site*. The stylized apple tree contrasted sharply against the realistic wooden shack called "The Last Nail," and some of the stage properties countered the attempt at modernization in the style of *The Studio*.[227] But there was also atmosphere.

Then came *Thunder in the Air*. For the first time, the Intimate Theatre proved lacking in providing adequate sets on stage. I had warned Falck, but he tried and failed in his attempts in Acts I and III; in Act II, however, he managed to create a room in which one could live and feel at home; it was a home that was more home-like than any I had ever seen on stage before. Ordinary rooms are usually failures, mainly because of the difficulty in constructing windows and tile stoves. Falck eliminated both the windows and the tile stove, and achieved something that was complete and enclosed, which breathed tranquillity and comfort. No warped window arches with fly screens in them, no leaning tile stove with dark cracks between the tiles. Only a buffet, a piano, and a dining room table, but arranged so that one did not miss any of the other details that often clutter the stage and take up space. It was successful in its simple beauty, and with it, we left the preface and *Miss Julie* behind. I also discovered that Falck *was* a director, had the gift of inventiveness, was a painter, had taste, and could produce on stage what one is seldom able to get: atmosphere, another word for poetry. The first and last acts were unsuccessful only because of lack of space. But we should have simplified and deleted, and not given in to constructing sets on stage.

*The Ghost Sonata* immediately proved to be impossible to stage as it was. Falck, however, liked challenges but he could not overcome the difficulties because they were simply too great to surmount. The play belongs to our theatre, however, and we'll put it on again in a simplified form.

Falck created a masterpiece when he produced *Sir Bengt's Wife*. His simple and attractive Hall of Knights would have honored a larger theatre; the costumes were tasteful in beautiful soft harmonizing colors.

Then came the miracle of *Kristina*, accompanied by the discovery that scenery could be scrapped without making the production monotonous or shabby. With this production we had found our way through our apprenticeship year, and now we are going to apply what we have learned!

Since I wrote the above, Falck has attempted to simplify the scenery even further, and he has succeeded, this time with *Crimes and Crimes*. The sides, painted as columns in neutral tints and an unknown style, remained standing throughout the whole play, and he also used backdrops, a few props, and varied lighting. I attended a private performance for artists. After the play, I asked if the columns had been distracting. Several people did not understand what I meant, because they had not even noticed the novelty. And now I myself could neither honestly remember whether the columns were still there in the night café nor whether the room was closed. That is how little the scenery can signify in a play whose content completely captures one's attention.

With the abstract plush draperies in *Swanwhite* and by not using the available newly painted scenery, Falck succeeded once again in his attempt at simplification. An effect that I found wonderful was achieved merely through lighting and a simple color tone. [-]

I know what is meant by stylization on stage, but I cannot put it into words until I have thought it over a little. The term became better known after Maeterlinck's first splendid dramas (but not after *Monna Vanna*, at which point his work had begun deteriorating). Maeterlinck's secret is this: His characters are active on a plane other than the one on which we live. He is in communication with a higher world. [-] I still do not understand why innocent little children are tormented in his dramas; perhaps they represent the innocent sufferers.

When Maeterlinck first appeared somewhere around 1890 in the latter days of naturalism, I read a review of one of his plays. We know, of course, that when a simpleton reviews a clever play, even the cleverest passages end up sounding stupid. The review seemed to be either a satire or pure rubbish. When I later came to read Maeterlinck in Paris, he was like a closed book to me, so thoroughly had I become immersed in materialism. But I felt a certain uneasiness and sorrow about not being able to grasp what he had to say, the beauty and profundity of which I sensed and longed for, the way a damned person longs for the company of good people.

It was only after I had passed through my Inferno years (1896-99) that I sought out Maeterlinck again, and then he impressed me like a newly discovered country in a new age.

He called his finest dramas marionette plays and considered them unactable. By marionette he did not mean what we call Punch and Judy shows but life-size figures manipulated by means of wires, which make such scenes as the black dog's or the little lamb's possible, but also lead to an angularity of gestures that seems conventional.

This made people feel that when actors performed Maeterlinck in the theatre, another type of acting was called for. It was not enough to merely depart from reality; one had to do something beyond that as well. This resulted in something like the abstract gestures of opera or of old tragedies that still survive at Théâtre Français.

I cannot sense anything else in this new stylization concept other than what we use when a high or exalted style is called for. And that was appropriate here. [-]

I believe, however, that Maeterlinck is best left unperformed. His infernal world is in the spirit of Swedenborg, but there is light in the darkness, beauty in the suffering, and compassion for all living things. But it is a desperate, fateful and heavy world.

If Materlinck is already part of the repertoire, it is better to forget the word stylization and instead request that the actors enter this author's marvelous world, where everything has a strange new sense of proportion, tone and light. If the actor can do this, then he will have succeeded. Otherwise, he remains outside this world; it remains closed to him. It cannot be learned, perhaps it can be acquired – but only by wandering through the inferno.

The word stylization must go. We have the older concepts high style and exalted style, and we understand those well!

History and ballads have always and rightly been considered common property, which the writer has been permitted to use and exploit. Fryxell, Afzelius, and Starbäck[228] have been employed most advantageously for this purpose, since they have included more human details than the dry chronicles and official histories. Fryxell, in a lively fashion, narrates with a rather colorless but flowing style. Starbäck and Bäckström, meanwhile, have amassed an amazing amount of material, which however is poorly worked out and arranged, so that one has to approach it with a drill and pickax to get at its gems.

Starbäck's (and Bäckström's) *Stories from Swedish History,* which are not really stories but consist of a rather dry history of Sweden, is common property, and from it I have taken most of the raw material for my historical dramas.[-]

When I wrote *Earl Birger of Bjälbo,* I proceeded as usual. I read Starbäck's history [-]. I made the major characters come alive by including blood and nerves from my own life, so that they became my own property. But in order to create atmosphere and to retreat into the remote past, I did as I usually do when writing historical dramas. I read Walter Scott. There was no Earl Birger here, but there were ingredients, decorations, and props from the Middle Ages, tournaments and displays of weapons, because Walter Scott was a great antiquarian, and *Ivanhoe* is particularly rich in antiquities. But there is also the fool Wamba, about whom I don't remember anything more than that he lost his collar. I read the novel last fall, but ten years earlier I had intended to include in *The Saga of the Folkungs* a man who had sold himself into thralldom. In that play I suggest that Birgitta's brother was a hostage or had given himself up as security for a major loan. However, I didn't have room in the play for that character but let King Magnus summarily set free a host of thralls. When *Earl Birger of Bjälbo* was taking shape I was fed up with exalted rhetoric on stage. Instead I nourished the plan that in the court, the fool would say what others dared not say. But my fool, unlike other fools [-], developed as a more complex character and became a representative of the voluntary thralls and a living image of Earl Birger's legal proceedings, which ultimately led to the abolition of imprisonment for debt. I had made the first sketch of my fool some thirty years earlier in *The Secret of the Guild.* There, too, the fool has a past and is not just a clown. Now, when I came across Wamba's collar, I found it picturesque and borrowed that detail, which is an author's right, because here I could simply show what otherwise would have to be narrated. The fool in *Earl Birger of Bjälbo* is *my* property. [-]

The Earl is mine, as well. He is not an instructor in declamation but a politician and a plotter as he was in real life. [-]

For a long time I had considered skimming our most beautiful ballads for knights [-] and using them in my plays. Then Maeterlinck got in my way, and influenced by his marvelous marionette plays, which were not intended for the stage, I wrote my Swedish stage play *Swanwhite.* You can neither borrow nor steal from Maeterlinck, and it is difficult to become his disciple [-], because there is no easy entry into his world of beauty. But he can inspire you to hunt for gold in your own refuse heaps, and in that I admit my ties to the master.

Impressed by Maeterlinck and borrowing his divining rod, I searched in sources such as Geijer,[229] Afzelius, and Dybeck's *Runa.*[230]

There were princes and princesses galore. I had already discovered the stepmother motif as a constant in twenty-six Swedish folktales, and the theme of rising from the dead could also be found here [-]. [-] So I put everything into the separator with maidens and the green gardener and the young king, and so the cream was tossed out, and in this way the end product has become mine.

But it's also mine because I've lived that tale in my imagination! One spring in the midst of winter .


To August Falck.


February 8, 1909. I am very curious about *Swanwhite* being performed with a drape [-]. Let's now try it with *Sir Bengt's Wife.*[231]

This is the new road that leads to the liberation of drama and frees the audience from painful intermissions. [-]

If *The Ghost Sonata* could be transformed with a drape, we can perform it for specially invited people, as we did last time. And it can be done! [-] The Mummy for instance could sit in the slit of the back drapes, as if in a closet. That would raise the piece to its proper level, which is not the tangible one. And now I see hyacinths on the barrier, see *Toten-Insel* (which you must paint large and grandiose) when the back drape is pulled apart. If you would like, I can transpose the piece for drape and barrier [-]. [-]

To August Falck.

March 8, 1909. [-] The deep stage you were looking for in a bigger theatre can be compensated for at the Intimate Theatre in this way: softer lighting and performing only behind the first wing. Perhaps the footlights should be removed. Next time try an experiment for me by using no footlights for one act. [-]

Furthermore, the set designer should apply a thin coat of paint; landscape painters achieve distance by spreading out the color with a spatula. He has to break with tradition and paint the foreground in thin soft colors that are mixed in half-shades and watered down, avoiding the primary colors. Mix the colors neutrally! And not like Grabow, who uses blazing colors. Also the actors should not use too much make-up. [-]

Are you going to have more than one set in the back? If not, open up the back wall. You know that I always prefer depth on stage. At least an open window where one can see a green tree. [-]

To August Falck.

September 8, 1909. [-] Since you are actually too young for your part [as the Captain in *The Dance of Death*], you have to use make-up to make yourself look older and should avoid moving like a young man. A gray wig would be too radical.

If you were always to speak in your own tone of voice, you would position yourself firmly in your role. And if you do not waver, you will not sound false or as if you were merely reading your part. If you could change your voice, this would be good. Just sit in the chair, bragging!

The pantomime should be omitted. It was misunderstood and it delayed the action.

The room is fine, perhaps a little cluttered.

The pauses in the beginning, up to the first explosion, must be extremely short, for the exposition is long and tiring. [-]

Don't forget the effect of the helmet at the [Captain's] exit, which I mentioned yesterday. And make the telegraph apparatus more visible! [-]

To August Falck.

January 31, 1910. [-] If the scene with the children in *The Great Highway* worries you or if children are not allowed [on stage], don't cut it but instead use a monodrama method:

You[232] say: "Here comes the mistress of the house (in this case she doesn't enter).

Then you say: "I've been through this scene before somewhere." There she is about to enter, and she says: "Walk silently, etc."

Then *you* describe the whole scene, in part as you imagine it would happen, in part as 'you' have experienced it! But no *babbling*!!! [-]

This is, you understand, a resource, and the question is whether the scene would not seem better, greater, more mystical if you were completely alone on stage.

Don't cut it under any circumstances. [-]


"Mine and Yours," *Afton-Tidningen*, September 5, 1910.

[-] As for *Easter* and the *Easter* girl, August Palme, among others, knows where in my life I found the Eleonora type, which, moreover, I prepared in both *Advent* and *Inferno*: a person who suffers for another (*satisfactio vicaria*). The second motif – Nemesis, well-meaning fate or a good deed paid back – I got from the Reverend K. on Värmdö [outside Stockholm]. The tension in the drama or the incident at the florist's I observed in a town [Lund] in South Sweden, where this unusual way of buying flowers has occurred at least once.

I took the mood from Haydn's *Sieben Worte*, which is purely Christian. The form, the three days of Easter, is my invention, corresponding to the three acts in the Passion drama. [-]

My allegorical attributes, the Easter lily and the scourge need no explanation.[233]

What I've taken from the riches of life itself, my own as well as that of others, becomes mine because I have given it a shape of my own and I have filled it with my wine, whether it's bitter or sweet. [-]

"The Beauty of It All,"[234] *Afton-Tidningen*, June 25, 1910.

[-] In *The Secret of the Guild* [-] agonizing doubt was symbolized by the collapse of the church vault, and the loss of faith by the guild's lost secret. Saul's journey and the journey of life itself were symbolized in *To Damascus* and in *The Great Highway*. These were obvious things. But symbolism is often confused with allegory, which in its meager, oldfashioned form embodies abstractions such as vice, foolishness, injustice, etc. [-]

"Guilt-Ridding," *Afton-Tidningen*, July 17, 1910.

[-] This play [*Lucky Peter's Journey*], which I myself don't appreciate since it lacks both artistic form and living characters, was written for my children in moments of leisure during the stormy periods when *The Swedish People* and *The New Kingdom* were being developed. [-]

To August Falck.

September 14, 1910. If I am to continue taking an interest in the Intimate Theatre, its original agenda must first be realized, that is, my unperformed plays must be performed first and not some stranger's!

I can't afford to make sacrifices to Maeterlinck[235] although I do admire him! [-]

I shall probably abstain from the Anti-Nobel Prize[236] and suggest that a foundation be set up instead to benefit the Intimate Theatre on one simple condition: that they perform me! [-]

You have *The Dream Play, Damascus* (both including roles for your wife), as well as *The Black Glove,* which you insultingly refused!

"January 22," *Afton-Tidningen*, January 15, 1912.

I have just gotten out of my sickbed to learn of a discussion about the celebration of my birthday. I have nothing against the idea that both I and the general public are reminded of my dramatic work by having my plays performed; for there have been many attempts to silence, ignore, suppress, devalue, and bury this, the most important part of my authorship. There will be a referendum or plebiscite in the entire country, and since most of my plays have been performed earlier and thus have stood the test of time and proven themselves stageworthy, I see this as a recognition of my *dramatic art*, which I have practiced now for over forty years.

# Strindberg's Plays

The plays are listed chronologically with respect to when they were written. The Swedish title is followed by the traditional/preferred English,[237] German and French titles.

p = first publication, pr = world premiere

1869    *Fritänkaren* (The Freethinker, Der Freidenker, Le Libre-penseur), comedy in three acts, p 1870 (pseudonym Härved Ulf), pr April 15, 2000 as a radio play (Swedish Radio), March 3, 2003 as a stage play at Strindberg's Intimate Theatre, Stockholm. *Det sjunkande Hellas* (The Sinking Hellas, Das sinkende Hellas, Hellas déclinant), dramatic study in three acts (pseudonym Härved Ulf), p 1960, revised into the five-act verse tragedy **Hermione**, p 1871 (anonymous), unperformed.

1870    *I Rom* (In Rome, In Rom, À Rome), verse drama in one act; p 1870, pr Dec. 13, 1870 at the Royal Dramatic Theatre, Stockholm.

1871    *Den fredlöse* (The Outlaw, Der Geächtete, Le hors-la-loi), tragedy in one act, p 1881, pr Oct. 16, 1871 at the Royal Dramatic Theatre, Stockholm.

1872    Prose version of *Mäster Olof* (Master Olof, Meister Olof, Maître Olof), historical drama in five acts, p 1881, pr Dec. 30, 1881 at the New Theatre, Stockholm.

1874    Revised version of *Mäster Olof*, historical drama in five acts, p 1948, pr Jan. 6, 1959 at Gothenburg City Theatre.

1876    Verse version of *Mäster Olof*, including the Epilogue (fragment), historical drama in five acts, p 1878, pr (without the Epilogue) March 15, 1890 at the Royal Dramatic Theatre, Stockholm.

1876-77 *Anno fyrtioåtta* (Anno Forty-eight, Anno Achtundvierzig, En L'an quarante-huit), comedy in four acts, p 1881, pr 1922–23 in Germany.

1877   *Efterspelet* (The Epilogue) to *Mäster Olof* (fragment), p 1878, pr Jan. 20, 1920 at the Lorensberg Theatre, Gothenburg.

1880   ***Gillets hemlighet*** (The Secret of the Guild, Das Geheimnis der Gilde, Le Secret de la guilde), four-act comedy, p 1880, pr May 3, 1880 at the Royal Dramatic Theatre, Stockholm.

1882   *Lycko-Pers resa* (Lucky Peter's Journey, Glückspeter's Reise, Le Voyage de Pierre l'Heureux), fairy-tale play in five acts, p 1882, pr Dec. 22, 1883 at the New Theatre, Stockholm. *Herr Bengts hustru* (Sir Bengt's Wife, Herr Bengts Gattin, La Femme de Sire Bengt), historical drama in five acts, p 1882, pr Nov. 25, 1882 at the New Theatre, Stockholm.

1886   *Marodörer* (Marauders, Marodöre, Maraudeurs), comedy in five acts, p 1886, pr. Feb. 14, 1953 by the Student Theatre, Uppsala.

1887   *Fadren* (The Father, Der Vater, Père), tragedy in three acts, p 1887, pr Nov. 14, 1887 at the Casino Theatre, Copenhagen. *Kamraterna* (Comrades, Die Kameraden, Camarades), comedy in four acts, p 1888, pr Oct. 23, 1905 at the Lustspieltheater, Vienna.

1888   *Fröken Julie* (Miss Julie, Fräulein Julie, Mademoiselle Julie), incl. "Preface," naturalistic tragedy in one act, p 1888, pr March 14, 1889 at private performance in the Student Society, Copenhagen. *Fordringsägare* (Creditors, Gläubiger, Créanciers), one-act drama, p 1889, March 9, 1889 at the Dagmar Theatre, Copenhagen.

1889   *Den starkare* (The Stronger, Die Stärkere, La plus forte), *quart d'heure*, p 1890, March 9, 1889 at the Dagmar Theatre, Copenhagen. *Paria* (Pariah, Paria, Paria), one-act drama based on a short story by Ola Hansson, p 1890, March 9, 1889 at the Dagmar Theatre, Copenhagen. *Hemsöborna* (The People of Hemsö, Die Hemsöer, Les Gens de Hemsö), folk comedy in four acts, based on S's novel of the same title (1887), p 1905 (in German trans.), pr May 29, 1889 at the Djurgård Theatre, Stockholm. *Samum* (Simoom, Samum, Simoun), one-act drama, p 1890, pr March 25, 1890 at the Swedish Theatre, Stockholm.

1892    *Himmelrikets nycklar* (The Keys of Heaven, Die Schlüssel des Himmelreichs, Les Clefs du ciel), fairy-tale play in five acts, p 1892, pr March 13, 1927 at the Schauspielbühne, Bad Godesberg. *Första varningen* (The First Warning, Die Erste Warnung, Premier avertissement), one-act drama, p 1893, pr Jan. 22, 1893 at the Residenz-Theater, Berlin. *Debet och kredit* (Debit and Credit, Debet und Credit, Doit et avoir), one-act drama, p 1893, pr May 13, 1900 at the Residenz-Theater, Berlin. *Inför döden* (Facing Death, Vorm Tode, Devant le mort), one-act drama, p 1893, pr Jan. 22, 1893 at the Residenz-Theater, Berlin. *Moderskärlek* (Motherly Love, Mutterliebe, Amour maternel), one-act drama, p 1893, pr 1894 Tour Messthaler, Germany. *Leka med elden* (Playing with Fire, Mit dem Feuer spielen, Il ne faut pas jouer avec feu), one-act comedy, p 1893, pr Dec. 3, 1893 at the Lessing-Theater, Berlin. *Bandet* (The Bond, Das Band, Le Lien), one-act drama, p 1897, pr March 11, 1902 at the Kleines Theater, Berlin.

1898    *Till Damaskus I* (To Damascus, Nach Damaskus, Le Chemin de Damas) pilgrimage drama in five acts, p 1898, pr Nov. 19, 1900 at the Royal Dramatic Theatre, Stockholm. *Till Damaskus II*, pilgrimage drama in four acts, p 1898, pr June 9, 1916 (together with Part III) at the Kammerspiele, Munich. *Advent* (Advent, Advent, L'Avent), mystery play in five acts, p 1899, pr Dec. 28, 1915 at the Kammerspiele, Munich.

1899    *Brott och brott* (Crimes and Crimes, Rausch, Crime et crime), comedy in four acts, p 1899, pr Feb. 26, 1900 at the Royal Dramatic Theatre, Stockholm. *Folkungasagan* (The Saga of the Folkungs, Folkungersage, La Saga des Folkungar), historical drama in five acts, p 1899, pr Jan. 25, 1901 at the Swedish Theatre, Stockholm. *Gustav Vasa*, historical drama in five acts, p 1899, pr Oct. 17, 1899 at the Swedish Theatre, Stockholm. *Erik XIV*, historical drama in four acts, p 1899, pr Nov. 30, 1899 at the Swedish Theatre, Stockholm.

1900    *Gustav Adolf*, historical drama in five acts, p 1900, pr Dec. 4, 1903 at the Berlin Theatre. *Midsommar* (Midsummer, Mittsommer, La Saint-Jean), serious comedy in six tableaux, p 1901, pr Apr. 17, 1901 at the Swedish Theatre, Stockholm. *Kaspers Fet-tisdag* (Casper's Shrove Tuesday, Kaspers Fastnacht, La Mardi-gras de Polichinelle), one-act comedy, p 1916, pr Apr. 16, 1901 at the Royal Dramatic Theatre, Stockholm. *Påsk* (Easter, Ostern, Paques), passion drama in three acts, p 1901, pr March 9, 1901 at the Schauspielhaus, Frankfurt. *Dödsdansen I* (The Dance of Death, Der Todestanz, La Danse de Mort), drama in four acts, p 1901, pr Sept. 29, 1905 at the Old City Theatre, Cologne. *Dödsdansen II*, drama in three acts, p 1901, pr Sept. 30, 1905 at the Old City Theatre, Cologne.

1901    *Kronbruden* (The Crown Bride, Die Kronbraut, La Mariée couronnée), drama in six parts, p 1902, pr Apr. 24, 1906 at the Swedish Theatre, Helsinki. **Svanevit** (Swanwhite, Schwanenweiss, Blanche-Cygne), fairy-tale drama in three acts, p 1902, pr Apr. 8, 1908 at the Swedish Theatre, Helsinki. *Carl XII* (Charles XII, Carl XII, Charles XII), historical drama in five parts, p 1901, pr Feb. 13, 1902 at the Royal Dramatic Theatre, Stockholm. *Till Damaskus III* (To Damascus, Nach Damaskus, Le Chemin de Damas), pilgrimage drama in seven tableaux, p 1904, pr Nov. 16, 1922 at the Kammerspiele, Munich (together with Part II). *Engelbrekt,* historical drama in four acts, p 1901, pr Dec. 3, 1901 at the Swedish Theatre, Stockholm. *Kristina* (Queen Christina, Königin Christine, Reine Christine), historical drama in four acts, p 1903, pr March 27, 1908 at the Intimate Theatre, Stockholm. *Ett drömspel* (A Dream Play, Ein Traumspiel, Le Songe), drama in fifteen tableaux, p 1902, pr Apr. 17, 1907 at the Swedish Theatre, Stockholm.

1902    *Gustav III*, historical drama in five acts, p 1903, pr Jan. 25, 1916 at the New Theatre, Stockholm. *Holländarn* (The Dutchman, Der Holländer, Le Hollandais), fragment in four parts, p 1918, pr Apr. 5, 1923 at the Lorensberg Theatre, Gothenburg.

1903    *Näktergalen i Wittenberg* (The Nightingale of Wittenberg, Die Nachtigall von Wittenberg, Le Rossignol de Wittenberg), Luther drama in fourteen tableaux, p 1903, pr Dec. 5, 1914 at the German Artists' Theatre, Berlin. *Genom öknar till arvland, eller Moses* (Through Deserts unto the Beloved Country or Moses, Durch Wüsten ins gelobte Land oder Moses, Par Déserts à pays patrimoniale ou Moses), fragment, p 1918, pr Jan. 14, 1923 at the City Theatre, Hannover. *Hellas, eller Sokrates* (Hellas or Socrates, Hellas oder Sokrates, Hellas ou Socrate), fragment, p 1918, pr Jan. 14, 1923 at the City Theatre, Hannover. *Lammet och vilddjuret, eller Kristus* (The Lamb and the Beast or Christ,

Das Lamm und die Bestie oder Christus, L'Agneau et la bête ou le Christ), fragment, p 1918, pr Apr. 12, 1922 at the City Theatre, Hannover.

1907    *Oväder* (Thunder in the Air, Wetterleuchten, Orage), chamber play in three parts, p 1907, pr Dec. 30, 1907 at the Intimate Theatre, Stockholm. *Brända tomten* (The Burned Site, Die Brandstätte, La Maison brulée), chamber play in two parts, p 1907, pr Dec. 5, 1907 at the Intimate Theatre, Stockholm. *Spöksonaten* (The Ghost Sonata, Die Gespenstersonate, La Sonate des spectres), chamber play in three parts, p 1907, pr Jan. 21, 1908 at the Intimate Theatre, Stockholm. *Toten-Insel* (The Isle of the Dead, Toten-Insel, L'Ile des morts), chamber play (fragment), p 1918, pr spring 1960 at École des Arts Décoratifs, Paris. *Pelikanen* (The Pelican, Der Pelikan, Le Pélican), chamber play in three parts, p 1907, pr Nov. 26, 1907 at the Intimate Theatre, Stockholm.

1908    *Siste riddaren* (The Last Knight, Der letzte Ritter, Le dernier chevalier), historical drama in five acts, p 1908, pr Jan. 22, 1909 at the Royal Dramatic Theatre, Stockholm. *Abu Casems tofflor* (Abu Casem's Slippers, Abu Casems Pantoffeln, Les Babouches d'Abou Kassem), fairytale drama in five acts, p 1908, pr Dec. 28, 1908 in Gävle, as part of a tour. *Riksföreståndaren* (The Regent, Der Reichsverweser, Le Regent), historical drama in five acts, p 1909, pr Jan. 31, 1911 at the Swedish Theatre, Stockholm. *Bjälbojarlen* (The Earl of Bjälbo, Der Jarl von Bjälbo, Le Jarl de Bjælbo), historical drama in five acts, p 1909, pr March 26, 1909 at the Swedish Theatre, Stockholm. *Svarta handsken* (The Black Glove, Der schwarze Handshuh, Le Gant noir), lyrical fantasy (for the stage) in five acts, p 1909, pr Christmas 1909 in Sweden as part of a tour.

1909    *Stora landsvägen* (The Great Highway, Die grosse Landstrasse, La Grand-Route), pilgrimage drama in seven tableaux, p 1909, pr Feb.19, 1910 at the Intimate Theatre, Stockholm.

# Notes

1     S spent several months during 1870 working on a five-act historical drama in verse about Erik XIV, the sixteenth century. Swedish king who murdered some of his nobles in Uppsala Castle.

2     Inspired by Old Norse culture, S actually refers to the month as "Butchering Month."

3     Adam Oehlenschläger was the leading Danish poet and dramatist during the first part of the nineteenth century. In 1871, S made Oehlenschläger's tragedy *Earl Haakon* the subject of his seminar paper in aesthetics, later published in vol. 2 of *The Son of a Servant.*

4     A revised version, in five acts, of his three-act play in blank verse, *The Sinking Hellas*, written in 1869, which S at this time submitted to (the eighteen members of) the Swedish Academy as his entry in a competition for new plays. It received an honorable mention but no prize.

5     S actually refers to the month as the Month of Autumn.

6     Verse drama (1863) by the Finland-Swedish writer Johan Ludvig Runeberg.

7     Play (1876) by Alexandre Dumas fils.

8     The Royal Dramatic Theatre in Stockholm.

9     On the prose version of *Master Olof* Josephson had written: "[-] I have not for many years read a play which has made such an overwhelming impression on me; [-] it must have been the most short-sighted, inartistic, lazy and un-Swedish theatre board to have had the nerve to refuse acceptance of this piece for performance."

10     *Hamlet*, Act III.1.

11     The Swedish two-chamber parliament.

12     The Royal Swedish Dramatic Theatre was founded by Gustav III (1746–92) on May 10, 1788.

13     Standart properties in drawing-room comedy at the time.

14     A machine to roll cigarettes.

15     As an envoy.

16     Theatre boxes closest to the stage.

17     *Lucky Peter's Journey.*

18     In this autobiography S's alter ego is called Johan, the author's first given name.

19  Axel Lamm who acted as Strindberg's protegé and for whose children Strindberg was a private teacher.

20  The protagonist in Schiller's drama *The Robbers* (1782).

21  The main character in *Lucidor*, a historical play (1854) by Oskar Wijkander.

22  Parisian daily.

23  Also named Comédie Française, the foremost theatre in France, founded in Paris in 1680.

24  Hyltén-Cavallius was head of the Royal Theatre 1856-60.

25  Anders Willman who was head of the royal theatres 1883-88.

26  A play (1857) by Friedrich Halm, pseudonym for E.F.J. von Münch Bellinghausen.

27  One who adapts literature as a profession.

28  Historical play (1865) by Frans Hedberg.

29  Historical play (1864) by Bjørnstjerne Bjørnson.

30  James Hepburn, Earl of Bothwell, Mary Stuart's third husband.

31  Waterway in Stockholm, close to the (old) Royal Dramatic Theatre.

32  The leader of the revolutionary fishermen in D.F.E. Auber's opera *La Muette de Portici* (1828).

33  Old-fashioned couple dance in 2/4 or 4/4 time.

34  Swedish daily, founded in 1830.

35  Income in addition to a fixed salary for actors at the royal theatres.

36  Opera by the Belgian composer F.A. Gevaërt, produced at the Stockholm Opera in 1865-66.

37  Theatre director J.F.I. Högfeldt.

38  Theatre director C.M. Boberg.

39  Verse drama by Henrik Ibsen.

40  The God of Charity.

41  Followers of the Norwegian revivalist preacher H.N. Hauge (1771–1824) who advocated a form of severe pietism.

42  Brand is killed in an avalanche at the end of the drama.

43  The Danish sculptor Bertel Thorvaldsen is the main character in *In Rome*. His statue of Jason (1803) represents one of the heroes in Greek mythology.

44  At the University of Uppsala in aesthetics.

45  In his seminar paper, only a brief passage of which is included here, S pits the idealist A against the realist B who has his sympathy.

46  V. F. Palmblad's translation of Sophocles's dramas was published in 1838-41.

47  Historical drama (1864) by Henrik Ibsen.

48 Later renamed *Master Olof.*

49 The Royal Library which until 1878 was located in the north-eastern wing of the Royal Palace.

50 Goethe's *Götz von Berlichingen* (1771) comprises 57 tableaux.

51 Anders Fryxell's *Tales from Swedish History* (1823-79).

52 Arvid Afzelius's *The Folklore Tales of the Swedish People* (1839-70).

53 Olaus Petri (1493–1552), the foremost Lutheran reformer of the Swedish church.

54 Gustav I (1496–1560), Swedish king, founder of the Vasa dynasty.

55 Member of a revolutionary movement during the Reformation that rejected the baptism of children.

56 Member of the Paris Commune 1871; a revolutionary person.

57 Henry Thomas Buckle, English historian, author of *History of Civilization in England* (1857-61).

58 Hans Brask (1464-1538), bishop in Linköping.

59 The legal system instituted by the Catholic church.

60 Otto von Bismarck (1815-98), German Chancellor.

61 Allusion to the New Testament, John 8:7.

62 Swedish king (1826-72).

63 By the mid-1880s S's marriage to Siri von Essen had become problematic. This colors his description of Kristina and her marriage to Olof in the autobiography.

64 Scientifically founded philosophy that rejects metaphysical speculations.

65 Olaus – S, using the Latin version of the name, here and elsewhere actually means Olof – is putting on *The Comedy of Tobias* with his pupils.

66 Schoolboy, a minor character in *Master Olof.*

67 The first part, written next, was *The Father*. The third part remained unwritten.

68 William Engelbrecht was touring the provinces and other parts of Scandinavia with his own company.

69 Short comedy based on a proverb.

70 Two collections of short stories, published in 1884–85, which laid the basis for S's reputation as a woman hater. For one of the stories, propagating sexual freedom and ridiculing the Holy Communion, he was even sued in court. Although he was acquitted, he was made aware of the controversial nature of the stories.

71 A neurologist in Paris whose work, using hypnotism in the study of dual personality and hysteria, was widely known in the 1880s.

72   Professor of Internal Medicine in Nancy. Examples of Bernheim's suggestion in a waking state made a deep impression on S and figures prominently in his major plays of the 1880s.

73   S has Zola's formula for modern drama as outlined in *Le Naturalisme au théâtre* in mind.

74   At the rehearsal of *The Father* in Copenhagen.

75   The Casino Theatre in Copenhagen, where *The Father* had its world premiere.

76   Well-known actress (1843–1922) at the royal theatres in Stockholm.

77   S's allusions are to *Hamlet, The Robbers* and *Ghosts* respectively.

78   Comedy (1723) by the Norwegian-Danish playwright Ludvig Holberg.

79   A "poor man's Bible," a medieval work of edification richly illustrated with pictures from the Bible aimed at those with little or no education.

80   Derived from the Greek *khoros* (dance) to describe a disorder of the central nervous system characterized by uncontrollable, irregular, brief, and jerky movements.

81   An often repeated phrase in the play *No Harm Done!* by Frans Hedberg.

82   Barki's recurring phrase in *David Copperfield* by Charles Dickens.

83   The protagonist of Molière's comedy *L'Avare*.

84   Italian philosopher (1548–1600).

85   Francis Bacon (1561–1626), English statesman and philosopher.

86   Thought-transference, telepathy (German).

87   Anton Mesmer (1734–1815), German doctor and practitioner of hypnotism.

88   The idea of a pure Aryan race was a central notion in nineteenth century ethnic theory.

89   The hero of Miguel de Cervantes's (1547-1616) famous novel.

90   S describes Jean as a *statbarn*, that is the child (*barn*) of an agricultural laborer hired annually by a large estate and principally paid in kind (*stat*). These laborers were at the bottom of the social ladder.

91   A reference to Zola's reaction to *The Father*.

92   Edmond (1822-96) and Jules (1830-70) de Goncourt who together wrote several novels of psychological realism focusing on a central female character.

93   The correct date is actually 1871.

94   In Greek tragedy an ode sung by a single actor; subsequently a style of musical composition for a single voice, originally without accompaniment, later (*c*.1600) with the support of a figured bass or continuo.

95   Opera (1871) by Giuseppe Verdi.

96    The acting style associated with André Antoine's newly opened Théâtre Libre in Paris.

97    As S may have known, Richard Wagner had already covered the orchestra pit at the Festival Theatre in Bayreuth, which opened in 1876.

98    Sir Henry Irving had already introduced this practice at the Lyceum in London.

99    Refers to *Creditors*. The sunrise occurs at the end of *Ghosts* and *Miss Julie*.

100   *The Red Room.*

101   An ad for Victoria Benedictsson's novel *Money*. The text notes: "There can be no doubt that the tale is partly colored by *descriptions of her own life.*" The emphasis is S's, having here inserted the words "but mostly her husband's" after "*own.*"

102   S had lent Brandes a manuscript copy. In a letter dated September 28, Brandes had told S that he found the play "generally speaking excellent – up to the end. I have my doubts about that. You don't kill yourself when there is no danger in sight, and here there is no danger. Perhaps five months from now but not tonight. The ending is romanticism, determined by the need to end the play impressively."

103   Fashionable restaurant in Stockholm.

104   Greek for 'necessity.'

105   In *The Wagner Case* (1888), which Strindberg had just read.

106   Miss Julie's siskin, which Jean kills.

107   In his letter of November 27, 1888 to S, Nietzsche had commented on the way *The Father* reflected his own conception of "*der Todhass der Geschlechter*" as its fundamental law.

108   Brandes replied the day after that S's explanations "*almost* persuade me."

109   To Copenhagen, where Strindberg attended a rehearsal of *Creditors*.

110   In a letter to *Politiken* on January 28, Henrik Pontoppidan had ridiculed *The Stronger*, in which "the heroine doesn't say one word."

111   Peter Nansen was a journalist and a publisher who translated the first part of *A Son of a Servant* into Danish.

112   Gustav Wied was to perform the part of Adolf in *Creditors*.

113   "Here I lie making literary history."

114   Originally intended as a lecture at the premiere of the three one-act plays at the Dagmar Theatre on March 9, 1889. The lecture was never given.

115   In classical mythology the ferryman who conveyed souls of the dead across the river Styx.

116   Eugène Scribe (1791–1861), Emile Augier (1820–89) and François Ponsard

(1814–67) are here treated with respect. Victorien Sardou (1831–1908) was best known for his effective and well-crafted vehicles.

117  A drama in three acts by Zola, based on his novel published in 1867.

118  Though written in 1872–73, this play was not produced until 1882.

119  A paraphrase of Zola's celebrated formula *"Un œuvre d'art est un coin de nature vu à travers un tempérament."*

120  Edouard Pailleron (1834–99).

121  The play was being revived at the Comédie Française with Sarah Bernhardt as Césarine.

122  In *The Repetition* (1843).

123  In *To Damascus I*, the final eight scenes show the protagonist retracing the path he has taken during the first eight, the journey out and back pivoting upon the Asylum scene which is the only one not duplicated.

124  Following his 70th birthday on March 3, 1898, Ibsen visited Stockholm, where he was received with great acclaim.

125  The stage directions for Act II.1 of *Crimes and Crimes* specify a pianist in an adjoining room practicing the finale of Beethoven's Piano Sonata Opus 31, No. 2, known as "The Tempest" but often called "The Ghost Sonata" by S.

126  "Common woman," "prostitute," "these women." Refers to Act III.2, where Henriette is shadowed by two detectives and accused of being a whore.

127  This note, first published in Strindberg (1919, 172) in the section "Pensées détachées," may well have been written earlier or later.

128  Something for something; dramatic term referring to a character's mistaking one thing for another.

129  The role in *Easter* that Harriet Bosse was to play at the Royal Dramatic Theatre premiere on April 4, 1901.

130  The title figure in *Séraphita* (1834-35), one of Balzac's *Études philosophiques.*

131  The protagonist of *The Crown Bride* allows her own baby to be taken away.

132  Maeterlinck's first play, published in 1889.

133  It is a common belief in Scandinavian folklore that trolls burst at sunrise.

134  Arvid Ahnfelt's *History of World Literature* (1875).

135  This was an early title of what was later called *A Dream Play*. It also referred to an actual building, the Horseguards' Barracks, built in 1897, which S could see from his Stockholm apartment.

136  Goethe's *Götz von Berlichingen.*

137  Historical drama by Gerhardt Hauptmann, written in 1896 and revised in 1902.

138  'Rus' in Swedish. Later called *Crimes and Crimes*, which Max Reinhardt

was rehearsing at the Kleines Theater in Berlin with Gertrud Eysoldt as Henriette.

139    Greek poet (sixth century B.C.) whose cart formed an improvised stage.

140    August Falck's successful Swedish premiere of *Miss Julie* took place in Lund in September1906 and had its Stockholm premiere on December 13 the same year.

141    Derived from Sanskrit, *Kama Loka* is the name given by the theosophists to the first stage which the soul enters after death, where it is released from the 'ghosts' of earthly life, the animal desires by which it has been possessed.

142    Immanuel Kant's 'The Thing-in-itself.'

143    The veil of illusion which, according to Schopenhauer, conceals the true nature of reality.

144    *Scheol*, from Hebrew, in the Old Testament, denotes the kingdom of death, where the dead live a shadowy existence in a kind of torpor.

145    S at times suffered from psoriasis.

146    Contact with the beyond.

147    German *Gespenst*, here in the plural, means 'ghost' in the sense of 'spirit.'

148    The Piano Sonata Opus 31, No. 2, and the Piano Trio Opus 70, No. 1, traditionally known as "The Ghost Trio."

149    German *Spuk* means 'ghost' in a more literal sense than *Gespenst*.

150    Thunder and storm, the fourth movement.

151    Refers to Jesus's words in Matt. 26:42: "If this cup may not pass away from me, except I drink it, thy will be done."

152    The Isle of the Dead. At the close of *The Ghost Sonata* a reproduction of the painting *Toten-Insel* by the Swiss artist Arnold Böcklin (1827–1901) appears in the background. S had arranged to have a copy of it hung to the side of the proscenium in the Intimate Theatre.

153    A bottle of soy sauce carried by the Cook in *The Ghost Sonata*.

154    This part of the "Author's Note" was probably written in connection with the first production of the play.

155    An allusion to Pedro Calderón de la Barca's play *La vida es sueño* (*Life is a Dream*, 1673).

156    S's second daughter by his first wife.

157    Albert Ranft, actor and theatre manager, controlled many theatres in Stockholm. One of them was the Swedish Theatre, where some fifteen of S's plays premiered.

158    Both plays by Goethe.

159 The so-called Shakespeare stage was introduced in Munich in 1889 by Karl von Perfall, Karl Lautenschläger, and Jocza Savits.

160 In response to Schering's wish to dramatize S's story "Karl Ulfsson and his Mother" from the collection *Memories of the Chieftains* (1906).

161 Against the will of Minerva, the Roman goddess of wisdom; against the grain.

162 No day without its line.

163 Situated close to what was to become the Intimate Theatre.

164 Refers to Hugo Philp, married to S's sister Anna, who died on January 18, 1906. Model for the recently deceased father in *The Pelican*.

165 Played the Baroness in *The Bond*.

166 In Stockholm, renowned for its light repertoire.

167 Allusion to Marc Antony's speech in Shakespeare's Julius Caesar, Act III.2.

168 Johan Ljungqvist who played the Friend.

169 Falck around this time played Mr. Y *in Pariah* and the Baron in *The Bond*.

170 In *Kristina*, a play about the highly cultivated Swedish queen (1626–89) who abdicated in connection with her conversion to Catholicism.

171 Claes Tott (1630–74), the Queen's favorite.

172 In Greek mythology, a beautiful woman sent by Zeus to bring misery to mankind.

173 A garment worn by both sexes.

174 The former has four lines in the printed text, the latter none.

175 Karl Michaelson, theatre manager.

176 At the Intimate Theatre situated at Norra Bantorget, about one-half mile downhill from S's apartment in the so-called Blue Tower, Drottninggatan 85.

177 Karin Alexandersson as Laura in *The Father*, had played Mrs. Heyst in *Easter*.

178 Refers to a powerful thirteenth century Swede, Ivar Blå, who is said to have claimed that he was able to "shake a king out of his coat," a statement that has become proverbial.

179 Anna-Lisa Hwasser-Engelbrecht was an actress known for her excellent voice training.

180 Bjørnstjerne Bjørnson (1832–1910), Norwegian writer, pioneer of realistic drama and winner of the Nobel Prize for literature in 1903.

181 Refers to August Falck who fulfilled both functions.

182 Manda Björling played Henriette in *Crimes and Crimes* at the premiere on January 21, 1909.

183 At the world premiere in Copenhagen.

184 Velour drapes at the back of the stage instead of a realistic decor.

185 John Gunnarsson, set designer, made sketches of backdrops for *To Damascus I* at the Intimate Theatre in the summer of 1908.

186 A stylized balustrade with emblematic objects placed on it.

187 In a letter to S, Knut Michaelson had suggested that Gösta Hillberg play Sten Sture Jr. (circa 1492 – 1520) in *The Last Knight*.

188 As director August Lindberg's prima donna she had played, among other roles, the King's Catholic Mother-in-law at the premiere of *Gustav Vasa*.

189 During his stay in Lund in late 1898 and well on into 1899, S resumed his private study of Shakespeare.

190 In 1873–74 S reviewed plays performed at the Stockholm theatres for *Dagens Nyheter*.

191 Swedish king (1316–74).

192 Fritz von Uhde (1848–1911), German painter whose paintings with biblical motifs were widely known.

193 *Axel and Valborg* (1810) is a tragedy by Adam Oehlenschläger.

194 Shakespeare's protagonists of respectively *King Lear* and *Timon of Athens*.

195 High, thick-soled shoe worn by ancient Greek and Roman tragic actors.

196 Light, low-soled shoe worn by ancient Greek and Roman comic actors.

197 *Rome conquered*, play by Dominique-Alexandre Parodi, staged in 1876 at the Théâtre Français.

198 Refers to *Regeln für Schauspieler* (*Rules for Actors,* 1803) published by Goethe's friend J.P. Eckermann.

199 Refers to Darwin's theory of evolution.

200 The famous American dancer Isadora Duncan had given a guest performance in Stockholm in 1906.

201 List of hymns to be sung during a church service.

202 Josephson staged *Master Olof* in 1881 after it had been rejected for almost ten years.

203 Dynasty reigning in Sweden 1250–1363.

204 'Smek' meaning caressing, a nickname presumably reflecting the debauchery at his court.

205 Birgitta Birgersdotter (1303–73) was canonized as Saint Birgitta in 1391.

206 Engelbrekt Engelbrektsson, Swedish regent murdered in 1436, is the protagonist in *Engelbrekt*.

207 Protagonist of the play *Wilhelm Tell* (1804).

208 A rebellion against Gustav Vasa 1542–43 led by the peasant Nils Dacke.

209 Swedish king 1560–68, son of Gustav Vasa.

210 King Erik's powerful confidant.

211 High-ranking noble family.

212 King Erik's brother, later to replace him as Johan III.

213 Carl August Hagberg's Swedish translation of Shakespeare's plays was published in 12 vols. 1847–51.

214 Drama (1779) by Gotthold Ephraim Lessing.

215 A political and military alliance 1609-35 between Catholic sovereigns and prelates in Roman Catholic Europe.

216 Jacob Johan Anckarström, Gustav III's assassin.

217 Norwegian fortress, besieged by the Swedes. Carl XII was killed here either by a bullet that came from the fortress or by an assassin from the Swedish side.

218 Carl XII returned to Sweden in 1714 after having spent several years as the 'guest' of the Turkish sultan.

219 As the subject for *Earl Birger of Bjälbo*.

220 Jutta (circa 1245–84) was said to have committed adultery with her brother-in-law. Mechtild (died 1288) was first married to the Danish king Abel (died 1252), who was said to have been murdered, then to Earl Birger.

221 Valdemar Birgersson, son of Earl Birger, Swedish king (died 1302), forced to resign in favor of his brother Magnus Ladulås (1240–90).

222 Carl Grabow (1847–1922) painted realistic scenery for several Stockholm theatres.

223 Popular singer who was also a photographer and a drawing instructor.

224 German for 'Beauty' and 'Truth,' presumably a reference to Goethe.

225 Appeared in several S plays including *Miss Julie*.

226 Pierre-Augustin Caron de Beaumarchais' *Le Mariage de Figaro* (1784).

227 English interior design magazine.

228 Carl Georg Starbäck's popular *Stories from Swedish History* (1860–75) was continued by Per Olof Bäckström.

229 Erik Gustav Geijer (1783–1847), poet and historian.

230 Richard Dybeck (1811–77), ethnologist and poet, published the journal *Runa* which was devoted to Swedish folklore.

231 The idea was to get *Sir Bengt's Wife* produced at Albert Ranft's Swedish Theatre.

232 August Falck appeared as the Hunter in the play.

233 Easter lily is a literal rendering of Swedish *påsklilja*, daffodil. The Shrovetide scourge, derived from the biblical one, still figures in Sweden in the

penitential period from Ash Wednesday to Easter in a decorative form as twigs 'dressed' in bright-colored hen feathers.

234    The untranslatable Swedish title is "Kråksång", literally 'Crow Song.' S is alluding ironically to a well-known Swedish saying: "*det är det fina i kråk-sången*" (that's the beauty of the crow song).

235    Refers to Falck's intention to produce Maeterlinck's *L'Intruse* at the Intimate Theatre.

236    Well aware that the Swedish Academy was not likely to award S the literary Nobel Prize, some 20,000 Swedes honored him with an "Anti-Nobel Prize" amounting to 20,000 crowns. This was presented to him on March 2, 1912 by Hjalmar Branting, leader of the Social Democratic party and later prime minister.

237    For other titles in English, see Törnqvist 1982, 250-51.

# Select Bibliography

Only books are listed.

Adamov, Arthur. 1955. *August Strindberg, dramaturge*. Paris: L'Arche.

Bandle, Oskar, Walter Baumgartner and Jürg Glauser, eds. 1981. *Strindbergs Dramen im Lichte neuerer Methodendiskussionen*. Basel and Frankfurt am Main: Helbing & Lichtenhahn.

Bayerdörfer, Hans-Peter, Hans Otto Horch, and Georg-Michael Schulz, eds. 1983. *Strindberg auf der deutschen Bühne: Eine exemplarische Rezeptionsgeschichte der Moderne in Dokumenten (1890 bis 1925)*. Neumünster: Karl Wachholtz.

Bentley, Eric. (1946) 1955. *The Playwright as Thinker*. New York: Meridian.

Bergman, Gösta M. 1966. *Den moderna teaterns genombrott 1890–1925*. Stockholm: Bonnier.

Blackwell, Marilyn Johns, ed. 1981. *Structures of Influence: A Comparative Approach to August Strindberg*. Chapel Hill: University of North Carolina Press.

Boëthius, Ulf. 1969. *Strindberg och kvinnofrågan till och med Giftas I*. Stockholm: Prisma.

Brandell, Gunnar. 1974. *Strindberg in Inferno*. Trans. Barry Jacobs. Cambridge, MA: Harvard University Press.

—. 1983-89. *Strindberg - ett författarliv*. 4 vols. Stockholm: Bonnier.

Brustein, Robert. 1964. *The Theatre of Revolt: An Approach to the Modern Drama*. Boston: Little, Brown and Company.

Carlson, Harry G. 1982. *Strindberg and the Poetry of Myth*. Berkeley, CA: University of California Press.

Dahlström, Carl. 1965. *Strindberg's Dramatic Expressionism*. Ann Arbor: University of Michigan.

Delblanc, Sven. 2007. *Strindberg – urtida, samtida, framtida*. Lars Ahlbom and Björn Meidal, eds. Stockholm: Carlsson.

Edqvist, Sven-Gustav. 1961. *Samhällets fiende: En studie i Strindbergs anarkism till och med Tjänstekvinnans son*. Summary in French. Stockholm: Tiden.

Eklund, Torsten. 1948. *Tjänstekvinnans son: En psykologisk Strindbergsstudie*. Stockholm: Bonnier.

Ekman, Hans-Göran. 2000. *The World of Illusions: Studies in Strindberg's Chamber Plays.* London: Athlone Press.

Falck, August. 1935. *Fem år med Strindberg*, Stockholm: Wahlström & Widstrand.

Gassner, John. 1965. *Directions in Modern Theatre and Drama.* New York: Holt, Rinehart and Winston.

Gierow, Carl-Olof. 1967. *Documentation – Evocation: Le Climat littéraire et théâtral en France des années 1880 et Mademoiselle Julie de Strindberg.* Stockholm: Almqvist & Wiksell.

Gran, Ulf and Ulla-Britta Lagerroth, eds. 1971. *Perspektiv på teater: Ur svensk regi- och iscensättningshistoria.* Stockholm: Rabén & Sjögren.

Hagsten, Allan. 1951. *Den unge Strindberg.* 2 vols. Lund: Bonnier.

Hedén, Erik. 1926. *Strindberg: En ledtråd vid studiet av hans verk.* Stockholm: Tiden.

Hockenjos, Vreni. 2007. *Picturing Dissolving Views*: August Strindberg and the Visual Media of His Age. Stockholm: Stockholm Cinema Studies 7.

Jacobsen, Harry. 1948. *Strindberg i firsernes København.* København: Gyldendal.

Janni, Thérèse Dubois. 1973. *August Strindberg: En biografi i text och bild.* Stockholm: Bonnier.

Johnson, Walter. 1963. *Strindberg and the Historical Drama.* Seattle: University of Washington Press.

—. 1978. *August Strindberg.* Boston: Twayne.

Jolivet, Alfred. 1931. *Le théâtre de Strindberg.* Paris: Bibliothèque de la Revue des cours et conferences.

Josephson, Lennart. 1965. *Strindbergs drama Fröken Julie.* Stockholm: Almqvist & Wiksell.

Kvam, Kela. 1974. *Max Reinhardt og Strindbergs visionære dramatik.* København: Akademisk forlag.

—, ed. 1994. *Strindberg's Post-Inferno Plays.* København: Munksgaard.

Lagercrantz, Olof. 1984. *August Strindberg.* Trans. Anselm Hollo. New York: Farrar, Straus and Giroux.

Lamm, Martin. 1924-26. *Strindbergs dramer.* 2 vols. Stockholm: Bonnier.

—. 1953. *Modern Drama.* Trans. Karin Elliott. Oxford: Blackwell.

—. 1971. *August Strindberg.* 2 vols. Trans. and ed. Harry G. Carlson, New York: Benjamin Bloom.

Lindström, Hans. 1952. *Hjärnornas kamp: Psykologiska idéer och motiv i Strindbergs åttiotalsdiktning*: (diss.). Uppsala.

—, ed. 1977, 1990. *Strindberg och böckerna*, 2 vols. Uppsala: Svenska Litteratursällskapet.

Lunin, Hanno. 1962. *Strindbergs Dramen*. Emsdetten: Lechte.

Madsen, Børge Gedsø. 1962. *Strindberg's Naturalistic Theatre: Its Relation to French Naturalism*. København: Munksgaard.

Meyer, Michael. 1987. *Strindberg: A Biography*. Oxford and New York: Oxford University Press.

Morgan, Margery. 1985. *August Strindberg*. London: Macmillan.

Mortensen, Brita and Brian Downs. 1949. *Strindberg: An Introduction to His Life and Work*. Cambridge: Cambridge University Press.

Ollén, Gunnar. 1982. *Strindbergs dramatik*. Stockholm: Sveriges Radio.

Paul, Fritz. 1979. *August Strindberg*. Stuttgart: J.B. Metzlersche Verlagsbuchhandlung.

Quigley, Austin E. 1985. *The Modern Stage and Other Worlds*. New York and London: Methuen.

Rokem, Freddie. 1986. *Theatrical Space in Ibsen, Chekhov and Strindberg: Public Forms of Privacy*. Ann Arbor: UMI Research Press.

Robinson, Michael. 1986. *Strindberg and Autobiography: Writing and Reading a Life*. Norwich: Norvik Press.

—, ed. 1991. *Strindberg and Genre*. Norwich: Norvik Press.

—. 1998. *Studies in Strindberg*. Norwich: Norvik Press.

Schütze, Peter. 1990. *August Strindberg: Mit Selbstzeugnissen und Bilddokumenten*. Hamburg: Rowohlt.

Smedmark, Carl Reinhold. 1952. *Mäster Olof och Röda rummet*. Stockholm: Almqvist & Wiksell.

—, ed. *Essays on Strindberg*. Stockholm: The Strindberg Society.

Sprinchorn, Evert. 1982. *Strindberg as Dramatist*. New Haven and London: Yale University Press.

Steene, Birgitta. 1982. *August Strindberg: An Introduction to his Major Works*. Stockholm: Almqvist & Wiksell International/ Atlantic Highlands, NJ: Humanities Press Inc.

—, ed. 1992. *Strindberg and History*. Stockholm: Almqvist & Wiksell International.

Stockenström, Göran. 1972. *Ismael i öknen: Strindberg som mystiker*. With a summary in English. *Acta Universitatis Upsaliensis: Historia Litterarum*, 5. Uppsala.

—, ed. 1988. *Strindberg's Dramaturgy*. Minneapolis: University of Minnesota Press.

Strindberg, August. 1912–21. *Samlade skrifter av August Strindberg*. John Landquist, ed. 55 vols. Stockholm: Bonnier.

—. 1918-19. *Samlade otryckta skrifter*. 2 vols. Stockholm: Bonnier.

—. 1948–2001. *August Strindbergs Brev*. Torsten Eklund and Björn Meidal, eds. 22 vols. Stockholm: Bonnier.

—. 1964. *Théâtre cruel et théâtre mystique*. Trans. Marguerite Diehl. Introd. Maurice Gravier. Paris: Gallimard.

—. 1965. *From an Occult Diary: Marriage with Harriet Bosse*. Torsten Eklund, ed., trans. Mary Sandbach. New York: Hill and Wang.

—. 1966. *Open Letters to the Intimate Theater*. Ed. and trans. Walter Johnson. Seattle and London: Washington University Press.

—. 1966. *August Strindberg über Drama und Theater*. Marianne Kesting and Verner Arpe, eds. Köln: Kiepenheuer & Witsch.

—. 1968. *Strindberg om drama och teater. Programskrifter och öppna brev med inledning och kommentarer av Göran Lindström*. Stockholm: Gleerup.

—. 1977. *Ockulta dagboken: 1896-1908*. Stockholm: Gidlund.

— 1981-. *Samlade Verk*. Lars Dahlbäck, chief ed. Circa 72 vols. Stockholm: Almqvist & Wiksell / Norstedt.

—. 1991. *Katalog över "Gröna säcken": Strindbergs efterlämnade papper i Kungl. biblioteket SgNM 1-9*. Barbro Ståhle Sjönell, ed. Stockholm: Kungliga biblioteket.

—. 1992. *Strindberg's Letters*. Ed. and trans. Michael Robinson, 2 vols. Chicago and London: University of Chicago Press.

—. 1996. *Selected Essays*. Ed. and trans. Michael Robinson. Cambridge: Cambridge University Press.

—. 1998. *Miss Julie and Other Plays*. Ed. and trans. Michael Robinson. Oxford: Oxford University Press.

Szondi, Peter. 1987. *Theory of the Modern Drama*. Ed. and trans. Michael Hays. Cambridge: Polity.

Söderström, Göran. (1972) 1990. *Strindberg och bildkonsten*. With a summary in English. Stockholm: Bonnier.

Törnqvist, Egil. 1982. *Strindbergian Drama: Themes and Structure*. Stockholm: Almqvist & Wiksell International / Atlantic Highlands, NJ: Humanities Press.

—. 1999. *Ibsen, Strindberg and the Intimate Theatre: Studies in TV Presentation*. Amsterdam: Amsterdam University Press.

—. 2000. *Strindberg's The Ghost Sonata: From Text to Performance*. Amsterdam: Amsterdam University Press.

—. 2001. *Det talade ordet: Om Strindbergs dramadialog*. Stockholm: Carlsson.

Törnqvist, Egil and Barry Jacobs. 1988. *Strindberg's Miss Julie: A Play and Its*

*Transpositions*. Norwich: Norvik Press.

Valency, Maurice. 1963. *The Flower and the Castle: An Introduction to Modern Drama*. New York: Grosset & Dunlap.

Vogelweith, Guy. 1972. *Le psychothéâtre de Strindberg*. Paris: Librairie C. Klincksieck.

Ward, John. 1980. *The Social and Religious Plays of Strindberg*. London: Athlone.

Williams, Raymond. 1966. *Modern Tragedy*. London: Chatto & Windus.

—. 1973. *Drama from Ibsen to Brecht*. Harmondsworth: Penguin.

# Name and Title Index

Carl XII, 161, 190
Casino Theatre (Copenhagen), 59, 176, 184
Castegren, Victor, 111, 139, 163, 164
Cervantes, Miguel de,
    *Don Quixote*, 67, 184
Charcot, Jean-Martin, 56, 183
Christina, Queen, *see* Kristina
City Theatre Hannover, 178, 179
Comédie Française, *see* Théâtre Française
Corneille, Pierre, 126
Court Theatre (Munich), 22, 23, 112, 113, 140,
    188
Craig, Gordon,
    *The Mask* (journal), 22

Dacke, Nils, 160, 190
*Dagens Nyheter* (Swedish daily), 85, 189
Dagmar Theatre (Copenhagen), 99, 176, 185
Darwin, Charles, 14, 65, 73
Dickens, Charles, 146
    *David Copperfield*, 146, 184
Diderot, Denis, 80
    *Paradox of Acting*, 24
Djurgård Theatre (Stockholm), 176
Dörum, August, 27
Dramatic Theatre (Stockholm), *see* Royal
    Dramatic Theatre
Dumas fils, Alexandre, 12, 80, 81
    *Les Danicheff*, 29, 181
    *La Femme de Claude*, 86
Duncan, Isadora, 155, 189
Dybeck, Richard, 190
    *Runa*.(Swedish journal), 169, 190

*L'Écho de Paris* (Parisian daily), 87
Eckermann, J.P., 189
École des Arts Décoratifs (Paris), 179
Engelbrecht, Anna-Lisa, 125, 188
Engelbrecht, William, 86, 183
Engelbrektsson, Engelbrekt, 54, 160,189
Erik XIV, 160, 181, 190
Eriksson, Magnus, 159, 189
Essen, Siri von, 21, 78, 183
Eysoldt, Gertrud, 96

Falck Jr., August, 11, 18, 19, 21, 24, 59, 93, 103,
    104, 113, 114, 115, 119, 120, 121, 122, 123, 124,
    125, 127, 135, 137, 139, 141, 142, 155, 156, 157,
    164, 165, 166, 169, 170, 171, 172, 187, 188,
    190, 191
Falck Sr., August, 59
Falkner, Fanny, 124, 125
*Le Figaro* (Parisian daily), 41, 86, 155
Flygare, Anna, 115, 118, 124, 125, 142, 155
Frederick the Great, 161
French Academy, 72, 73
Fryxell, Anders, 168
    *Tales from Swedish History*, 183
Fuchs, Georg, 50
    *Die Schaubühne der Zukunft*, 22

Geijer, Erik Gustav, 169,190
Geijerstam, Gustaf af, 76, 87, 88, 89
Gernandt, Christian Emanuel, 76, 156
Gevaërt, F.A., 182
Goethe, Johann Wolfgang, 12, 20, 24, 28, 134,
    150, 153, 190
    *Clavigo*, 111, 188
    *Faust*, 21, 44, 128, 153, 164
    *Götz von Berlichingen*, 50, 95
    *Rules for the Art of the Stage*, 150, 189
    *Stella*, 111, 188
Goncourt, Edmond de, and Jules de, 69, 184
    *Henriette Maréchal*, 80
    *Sœur Philomène*, 82
*Göteborgs Handels- och Sjöfartstidning*
    (Swedish daily), 87
Gothenburg City Theatre, 175
Grabow, Carl, 163, 164, 190
Grandinson, Emil, 22, 93, 138, 163, 170
Guiches, Gustave,
    *Entre frères*, 83
Gunnarsson, John, 137, 189
Gustav I, *see* Gustav Vasa
Gustav II Adolf, 160-61
Gustav III, 161
Gustav Vasa, 50, 160, 183, 190

Hagberg, Carl August, 160, 190
Håkansson, Julia, 138, 189

Voltaire, Francois-Marie Arouet, 161
    *Candide*, 32

Wagner, Richard, 185
Wahlgren, Helge, 117, 138, 142
Waldteufel, Emil, 155
Widholm, Gunnar, 105
Wied, Gustav, 185
Wijkander, Oskar,
    *Lucidor*, 40, 182

Willman, Anders, 182
Wrangel, Carl-Gustaf, 78

Young Sweden, 76

Zola, Émile, 16, 57, 126, 184, 186
    *L'Assommoir*, 82
    *Germinal*, 82
    *Le Naturalisme au théâtre*, 184
    *Thérèse Raquin*, 80, 81, 82, 127, 186

# Subject Index

conflict, 16, 48, 84, 94

conglomerate, 15, 65

costume, 22, 23, 30, 35, 56, 59, 78, 120, 128, 133, 154, 164, 166

counterpoint, 139, 163

crescendo, 145

critic, see theatre critic

crowd scene, 31, 70

curtain, 16, 29, 79, 81, 127, 140

curtartin line, 110

cut, see deletion

dance, 28, 70

dancer, 155

Darwinism, 65, 73, 150

decor, see scenery

deletion, 14, 31, 60, 88, 119, 121, 126, 140, 141, 154, 170, 171

dematerialization, 164

*denouement*, 94, 140

determinism, 52, 74

*deus ex machina*, 79

dialect, 159

dialogue, 35, 49, 50, 68-69, 80, 93, 112, 113, 126

diction, 23, 24, 28, 116, 124, 135

diminuendo, 145

director, see stage director

discovery, 91

drama structure, 18, 19, 31, 45, 69, 80, 82, 87, 93, 109-110, 134, 139, 140, 159, 163, 171

drama text, 23, 113, 140

dramatis personæ, 17, 112

drapery, 113, 121, 137, 141, 155, 156, 169

drawing-room drama, 12, 93, 126, 181

dream, 18, 59, 95, 109, 126, 163, 164

dream play, 12, 17, 94

dreamer, 95

dress circle, 78

dress rehearsal, 23, 105, 111, 118, 132, 148

dressing room, 44

duet, 72, 121

eavesdropping, 29, 38

emblem, 79, 100-101, 137, 138, 155-156, 164, 169, 171

emotion, 15, 23, 28, 30, 63

ending, 52-53, 74, 109

ensemble acting, 24, 30

entrance, 123, 141

enunciation, 22, 130, 150-151

environment, 15, 61, 66, 68, 71, 81

event, 82

evolution, 14, 50, 52, 53, 65, 76, 150

exit, 60, 71, 122, 135, 141

experimental theatre, 20, 75, 76

exposition, 133, 170

expressionism, 12

extra, 45, 84, 126

eye movement, 123

facial expression, see mimicry

fairy-tale, 112

fairy-tale play, 12, 13, 125, 139

fate, 66, 116, 171

fencing, 28

film, see movie

five-act play, 27, 69, 83, 107, 125, 126, 140, 181

folk music, 70, 92

folktale, 169

fool, 55, 159, 162, 168-169

footlights, 29, 43, 71, 131, 143, 170

foreshadowing, 140, 162

formalism, 140, 150

fourth wall, 13, 72

foyer, 29, 44, 113

frame, 140

free will, 15

French comedy, see drawing-room drama

full-length play, 82, 83, 125

furnishing, 140, 166

gender alternation, 91

gender relation, 34

gesture, 27-28, 29-30, 35, 38, 72, 77, 116-117, 122, 130, 131, 135, 138

guilt, 17, 110, 160

headgear, 119, 155, 170

heredity, 15

hero(ine), see protagonist

physiology, 64, 80

pietism, 46, 47, 92

pilgrimage drama, 12, 17

place, 94-95

plausibility, 74, 116

play reading, 11, 12, 13, 21, 22, 48, 85, 128, 133, 140, 141, 146

playing time, 16, 69, 160

playwriting, 11, 13, 20-21, 38, 45, 86, 152, 157-158

plot, 15, 19, 29, 61, 74, 75, 80, 82, 139

post-Inferno, 13, 23

positivism, 52

posture, 24, 60, 77, 115, 130

preface, 86, 165, 166

pre-Inferno, 13

production, see stage production

prompt box, 35, 46, 72

prompter, 112, 113, 151

proofs, 11

prop, see stage property

proscenium box, 72

protagonist, 13, 15, 17, 49, 51, 77

*proverbe*, 56, 84

providence, 154, 160

psychic murder, see soul murder

psychic suicide, 54

psychologicy, 17, 32, 53, 64, 69, 72, 80, 82, 84, 89

public character, 17

publication, 11, 12, 41, 85

punctuation, 124, 145

punishment, 89, 91


*quart d'heure*, 16, 77, 83

*quid pro quo*, 91


radiations of the ego, 17

radio, 16

*raisonneur*, 83

realism, 12, 13, 33-34, 48, 52, 56, 69, 80, 81, 121

rebuff, 91

reception, 85

recipient, 11

recitation, 28, 50

reconciliation, 91

rehearsal, 11, 23, 44, 58, 60, 111, 129, 144, 151, see also dress rehearsal

repertoire, 21, 23, 42, 55, 72, 75, 82, 86, 113, 167

repetition, 110

reporting, 150-151

resolution, 91

revelation, 140

revenge, 66

reversal, 91

review, 22, 49

reviewer, see theatre critic

rhythm, 135, 139

*ritardando*, 94, 115, 145, 151

role, 42, 56, 93, 96, 116, 117, 118, 119, 120, 126, 130, 132-133, 137, 139, 148, see also character

role alternation, 56, 125

role identification, 24, 30, 39, 40, 49, 50, 52, 61

romanticism, 39, 74, 75, 80

royal character, 17

run, 13


*satisfactio vicaria*, see vicarious sacrifice

scene, 126, 140

scene change, 32, 112

scenery, 22, 23, 58, 71, 80, 88, 89, 96, 102, 112, 124, 136, 139, 140, 141, 145, 162-163, 164, 165, 166, see also set(ting)

scenic time, 15, 16, 160

scenography, 24, 79

sciopticon, 22, 89, 142-143, 163-164

score, 133

screen, 96

season, 88

secret, 91, 94, 107, 113, 140

set(ting), 22, 55, 71, 87-88, 136, 137, 139, 141, 157, 162, 163, 165

set piece, 88, 96

Shakespeare stage, 89, 113, 140

short story, 56, 112

silent acting, 121, 131

slice of life, 13

soliloquy, 126

solo number, 110, 127

song, 70

*sotto voce*, 23